united states

CONTESTATIONS

A series edited by
WILLIAM E. CONNOLLY

A complete list of titles in the series
appears at the end of the book.

united states

Thomas L. Dumm

Cornell University Press

Ithaca and London

First published 1994 by Cornell University Press.

Printed in the United States of America

♾ The paper in this book meets the minimum requirements of the American National Standard for Information Sciences–Permanence of Paper for Printed Library Materials, ANSI Z39.48-1984.

Library of Congress Cataloging-in-Publication Data
Dumm, Thomas L.
    United states / Thomas L. Dumm.
        p.   cm. — (Contestations)
    Includes index.
    ISBN 0-8014-3002-X (alk. paper). — ISBN 0-8014-8190-2 (alk. paper).
    1. Liberalism—United States.   2. Political culture—United States.
3. Political psychology.   4. United States—Politics and government—
20th century.   5. United States—Social life and customs—1971–
I. Title.   II. Series
JA75.7.D78   1994
320.973—dc20   94-10146

For Nathaniel Herold

The last goliard

Contents

Acknowledgments

Writing is too often a pastime of idiots. I like to think I have been saved from my idiocy by the imaginary presence of those whom I eventually would need to thank.

First, not foremost but most necessary, are my thanks to corporate bodies. I thank the Trustees of Amherst College for providing me with sabbatical aid in the form of a Lowenstein Fellowship during the 1988–89 academic year. I spent that year living in East Los Angeles, where I first decided the broad theme of this book might not be too far beyond me. I also thank the following presses for permission to reproduce elements of essays from the following volumes. A short version of Chapter 3 appears as "George Bush, or Homosocial Politics" in *Body Politics*, ed. Michael Ryan, 1993, by permission of Westview Press, Boulder, Colorado. A part of "P.S. (I Love . . .) Television in Wartime," appears as "Telefear: Watching War News," copyright © 1993 by the Regent of the University of Minnesota, in *The Politics of Everyday Fear*, ed. Brian Massumi, by permission of the University of Minnesota Press. A large part of Chapter 4 appeared as "The New Enclosures," in *Reading Rodney King, Reading Urban Uprising*, ed. Robert Gooding-Williams, Routledge, 1993.

Permission from the University of Minnesota Press to reproduce the *Diagram of Foucault*, from Gilles Deleuze's *Foucault*, is also gratefully acknowledged. Finally, I thank the Mary Boone Gallery of New York City for permission to reproduce *Untitled (You construct intricate rituals which allow you to touch the skin of other men)* and *Untitled (We are astonishingly lifelike/Help! I'm locked inside this picture)* by Barbara Kruger.

People at several institutions invited me to speak while I was working on this book. I thank Alan Keenan and Tom Keenan for inviting me to participate in the conference "On Television," at the Johns Hopkins University in the spring of 1988. I also thank Michael Shapiro of the University of Hawaii for asking me to speak on the subject of homosocial politics early in 1989. I thank Eric Forsman and Maria Farland for the invitation to speak on Barbara Kruger and Andrea Dworkin to students at the Humanities Center at Johns Hopkins in the autumn of 1989. I am deeply grateful for a timely invitation in May 1992 from Tom Keenan and Pat Morton of Princeton University to discuss the Los Angeles riots at the ongoing seminar on homelessness, an interdisciplinary group composed of some very helpful people. Finally, thanks to Alice Jardine, Marjorie Garber, and Bonnie Honig for inviting me to participate in the conference "Forty Years After: The Rosenberg Case and the McCarthy Era" at Harvard University in the spring of 1993.

Among the people who have read parts of this manuscript and provided helpful comments are Jill Frank, Tom Keenan, Rosemary Coombs, Lisa Wedeen, Dick Flathman, James Der Derian, Karen Sanchez-Eppler, Kim Townsend, Andy Parker, Shin Chiba, Jane Bennett, Bill Chaloupka, Jon Flatley, T. L. Popejoy, Marianne Constable, Eric Forsman, Avital Ronell, Ted Pearson, Janet Gyatso, Diane Rubenstein, Michael Ryan, Stanley Cavell, and Steven White.

Several people read a very rough draft in its entirety and provided useful suggestions. I thank Cecilia Cancellero, Andrew Ross, and Michael Shapiro for substantive comments, some of which are reflected here. I am deeply grateful to George Lipsitz and to Anne Norton for their passionate and involved readings. At a crucial moment, their detailed reports on the manuscript provided much-needed encouragement. Andrew B. Lewis provoked me above and beyond the call of copyeditor. Roger Haydon, editor at Cornell University Press, was a great advocate.

Finally, there are some people who read all of this book, or some of it, or none of it, but whose critical presence and care allowed me to conjure them up as the second person in this confused narrative. Margaret Groesbeck and Michael Kasper are the secret weapons of scholarship at Amherst College's Frost Library. My conversations with Fred Dolan on the idea of America are reflected on every page of this book. Austin Sarat's boundless energy and critical commentary exhausted me and renewed me at every stage of this book's development. Bob Gooding-Williams provided an example of grace and intellectual even-temperedness and consistently asked the hardest questions. Marie-Hélène Huet invited me to teach two seminars with her and provided me with an extraordinary education, even though she found me an incorrigible student.

Four individuals were constant personal and telephonic presences during the composition of this book. Bonnie Honig took time from her own work on a remarkable book—*Political Theory and the Displacement of Politics*—to give me a keen ear and much advice on the presentation of self and argument. George Kateb has been a particularly useful irritant, not only shouting at me on the telephone but traveling all the way to Amherst College from his home in the wastelands of New Jersey to pound a few fundamentals about Emerson into my still-too-thick head. As a consequence, this book is more an argument with him than it once was. William E. Connolly, the general editor of this series, read every page of this manuscript and has listened patiently to my unformed thoughts on subjects present in this work for ten years now. I think of this book as a product of our friendship. Finally, Brenda Bright took me to the places, geographically and ontologically, that made it possible to write what is here.

As for the dedication, it is made to one of my teachers.

T.L.D.

Amherst, Massachusetts

united states

Introduction

Dream delivers us to dream,
and there is no end to illusion.

—Ralph Waldo Emerson

In this book I make a series of related claims about elements of popular desire and their expression in the words and acts of some representative citizens of the United States of America. I trace some connections between the American political unconscious and the governing representations of public culture. In what I hope is a contrast to the claims of those who represent power or who mirror the desires of those who are deemed powerful, I want to make visible the outline of a political ethics that resists the privilege of dispassionate judgment. I do so to suggest ways for those of us who are so inclined to explore the possibilities for a reinvigorated democratic life.

I want to pose a question, which I hope will lead to many others: How might we break down barriers to the reinvigoration of democracy in our corporate polity? For many advocates of democracy the task is primarily public in character. If we could make laws to break the dominance of corporate capital, if we could devise mechanisms to redistribute adequately the goods necessary for democratic life, if we could create policies to temper majoritarian impulses with love of neighbor, if we could endorse a pedagogy to teach how liberal values can cultivate a democratic culture that enables the fullest bloom of our potential as citizens and subjects, then we would be able to overcome the barriers presented by the power of factions and the corrosive effects of the cumulative inequalities of our age.

I am not unsympathetic to the work done and the positions held by these various and sometimes conflicting advocates of democracy. I am fortunate to have been an apprentice to the thinking of a few of the people responsible for advancing the democratic ethos in our time. But the path I have chosen to take in this book is premised on another aspect of the democratic impulse—that which begins as an intuition and only later finds its justification as a method. I intend to explore the possibility for democratic rejuvenation through a project of making the personal political, by emphasizing elements of our common experience in which the political is also personal. I think this project may be of particular value now, a tract of time when the boundaries between public and private spheres of life are effaced and reasserted in contemporary American political culture as a matter of explicit political strategy and tactic. Selective boundary crossing, I assert, is the primary strategy of corporate power brokers. But it also informs the variety of tactical responses to the damage inflicted on our lives by the commodification of private existence, which remains a signal achievement of late capitalism.

I believe that it is at the level of the tactical, in the spaces where the commonplace events that inform how we are obliged to one another occur, that the democratic ethos to which I aspire may most fully engage and energize liberal values. Liberalism, especially in its least fearful forms, has always placed individual rights over and above all other political values because liberals have believed not only that individuals are best able to live good lives when autonomous, but also that autonomy, freedom in its fullest sense, is what enables the development of a culture that is substantively democratic. But the mutual plight of liberalism and democracy is that each has failed to energize the other, as liberals have claimed could happen and democrats have hoped. In our united states, liberalism is but the triumph of privatism, and democracy a mere and unimaginative insistence upon equality.

As an aspiring liberal democrat I seek to reconnect liberalism and democracy to see if any sparks can still be generated from the contact of each with the other. I see this effort as another way of connecting the personal to the political.

In response to those who manage our phantom public sphere, some people have been preparing us to be more receptive to a form of criticism that would dare to describe how personal life is shaped by and gives shape to political life. Most who have done so, so far, have felt that they had little left to lose by remaining silent, and a world to gain by exposing private stratagems of power as enacted on them. We might recall that the passionate exposure of private life in our time, indeed the very slogan "The personal is the political," comes to us primarily from the feminist movement, and feminists of various persuasions have been most convincing in showing the need to take seriously the connections between private and public life.

But my exploration of the connections between the personal and the political differs from the similar explorations of many feminists, primarily as a consequence of my different position. The feminist writers I admire have, for the most part, operated from positions inferior to those whose positions of power they challenge. Although I share some of the political views of those who are relatively powerless in their approach to our united states (and here I think most readily of some of the work of Patricia Williams),[1] I understand my position to be one of relative power or complicity with the powerful. It seems to me to be of value to the democratic project to analyze the politics of power from inside, so to speak, from the perspective of men in the superior position.

In my pursuit of such a project I have learned that the lines of public and private power often become blurred and that the very idea of a meaningful separation of public and private spheres comes into question. Although the viability of a public sphere has been repeatedly subjected to skeptical appraisal in this polity since Walter Lippmann and other Progressives raised it as an issue early in this century,[2] less attention has been paid to the establishment of what might be dubbed the phantom *private* sphere. I seek to understand what has happened to render so fragile that private sphere, and yet also to understand how its imaginary force in contemporary life as a means toward a better democratic culture is so pervasive. I wish to conjure up an image of the private that might give you access to its fugitive meanings. Hence, this book is written by me for you, my imaginary companion in this exploration of our common culture, to pose to you my questions about how we have come to be who we are.

I am acutely aware that by mediating the private through my own experience of it, I risk appearing narcissistic, merely projecting onto you an image of who I think *I* am to achieve that peculiar self-validation some find by performing for an audience. I know that no disclaimer on my part can reassure you to the contrary. Moreover, paradoxically, I know of no other responsible way to represent the effects of a political culture that at this point in its history, could fairly be described as suffering from a sort of hegemonic narcissism. American narcissism, in its political effects, seems to consist of a studied ignorance of how representations of the (highly problematic) public sphere are effective to the extent that they refer to and stimulate private images of power, security, and the satisfaction of resentment for those who find themselves in superior positions.[3] So in projecting myself onto the material with which I work in this book, I hope to provide you with a way of thinking through the project of who you are in reference to those of us who share this dangerous condition.

If you read this book, then you will (unavoidably) learn something about me, perhaps more than you might wish. Of course, such is the risk one takes by reading any book. But I also would remind you that the "me" you will learn about is itself fictive and partial. I am fictive in the sense that I believe that my self-understanding is mediated through the representations that compose me. To vulgarize Lacan, there is no "me" without a mirror. That this experience of self is alienated I take as the starting point for a series of exercises in learning to (re)compose my self politically. I am partial first in the sense that I am incomplete, and I am incomplete because I am not yet dead, because (to use words I have drawn from reading Emerson) experience has kept the circle from closing, because compensation remains possible for me, and because, for all my striving, I can only touch on, not surround or fully illuminate the self that I still wish to know. I am a man, not a woman, I am straight, not gay, I am white, not black. For every part of me that is, there is another part that is not. And yet every one of these assertions is itself not completely true. Knowledge of this doubly incomplete character of my life (as an American, but also as a modern subject) informs whatever insights I might offer you. I think that this sense of incompletion is still available to all of us as a part of our cultural experience in united states. It is a part of the liberal-democratic heritage from which we might all draw.

Less important is the other element of my partiality, which is my political bias, as a member of the generic party of radical discontent. My sense of discontent limits my perspective. But I also see my political bias as an example of perspectivism in a deeper sense, as a phenomenon first made famous by Friedrich Nietzsche. The general philosophical problem raised by perspectivism is that of nihilism, or the deep meaninglessness humans confront as a consequence of being human. Perspectivism becomes a political problem especially for those who seek a universalist position from which to render judgments. And since the Enlightenment at least, this quest for position has been identified with the project of normative political thought. Hence, perspectivism has been under sustained attack of late, associated with such phenomena as multiculturalism and identity politics, and for some commentators linked causally to the excesses that lead to totalitarianism.[4] The claims recurrently made by those who repudiate perspectivism in the name of objective reality, who rail against the demons of multiculturalism and political correctness in the name of national unity and pledging allegiance to the flag of core values, strike me as disingenuous, advanced from the partial positions of political actors who end by claiming that their particular perspective is universal and commands obedience. In other words, perspectivism is a *shared* condition. We are *all* human, all too human. Hence, I work to oppose the political oppression that is the practical consequence of such pledges of allegiance to universalist principles, whether they are embraced by George Bush or Michael Walzer, Bill Clinton or Catharine MacKinnon. This book might be read as an exercise in opposition to the claims of those who would order the rest of us to be democrats rather than join in the fun and pain of learning how to be democrats.

In my opposition I am relieved to have the resources of a particular tradition of American letters available as a force of reassurance when I am scorned or ignored. I have chosen a phrase from Emerson as an epigraph, not because I would claim to be a latter-day saint of transcendentalism, but because I think that it might be possible for us to live in Emerson's America as an alternative experience of our culture. Although I think that we can be delivered from dream to dream, I do not think that such a possibility is necessarily comforting. Precisely because deliverance remains a possibility, I would not rely on Emerson as a voice of solace. I would not, for instance, focus on the uselessness of experience that seems to flow from his insight into it.[5] Or to be more awkward, but also more accurate, I would not believe that the uselessness of experience is as useless as I think he sometimes thought.

In contrast, it is on the surface of things that I believe we can learn how to be democrats. But this too is a lesson that one might learn from an encounter with Emerson. When he wrote, "I know better than to claim any completeness for my picture. I am a fragment, and this is a fragment of me," he gave form and words to the experience I wish to limn, even as he seemed to resist its import for himself.[6] But Emerson did not want to make himself ridiculous by trying to realize his ideas in the world of experience: he worried about becoming the worst sort of democrat, one who foams at the mouth and hates and denies. His reticence was, I think, unfortunate, even if he ultimately overcame it in times of crisis. I do not intend to be so quiet, in part because I think the American crisis continues and has spread to less readily identifiable sites than those Emerson was able to confront in overcoming his fear of abandoning the project of self-reliance.

In being so noisy, so hypothetically extreme, I may be going *too* far, as I was occasionally warned while I was composing this book. But I would argue that few of us who have taken upon ourselves the responsibility of thinking about the politics of American society have gone far enough in recent years toward identifying the maladies that have undermined democratic life. To go too far, what does that mean? How does one move past the boundaries that hold us so firmly in place, as we gradually melt under the heat of our troubles, without going too far? How does one begin to explore the rich possibilities of democratic life if one won't risk offending those who would pretend either that life is easily repaired, who would, I guess, suggest that we live in the best of all possible worlds, or who have decided that there is no remedy at all, that a mournful, knowing weariness is the most suitable posture in this drawn-out approach to the fin de millennium?

But it is my intention that the excesses you might find in this book be the result less of anger at complacence or resignation than of hope for, among other things, better laughter. I think that the imaginative project of representing the political experience of our united states, if undertaken without a sense of the absurd, both misses something essential about this culture (its humor) and contributes to its most dangerous pretension (its seriousness). If you find moments of truth in this book, I want them to occur when you are laughing, if not aloud, then to yourself, or at least when you are feeling something.

Even so, it is a complicated matter, this question of our laughter, because laughter is also a bridge to the violence that composes the plot through which we live together. I once thought this book would be about the character of our violence, that it would be no more or less than a study of how we love to hate. But now I know a bit better, and hence do not dare make such extravagant claims. Instead I would note only that our violence seems to be inevitably associated with a desire to create a coherent narrative of life, and that it intensifies as life becomes less comprehensible. In that sense, violence is not a theme of this book, but the atmosphere with which it is imbued.

The chapters of this book are intended to be read in sequence, but surely they will not be by all its readers. That's fair. I didn't write them in sequence, that is, not in this sequence, for the final arrangement of the book is not even mine, even though the pagination represents my last attempt to impose a narrative that will expose my partial understanding of the connections between public and private life. To the extent that I succeed in my efforts here, it will be not because you agree with what I have to say, but only because you recognize that what I have to say might contain an element of truth and what *that* might mean for all of us as we approach the end of the American century.

One last note. To the extent that it is consistent—even if small-minded, *pace* Emerson—this book is written, for better or worse, from the perspective of someone who has not tried to distance himself from certain stereotypes concerning American experience. Its meaning may thus be more of a puzzle the further from the stereotypical experience you might be. For those of you who are not American citizens or residents, or even better, who feel as though you somehow have evaded the American dream, I suggest that you read this as an introduction to American studies, as an explanation for our intrusion. You may be able to measure your distance from our dream by the extent of your estrangement from its more radical manifestations.

CHAPTER ONE

Dear Laurie Anderson

In our country, Goodbye looks just like Hello.

—Laurie Anderson

Dear Laurie Anderson,

I am writing to you about our united states.

I am writing to you because your united states have intersected mine. From your vision of our power and disconnection I have learned something that I want to share with you. When we are apart we oppose power to freedom. But when we reach united states, we shout about the power of freedom, even as we whisper secrets about the variety of crimes that freedom requires of us. We have failed in many ways. But I have learned from you that our worst offenses against ourselves and one another have been imaginary. There is no health in us. Our united states are the results of strange combinations and fearful disruptions. Because we pretend that we can unite through freedom, we are actually free to unite. And when we are united, we have trouble imagining what it would be like to be apart. But united states—yours, mine, ours, theirs—are always temporary; we live in constant fear that we will separate. The moments we fear that we could never survive being alone are the moments we discover that we have always been separate and alone.

I am writing to you because you have thought through the pun of this country. You have shown me how to think about how *united states* defines that which it names. We are united states, we seek to be united, we seek those states in which we can enjoy the illusion of being united. The power of united states derives in part from how we are exposed to the truth of fragility and temporality on the very surface of that to which we pledge allegiance.

I am writing to you because your voice is calm and electric.

I am writing to you because I worry that our pretense is killing us. There is an early death lurking in the heart of our states of attraction to one another and that early death becomes invisible when we enter our united states. We find ourselves tempted to kill to keep from dying. Yet we keep dying anyway.

I am writing to you because in this age of disenchantment we share a condition, and we share a state of mind. I have reached this common state of mind with you because I want to be a fan of yours, which means that in a peculiar sense, one unique to cultures of fanatic spectators, I seek to be you, that in seeking to escape who I am, I want to place myself inside your head. My fanaticism reflects my desire to return to a place of peace, and it has me seeking you out, seeking your approval. But as great as you are in my own peculiar imaginary, even my admiration and my fanatic fascination for you, my learned stupidity, doesn't help me overcome my fear. Every time I think about our united states I imagine that I am risking a literal enactment of early death. I am anxious, neurotic, just another narcissistic American man. Every time I want to face up to our problems I think that to do so would require an act of renunciation, a pious wish to expiate the secular sin of our imaginary flight from reality through the peculiar political intercourse that substitutes unification for interaction.

I am writing to you because, in imitation of you, I want to be brave. We live not really in a land of the brave, but in a brave land, and because the land is brave we have not needed to be brave ourselves. I think that to learn how to be brave we must be cut off from our means of escape, we must allow the fear that would dissipate in the force of our flight (from our selves, from one another) to build in intensity instead. I hope that by keeping you in mind I will not allow myself means of escape, that the power of your work will in fact serve to *prevent* me from becoming a fan of yours, that you will inspire this study of united states by teaching bravery.

I am writing to you because I think it is a good time for us to think about who we are, together, rather than apart.

I am writing to you because I want to be well, or at least better. I seek clues concerning our affliction. I read manuals of hope, I seek instruction on our plight. I seek a cure for this disease of symptoms.[1] I seek a chemotherapy for my soul. For we are living in a world where symptoms are diseases, where appearances are realities, where acts of constitution depend on fabulous assertions regarding past circumstances (which provide the confidence we need to assure their projection into the future). Hence, we never know who we are.

I am writing to you because your performances gesture toward the hope that if we could begin to see this latency in the words and phrases through which we constitute our selves, we might be able, if only momentarily, to step aside from the path of our most familiar thoughts, and begin to move to new states of independence.[2] You're not the first to try to tune in through the static of the quotidian to clarify a truth about our condition. It doesn't comfort me much to recognize that the attempt to do so is almost always initiated in those moments of confusion which have the potential to deepen into a more fundamental perplexity. We might, say some, be distracted by our confusion, when the answer is simple—move on, will yourself into being, or, as an alternative, follow a code, submit to a higher power, get into a twelve-step program.

I am writing to you because you evade the stability of our dominant codes of identity as you seek to open us to democratic possibilities. If we make statements that, in retrospect, we can identify as having started something (performatives that fabulously transubstantiate into constatives), in our moment of crisis we can offer our perplexity to one another. I want to work through my confusion, my perplexity as a student of politics. I begin with the hope that to be perplexed can lead one to the presence of paradox, and that if we can learn to inhabit the paradoxical, we might better understand how we unite.

I am writing to you because in your art you successfully evade identification, and many of our most urgent political paradoxes have arisen with attempts to fix identities.[3] The most urgent political activities are too often associated with remedial, not creative, gestures. Exhausted from our great visible moments of founding, we fail to acknowledge the politics of initiation in our own time. We struggle to fix things, but we do not understand how we might begin again other than by fixing things. What might it mean to "fix"? We might repair what is thought to be broken; we might try to stabilize, to set into place something that has been disordered; we might neuter something; we might take a fix, a dose of a drug or other addictive substance in order to feel good and defer the onset of withdrawal. Each way in which we might fix identity has advocates today. Each way of fixing might be known as a response to as well as a cause of our illness of symptoms. Each seeks to preserve something in the way we reach and sustain our united states. And of course because our lives overlap, so too do our ways of fixing things.

I am writing to you because you, perhaps more than most, know the violence that hides in voices urging repair and reconciliation. Within such voices there is a dangerous tension. The strains placed on our identities by our crisis seem to compel those who bear our most visible and powerful identities to intensify their efforts to maintain coherence. They thus precipitate all sorts of harmful exercises of repression as they seek to preserve the habits of life from which they once gained solace. They confuse life in general with their particular identification and do damage to both. In their earlier incarnations identities may have seemed coherent and full of purpose, may have issued forth a certain sovereignty, or at least adhered to a settled place within some order. Those who hold on to a past that ignored the pain on which those identities were built may seek no more than to maintain themselves, but in so doing they become something altogether different from what they putatively seek to preserve. In becoming defensive, they become reactionary. Rather than break from the ways of doing things that have taken them so far into the stories of their lives, they deepen their reliance on old ways. In so doing, they conjure up all sorts of symptoms, which come to constitute our disease. This is how our dissent became acquiescence, this is how radicals became neoconservatives. This is how the generation of the 1960s came to condemn the generation that arose after its bitter defeats, helping them turn into what their parents feared. This is how the children of the 1960s became the amnesiacs of the 1990s.

But not you. You have put the American identity crisis on display. The idea of an identity crisis is not unusual—who among all of us never doubts who he or she might be, and who among us does not, at some point, blame our parents, and then deny having done so?—but most of us are not performance artists like you, and most of us seek to distinguish between the personal sovereignty of individual identity and the political order we inhabit. I want to tell the people who think about these things in ignorance of your work about their poverty of imagination. I want to enlist you in an effort to reimagine and re(dis)cover democracy in America.

Many years ago when you posed as a skater on blocks of ice playing the violin, and played until the ice blocks melted, I was unsettled and comforted.[4] I did not know why then, but now I think I do. In a public square you alchemized a shining confidence from the darkest resources of the American constitutional soul. I was upset, I think, because the image you enacted violated a prime separation of private and public inscribed by those who founded our united states. Did you ever worry that someone would come along and carry you away? Did you ever worry that the ice would never melt? Constitutional government has had as one of its primary attractions the separation of public and private spheres in order to facilitate united states. Separation has been made to assure good citizens that a gap will always exist between the political and the personal, that the ice that separates them will never melt. Our politics has consisted of boundary maintenance, famously heroized in *Federalist* 10 and lamented by many political theorists. It has promised an unbounded freedom, as long as the ice remains frozen. This coldness is attractive to all of us, in part because each of us can understand (and undermine) it in our own ways. (Even postmodern porno-nihilistic plagiarists like Kathy Acker, another performance artist, seek shelter in our separations when the exercise of freedom is threatened by governments in other places, say, in Great Britain.)[5]

In the world of what they would call politics proper, defenders of the liberal art of separation still acknowledge the subtle connections between procedures of constitutional democracy and the "morals" of the citizenry.[6] In his most recent study of Constitutionalism, the legal philosopher Bruce Ackerman goes so far as to argue that our national government has undergone several transformations that have resituated the meaning of freedom in response to crises that deeply involved issues of personal identity.[7] The abolition of slavery was a disruption of contract, and the development of governmental regulation and direct intervention into the lives of individuals was enabled by further abridgement of the private sphere. Ackerman persuasively traces many of these changes through a reading of constitutional *law*. His claim for the theory of dualist democracy, that there are times in which constitutional politics takes precedence over "ordinary" politics, delimiting the range of future possibilities, makes a great deal of sense, after the last crisis has been resolved.

But those future halcyon days are never upon us. Ackerman, brandishing the Constitution, provides no guidance to how we are even to know when we are in crisis. He can't, I think, because we cannot remember days of peace. Crisis is normal. All crises of national security are reduced, eventually, to the normal. And because so many legal thinkers have absorbed the normalcy of crisis, of late they have tended to forget that the law is but one instrument among many for ordering life in a democratic culture, and that the law will do nothing to cure us of the disease that has no symptom. Nonetheless, we call on law to save us now. This dependence on law is yet another thing to worry about, because dependence devolves, and we shall end up relying on the most brutish elements of it. Law in its most blatantly repressive guise, law that can only say no.[8]

Why do these abstract formulations infuriate me so? Because you are sensitive to how abstractions cover for power, I think you might know why. And this is also why I want to enlist your help. I want to find a way to neutralize this resort to law. I want to be able to think about a different constitutionalism, one premised on the notion that we can experience the Constitution together best by acknowledging that although the dilemmas of representative democracy often appear to be resolved through legal processes, the law is but one of the registers, creative and destructive, through which constitution proceeds. Our boisterous civil society—you on skates frozen into blocks of ice, playing the violin on the streets of one of our great downtowns—is itself an argument against seeking an explanation for the meaning of politics in the narrow turf of officially politicized matters, especially in the exclusion of alternatives to right-wing corporatism that has marked the past two decades of official public life.[9] The life of democracy continues into the age of dysfunctional families from the hills of Arkansas, even if Bill Clinton left Hope behind long ago.

That so many of us have so often misconstrued Constitutional law as the hard core of the law of constitution might be attributable to the hegemony of liberalism in political life since independence. But that mistake has not impeded the flow of all sorts of constitutive activities in our democratic culture, in the culture of what George Kateb has called "democratic individuality."[10] You have explored precisely the realm of constitutional experience that exceeds positive law, that operates in confluence with and in opposition to law, and that most fully informs the current crisis in domestic life.

But even so, some things are easier for artists, I am convinced. The discipline of art, in our age, operates as a salve, if not a salvation for too many artists.[11] But you have been different, ruthlessly taking as your material the banalities of our domestic lives. Our puns, our prejudices, our cold desires compose the networks of meaning you guide us through. This why I write to you.

How are we to live together under the circumstances that tear us apart? That is our crisis, and that is what I am writing to you about. But it is also my topos, it is also my life and yours, which means that I have decided not to efface the turmoil I feel, or the turbulence that shapes whatever insight I can bring to these matters, in the name of political theory. I must address you, even as I know that most likely you will be constructed in my own image, a reflection of my distorted hopes. You will not be a neutral judge, a genderless being, even as you negotiate our gendered paths of desire and loathing. But perhaps you will be fuzzy on the edges, deformed, conglomerated, not quite a progeny of monstrous imagination, but close enough for me. I look and I see and I write this epistle on our crisis from an ambivalent political position, one that will unfold as you and I trade places, blend and separate, and, I hope, move slightly beyond our predetermined positions.

I apologize for waiting so long. It is a letter that has been too long in preparation for such transient conclusions as might be lodged here. But that is a risk I will take, and hope that whatever elements of this report that become dated will at least serve as a historical document from a particular time and place. After all, as you know better than I do, we live in a system of representation that depends for its efficacy on a secular faith in reality. Wired, our geography is a system of overlapping grids that steadily and unceasingly proffers electronic communion to each of us. Alexander Graham Bell hoped to reach the dead by telephone, but we know that the dead are potent ghosts.[12] Every telephone, every television monitor, every cable (of light) illuminates the presence of our ghosts, buried under layer after layer of unspeakable language. These grids succeed and supplement the Interstate Highway system, which is in turn the successor and supplement to the great railroad system, laid over Mr. Jefferson's townships, modeled in part on William Penn's city of brotherly love, Philadelphia having been the materialization of the imaginary desire of George Fox to represent an orderly soul who would welcome God's Inner Light, preparing our bodies as vestibules in the House of the Lord. These grids shape the warp and woof of our experience, they are the intersections that unite our states, the places where we find ourselves, and in due course, lose ourselves. Our landscape is marked as surely as our bodies by the history of an imaginary desire—e pluribus unum.

Sure, the personal is the political. Your art is premised on this deceptively straightforward thesis. But when thinking about these matters I can see you try to hold both person and politics up to question, asking how the meanings of both have migrated in our times, and have become suffused in shifts in the powers that they represent. Our bodies document the effects of such power, but we have not yet learned how to read the document.

(I see the electric bulb of light within your smile. I see its dangerous parody of blackface, the heat from within, shining through.)

The personal is political in another sense as well. We are pained into existence, we suffer our punishments, as it were, automatically, a result of being in the world. In fact, though it seems human to pretend otherwise, punishment precedes action. We become who we are through processes that separate us in order to make us known, even to ourselves. This quasi-fundamental element of coming into being as a self, a mode relied on to make sense of life, operates close to the surface in our united states, because as adults our range of mobility, the looseness of our connections, the possibilities for our retreats into a comfortable, less than desperate vagabondage lie close to the surface of experience. We know our violence viscerally, in the casual gestures of gangsters and cowboys, in the sinister flickering of smooth criminals, projected on screens in the dark, casting their shadows deep into our culture.

I am writing to ask you: What sort of innocence do we seek to protect?

It is a transitional question, I suppose. Have you ever heard of Louis Hartz, the great theorist of American exceptionalism, who believed that we Americans have always avoided the knowledge that might threaten to end our innocence?[13] Indeed, our most deeply reactionary sense of identity is cloaked in the (dis)guise of mobility and movement, activities not immediately associated with reaction. But Hartz understood that the liberal consensus of movement under which we have prospered and sometimes suffered was bought at a price that includes the repression of alternative voices and the stultification of what might be called a cosmopolitan worldview. In fact, his work is an extended lament concerning the naïveté or immaturity of his fellow citizens. In its most important arguments his major book, *The Liberal Tradition in America*, highlights the conditions under which a polity might be able to grow without maturing, expand while protecting a studied ignorance concerning the ends of power. In this sense, even the deeply illiberal politics of the past decade have been a part of the liberal tradition. The country in which you and I struggle to compose our lives, as it begins to decline in power on the stage of the world, is in a state of arrested development. Such an arrested development has not been wholly negative—it may have contributed to the end of chattel slavery, if one considers chattel slavery to be a decadent reflection of a particular kind of maturity. But the costs of arrested development are great, nonetheless.

It has been difficult to acknowledge the important consequences that follow from Hartz's suggestion that our fundamental innocence is a consequence of flight. We don't want to think of ourselves in that way. But there it is. For Hartz it was a quintessential part of our character. He emphasized that our English forbears fled Europe rather than stay and fight for their beliefs. And we haven't stopped running. The fate of our revolution has been constantly deferred because we haven't stopped running. He meant this when he wrote,

> Revolution, to borrow the words of T. S. Eliot, means to murder and create, but the American experience has been projected strangely in the realm of creation alone. The destruction of forests and Indian tribes— heroic, bloody, legendary as it was—cannot be compared with the destruction of a social order to which one belongs oneself. The first experience is wholly external and can be completed; the second experience is an inner struggle as well as an outer struggle, like the slaying of a Freudian father, and goes on in a sense, forever.[14]

What would it take to fold the experience of outward destruction inward? How might the decline that this confrontation represents be . . . declined? And then, how could we terminate the analysis of slaughter, complete our mourning for the loss of our beloved, and learn how to extricate ourselves from the melancholia that accompanies our violence? The colonizers of North America solved their first political problem by establishing distance from what they thought was its source. Hence, all subsequent political conflict might be said to have proceeded from strategies by which difference might be turned into distance. In this way, all perceived threats to the autonomy of the polity have been made external. So we have a long way to go once we stop running away. If we stop running away.

I am writing to you because you have stopped running. Of course, your fate and mine hinge on whom we consider the bearers of the innocence that emerges from guilt. Who killed off the Indian tribes? I didn't and you didn't, and yet because we reap the benefits of their slaughter, our responsibility inhabits the silence I maintain in the face of my advantage. Who is responsible for the blood profit of chattel slavery? Lincoln prayed for the nation that the death and suffering of the Civil War would be expiation enough, but we know better now than to pray, don't we? We also know that the responsibility rests lightly upon us, a consequence of our mobility, of the paradoxical lightness with which we wear our identities. Our complex innocence, our Americanness, is rooted in an impulse to keep fear outside our souls. In short, it would seem that to understand how we have avoided responsibility for the violence of establishing our sovereignty requires that we come to terms with the complex innocence that departs from guilt.[15] This complicated transformation of guilt into innocence is responsible for the particular texture of the freedom we share with other Americans, and is the model for the specific cruelty of the politics we practice.

Often our politicians make spectacular gestures toward revolution. But because they realize that revolution would put at risk the pleasures we derive from our united states, their gestures have a quality of unreality about them or, to be more specific, suffer from an absence of the reality principle. Although we want our politicians to make such gestures, we hope that they are empty promises, even when they are kept. We will kill rather than revolt. We like to think that if our soldiers don't die we will not suffer. We like to think we can forget about the bodies we bury alive in the desert. But that is not how the world works. No bodies remain buried in our united states. They come back to us as nightmares that never fail to incite more violence. After the recent war we prosecuted in the Persian Gulf—our most recent as I write, by the usual measurements of war—the hollowness of our incitement to violence has become more apparent. This is true even in the wake of (or perhaps especially because of) the devastation that we wrought on the people of Iraq. We have failed to understand what is at stake for those who would revolt, and those who would live after such revolutions.[16] Even those who attempt to resist such an epithet as "patriot" betray a peculiarly naive allegiance to our liberalism in refusing to consider the "trouble" that revolutionary aspirations might raise. In this our bearers of revolution engage in the same tactics as those of us who have been complacent in the face of our horrible acts. We are no revolutionaries, if ever we were. Our common inability to think about the consequences of slaying suggests that even in killing, we try to kill innocently.

But our murderous innocence is not limited to how we forget our cruelties in our ongoing celebration of the present. Innocence inhabits our diversions, our entertainments, our accidents and social lives. Sometimes, it seems that only performance artists like you and novelists like Don DeLillo enable us to traverse the separations that prevent us from connecting, or folding into, the variety of experiences that make up our domestic lives. In *White Noise*, DeLillo presents a character who teaches a seminar on car crashes. His students see these crashes as symbolic of the drive to suicide, but this professor—who specializes in the study of Elvis—imbues them with life. He says, "I see these car crashes as part of a long tradition of American optimism. . . . It is not decay they are seeing but innocence. . . . It is a conservative wish-fulfillment, a yearning for naïveté. We want to be artless again. We want to reverse the flow of experience, of worldliness and its responsibilities. . . . These are days," he says, "of secular optimism."[17]

DeLillo takes us to an intersection, a site where we unite, and evokes the bloody accidents that occur in the careless crossing of lines. He sketches, in miniature, the profound horror that underlies our complex innocence, which seems to take the form of nostalgia as we approach the end of the millennium.[18] Our secular optimism is achieved by overcoming a sacral investment. DeLillo thus implicitly connects us to Robert Johnson's great blues song "Crossroads," the urtext of all rock-n-roll, which is to say the fountain of our contemporary popular culture. Johnson's song provides a glimpse of the satanic exchange we have made, that which inspires all contemporary visions of wreckage by inciting us to destruction in the name of a beautiful death. Johnson's crossroads, DeLillo's intersection, suddenly, in the heart of the 1980s, became your home.

Thank you for receiving this. I know that I have gone on too long. But how else could I begin to think about united states, unless I wrote a letter to you, who so recently have broken the code through which it has preserved its mysteries?

So what is it I am sending? I would call it an experience-book. "An experience," Michel Foucault once said, "is, of course, something one has alone; but it cannot have its full impact unless the individual manages to escape from pure subjectivity in such a way that others can—I won't say re-experience it exactly—but at least cross paths with it or retrace it."[19] Whose experience is this? Of course it is mine. But perhaps it will touch a nerve in you as well. And I can imagine the possibility that you might not know who you are either. Indeed, I want to show you this process of discovery, I hope to entice you to read, if only out of curiosity. My wish is yours. I do not wish to remain unchanged, nor do I wish you to remain the same.

Are you there? I only know that I am writing as though you are. I need to connect with you, to share an uncertain yet intimate voice, to take the risk that we have failed to take. It is no small irony that our polity is so deeply committed to the idea that the personal is the political that we demonstrate it in every attempt we make to separate persons from politics. To break the barrier imposed by those blocks of ice need not mean that we must engage in the subjective solipsism that haunts the memoirs of our culture. Instead, it might mean that we should try to learn about each other as we undergo our changes. Such an effort entails a certain risk, but it is a small one, given the larger risks we take with each other every day, given the violence we do to each other and others in attaining united states.

So I will tell you as I begin that I want to neutralize the field of memory that presents the past nostalgically. I want to admit the violence inherent in our meetings, our collisions, the joy that attends our car crashes. I want to examine the darkness inherent in our imagination of unity. I want to examine some of the conditions that allow and disallow our attempts to connect. What does it matter that I have wanted to do this for a long time, and that I believe that the accumulated effects of our various attempts to unite have resulted in a crisis that has stirred in me this urgent wish to begin by writing to you? My voice is fictive, my technique a series of more or less imaginative leaps. It matters not at all that I have this desire. I am but one of millions, and as a friend has suggested, our theories are but mist and snow.

Are you there? I would like to think you are listening, and I will pretend, in my innocence, you are.

Goodbye. . . .

Hello.

CHAPTER TWO

Judith Shklar, or
Fear of Liberalism

We fear a society of fearful people.

—Judith Shklar

Liberalism and Condemning Judgments

What stigmatizes our vision, even as it has come to extend so widely, so deeply, and so powerfully? From time to time we experience dread. I believe this dread is a consequence of the conflict between our seemingly infinite capacity for vision and the anxiety that accompanies our knowledge of infinity. This observation is hardly original. One of the best political theorists of our time, Sheldon Wolin, has taken up the theme of vision as his subject in order to understand the sweep of "Western" political thought through the ages.[1] A multitude of thinkers have contributed to the writing about vision, for better and for worse. But perhaps the time of vision is coming to a close, even as time itself becomes more fungible.

Our success in the field of domination has enabled us to ignore the ways in which we cannot see. Although we become most confused when we look back for a place of origin and see nothing, our ignorance of the past is not the worst of our vision problems. More important, we are blind to the present. We are like Herman Melville's whales, blind to the great middle, even as we swim in it.

But it is also true that the extremity of our vision most obviously reveals the outline of our commonality. Our extremity is especially apparent in reference to those condemnations through which we evade what we have made. That condemnation is a technique of control. If liberal innocence departs from guilt, perhaps we should also keep in mind that there is a complex relationship between guilt and condemnation as well, that "condemnation keeps at a distance, along with the condemned, the question of what it is that made their guilt possible."[2] The blindness in the middle of liberalism is associated with its condemnatory judgments. Our judgments obscure the practices we have spawned. I do not want to claim that we are hypocrites, we liberals. We are not so subtle. But I do want to think about some of the consequences of our blindness.

We suffer from our blindness most obviously when we condemn cruelty. I want to look at our condemnation of cruelty closely. Judith Shklar condemns cruelty, especially in her famous formulations concerning the liberalism of fear.[3] Her writings illuminate the strongest possible case for what might be termed an unreconstructed version of liberalism. Moreover, her liberalism is American in yet another way. Her work focuses closely on the importance of slavery for understanding political experience; she argues powerfully about the persistence of injustice and its relationship to contingency; and she characterizes voting and earning as crucial components of democratic citizenship.[4]

This admixture of slavery, physical pain, and longing underlies almost all of our political representations and distributions. I believe that flowing through the constitution, running the tumultuous machinery of governance, are the hate and love shaped by these elements of experience. They are intertwined in a battle of opposition, as the character Radio Hakeem described with his fists in Spike Lee's movie *Do the Right Thing*.

So I want to think with Shklar even as I object to her voice. I realize that I come into conversation with Shklar late and begrudgingly, and I think she would oppose even my reconstruction of her voice here. But if I err in my criticism of her work, at least I criticize.[5] It is sad to realize that Shklar's work has not been criticized; in that silence her admirers have not honored her. But for those who think that this is a time when free individuality is being contested in new ways that confound older liberal aspirations, to think about the traditional mode of characterizing dangers to that individuality in an uncritical manner becomes an exercise in nostalgia. Nostalgia is possibly most acute in this most liberal society, where we have disseminated most widely the technological forms of expression that have so strongly influenced contemporary world culture, and have left our formulations concerning the autonomy of selfhood untouched.[6]

Shklar insists that fear, injustice, and citizenship stand at the heart of liberalism. She develops a unified argument concerning these different dimensions of liberalism. But because of her faith in the power of liberal unity, Shklar does not consider the possibility that the primary threat to citizenship might be found in the very forces that protect citizenship, techniques that undermine civil society even as they enable it by incorporating its practices into a political order that must deny what it claims to support. If what Michel Foucault has called governmentality persistently disrupts the field of freedom described by Shklar and other liberals, then we must think again, and again, until it hurts, about the cruelty that resides within the liberalism of fear. Although the issue is one of reflection on one's own practices, for me it is also one of the style of thought that encourages the politics of condemnation of what we have made. It may be that fear is driving us away from a freedom that would enable us better to live within and even modify the political ethics that govern us.

Tolerance/Justice/Citizenship

Shklar begins her most sustained discussion of the liberalism of fear with the suggestion that liberalism itself has but one overriding aim, "to secure the political conditions that are necessary for the exercise of freedom," by which she means that "every adult should be able to make as many effective decisions without fear or favor about as many aspects of her or his life as is compatible with the like freedom of every other adult."[7] But, she then notes, the conditions necessary for the exercise of freedom rarely have been given up to modern people.[8] For Shklar it is crucial to identify liberalism under the conditions of its historical emergence and stultification. Otherwise, one will remain ignorant of its resources and limits and confused about its relationship to other, sometimes closely linked, phenomena.

The most important mistake people make when thinking about the history of liberalism, Shklar thinks, is to identify liberalism with modernity. This mistake is common because one of the foundations of liberalism, toleration, emerged during the era that contemporary thinkers associate with the origins of modernity in the West. This error leads people to misconstrue the liberalism of fear, because the liberalism of fear is rooted in tolerance. But although the liberalism of fear originates in religious toleration, by itself toleration is not liberal. Thus it is axiomatic that until the bonds between theistic religion and individual conscience are severed, the liberal principle of respect for persons cannot fully emerge.

Toleration seems to operate instrumentally, in that it is a means for allowing freedom to flourish.[9] Shklar suggests that if toleration were an end in itself, the liberalism based on toleration would be justly accused of absolutism. But the toleration she espouses does not lend itself to such a nihilism. Instead, it suggests, as a modest counterpoint to the grand philosophical and religious traditions concerned with the possibility of truth (either revealed or reasoned), that in embracing toleration one simply need not choose one or another tradition of truth.[10] Hence she endorses political strategies that channel the requirements for truth to particular realms of power. These channels will be the products of the practice of toleration. From toleration develops the greatest of liberal innovations—namely, the institution of strong distinctions between public and personal spheres of life. The beginning and end of fearful liberalism's specific allegiances are defined in response to the threatening circumstances of the day, which are mostly associated with the breaching of public and private.[11] One must draw a line between public and private, and constantly redraw it. That the line is drawn is more important than where the line is drawn (which is a matter of historically conditioned factors—technical, military, productive). The practice of drawing this line is akin to what Michael Walzer has called liberalism's art of separation.[12]

Fearful liberals draw lines between public and private specifically to reduce the possibility of cruelty, which Shklar understands to be the worst, and thus the most important, of the ordinary vices. She suggests that public cruelty is worse than private cruelty. It tends to be more systematic and less episodic than private cruelty. It is made possible, if not caused, by differences in public power. It leads to the pervasive presence of fear in a polity, which is the most potent danger to freedom. And of all the things we fear, most important, "we fear a society of fearful people. . . . Systematic fear is the condition that makes freedom impossible, and it is aroused by the expectation of institutionalized cruelty as by nothing else."[13] Public cruelty is the reason for establishing minimal governments in the Lockean mode.

The minimal license that liberal citizens give to government to use its power of coercion is in response to fear; government acts to quell fear of incursions on freedom.[14] Governments can be cruel, but only to prevent greater cruelty. The ultimate role of government is to preserve the space of freedom. That space is endangered by a variety of abuses of power. But for Shklar all such abuses might be categorized as being either systematic and persistent or unsystematic and episodic. "The fear [that the liberalism of fear] does want to prevent is that which is created by arbitrary, unexpected, unnecessary and unlicensed acts of force and by habitual and pervasive acts of cruelty performed by military, paramilitary, and police agents in any regime."[15]

The liberalism of fear responds to injustice. It is also an argument about how to ameliorate it. Shklar notes that injustice is visited on some people as a consequence of their race, gender, class, or other contingent characteristics. Not only are such attributes outside of the control of individuals, they are shared by a category of persons and hence are likely to lead to systematic injustices. Promises are broken all the time, but when one is more likely to suffer a broken promise because of a systematically imposed subordinate status, then in all likelihood there is a public abuse of power.[16] The line separating injustice from misfortune is never clear or clean, but like the line between public and private, it must be continually drawn and redrawn.[17]

The most harmful consequence of injustice is the sense of injustice it produces in those who suffer it. Nowhere does Shklar better illustrate her concern for the problem of injustice than in a brief comparison of two works of fiction. Both are stories of terrorist responses to injustice, responses (almost) warranted on the part of those who have deeply suffered the sense of injustice, Heinrich von Kleist's *Michael Kohlhaas* and E. L. Doctorow's appropriation of the Kohlhaas story in his novel *Ragtime*.[18] Shklar sees these two tales as examples of "the translation of intensely felt personal injustice into political violence." They are important examples because the only difference between the otherwise identical experiences of injustice felt by Kohlhaas and Walker is historical circumstance.

In Kleist's story, a Junker unjustly confiscates and abuses Kohlhaas's two horses. No one listens to Kohlhaas's suit because the Junker has important connections at court. As Kohlhaas pursues his case, he is subjected to endless insults and injuries, until he finally raises a peasant band that terrorizes the whole region. After much travail, the Elector of Brandenberg goes over the record, puts the Junker in jail, and restores the horses to the owner. Kohlhaas, though, suffers the consequence of going outside the law: he is executed. He submits to his fate without resistance. He accepts the judgment as his due. He also gets revenge on one of his betrayers, the Elector of Saxony, by denying him knowledge of his predicted fate. For Shklar "this is a story of justice vindicated because a just political world of law-enforcing princes is taken for

granted, even by Kohlhaas in his fanatical quest for personal vindica-
tion." Social retaliation ends when one man's sense of justice is satisfied.

Coalhouse Walker, ragtime pianist, is not in the same situation at all,
because he is a black man in America. When his Model T is vandalized
by a racist fire chief, no lawyer will even take his case. He gathers a
band of youths that burns fire stations; eventually, they kill some
people. Ultimately, he and his gang take over J. P. Morgan's personal
library in New York City, finally forcing political authorities to acknowledge the injustice suffered by Walker. They make the fire chief
repair the car and apologize. When Walker turns himself in, he is shot to
death by police. "This is where the similarity between the two stories
ends," writes Shklar. Walker expects no justice. He and his cohorts
don't believe that they live in a just society. Walker's followers want him
to lead a social rebellion to secure their rights as citizens. But he refuses,
perhaps because he is an artist.

Shklar wants to know: How might the young terrorists following
Walker have tried to justify their actions? In asking this question, she
acknowledged the exhilaration that might be found in the "cleansing
violence" to which Jean Paul Sartre referred so enthusiastically in his
preface to Frantz Fanon's *Wretched of the Earth*. But more important for
Shklar is a notion that the terrorists themselves might advance: no one
whom they might kill is politically innocent if he or she has passively
allowed such injustice to occur. Shklar disagrees. "Passive injustice is a
civic failing, not a sin or a crime."

Shklar does not deny that Coalhouse Walker and his followers were
victims of injustice. But had they continued shooting, the logic of war
would have displaced the logic of right. In that situation, democracy
(and hence freedom) would be at risk, because in war, the powerful win
out over the powerless. In a situation like that, resistance intensifies the
power of the police. Thus, although terror may be important as a form
of political self-expression, in the long run it results in defeat, and hence
is profoundly stupid.

In place of terrorism, Shklar proposes constitutionalism. To work
toward a better public justice, which would reduce or eliminate the
temptation to terrorism, is also to work toward procedures that are
substantively democratic. Procedures are not mere formalities; they
animate the concern for justice. In establishing forums accessible to all,
they reinforce the public social standing of those who are members of
the polity. They civilize.[19] Procedural inclusion thus is crucial to the
healthy development of what she calls citizenship as standing.

Citizenship as standing embodies an internal tension that Shklar acknowledges. Its history and prospects are crucial to understanding how social stability and justice might more or less be achieved. Citizenship embodies the tension between the existence of social strata and the egalitarian demand for respect.[20] These conflicting poles of standing find symbolic expression through the rights to vote and to earn. Hence it is important "to recall that the disenfranchised and the excluded were members of a professedly democratic society that was actively and purposely false to its own vaunted principles by refusing to accept these people or to recognize their right to be voters and free laborers."[21] The "real" history of the citizens is to be found in the tensions between inclusion and exclusion uniting these disparate experiences.

For Shklar, the key threats to inclusion in our history have been slavery and sexual oppression, and the residues left by them after their juridical elimination and delegitimation. Chattel slavery and its abolition have informed decisively the problem of citizenship for all groups who have sought inclusion in our politics.[22] In her discussion of the histories of the expansion of suffrage and earning rights, she focuses on how disenfranchised voters and unemployed people have compared their respective states to that of slavery. For both, she reviewed debates about including otherwise excluded groups from the right to participate in citizen activity.

The right to citizenship as standing is most clearly and uncomplicatedly framed in reference to the right to vote. But even here it is not framed unambiguously. Although the right to vote is generally acknowledged to be fundamental because it serves to preserve other rights, it does not do so unless a voter votes as a member of a group of people joined by a common interest.[23] One might argue, however, that the right to vote is an end in itself, because its distribution, regardless of its exercise, gives to all who have it equal standing as citizens. Indeed, Shklar suggested that the central reason for voting's importance is not so much its exercise as its standing as a right, which is threatened as a consequence of its practical distribution.

But if voting gives each citizen, at least formally, an equal voice, the right to earn does not. "Modern citizenship is not confined to political activities and concerns," Shklar notes. And whereas voting may be part of citizenship, citizens are members of "two interlocking public orders, one egalitarian, the other entirely unequal. To be recognized and active as a citizen at all he must be an equal member of the polity, a voter, but he must also be independent, which has all along meant that he must be an 'earner,' a free remunerated worker, one who is rewarded for the actual work he has done, neither more nor less."[24] She develops this difficult theme through a discussion of democracy during the Jacksonian era and the coincident emergence of our work ethic. And she reinforces her point concerning the difficult relationship of citizenship to earning through testimony from W.E.B. Du Bois, Frederick Douglass, and Abraham Lincoln concerning the importance of free labor to political equality.[25] She does not want to reduce citizenship to nothing more than standing but to demonstrate that to think about citizenship as standing is to confront directly the problem that the heritage of slavery has presented to the American polity. So when she mentions the problem of forced idleness among southern plantation owners, she might have been thinking as well about the corrosive effects of forced unemployment now.[26] When those who advocate "workfare" claim that the idle poor have lost citizenship rights, we might think of the connection between the loss of work and a fall into the condition of slavery. This is doubly true when employment and general socioeconomic status is connected to minority status.[27]

When issues concerning citizenship gravitate toward the blurry, ill-defined boundary between public and private, standing becomes a test of the capacities of a liberal polity to rule justly. Shklar's insistence on the importance of citizenship as standing and its substantive degradation through the historical fact of slavery leads us back to prior questions concerning liberalism in relationship to government. Simply put, if one's standing is tied to one's self-respect, and if self-respect is an important *political* good in the United States, we must not truncate the relationship between civil society and government. The two public orders of voting and earning are related through civil society. And civil society is a constantly shifting space, sometimes combining the public and private domains of equality and hierarchy in surprising ways.[28] The rights to vote and to earn are equal requirements of "a society that is committed to political equality and the principle of inclusion."[29]

Shklar builds on the liberalism of fear to a larger vision of a civil society that might, through its laws, develop the dignity and individuality of its citizenry, insuring that the realm of justice increases in scope and depth. She carries forward a liberal tradition found wherever the principle of toleration has been present.[30] Much of her argument, as she herself suggests, depends on how civil society operates to balance public and private spheres of activity. But to recognize that civil society is closely tied to government, political economy, and a moral psychology of self-respect suggests other recognitions as well, concerning many different elements in the relationship of government to citizenship.

What are the various practices that straddle the separation of public and private? How do they support or undermine this practice of freedom? Why do we feel so strongly the need to separate in order to connect?

Civil Society as Incorporation

We might find answers to these questions in the study of civil society. Among those who have attempted to think about contemporary civil society in the context of united states is Michael Walzer, who offers this definition: " 'Civil society' names the place of uncoerced human associations and also the set of relational networks—formed for the sake of family, faith, interest and ideology—that fill this space."[31] Civil society is thus a site where we come together. But when we try to attain a civil society we often find that it eludes our grasp.

We might see how fraught with difficulty our civil society is if we think of an example of its enactment. The 1991 SuperBowl, I think, presents us with an enactment of precisely the sort of civil society Walzer defines. It was a moment when a network of relations provided us a united state of great intensity. The halftime show celebrated *us*: it showed, in most explicit terms, how we might achieve a unity through war against symbolic opponents. It was a great spectacle, presided over by President Bush and the people of Disney. Everyone "there" supported the war, even those at home. All of the elements of family, faith, interest, and ideology were woven into a seamless web. Whitney Houston lip-synched the national anthem (and later released it as a record and video. Her version of the "Star Spangled Banner" became a best-selling single). At halftime, children of troops serving in the Persian Gulf ran out onto the field, and George and Barbara Bush addressed the nation from the White House. A dialectic, with football as the copula, was unabashedly connected: to be patriotic is to be a fan of professional football, and to be a football fan is to understand and endorse the tactics of late modern war. It was a moment when we all were asked to pledge allegiance to a set of core values, and we did, in overwhelming numbers.

Walzer (inadvertently) suggests why so few of us explicitly consider the question of civil society when we think about such moments of unity. He does so while cataloging a variety of visions of civil society that inform and compete with the liberal model. Each model, he suggests, is wrong to the extent that it is singular, missing the complexity of human society, and promoting its own version of the good unequivocally against all other versions of civil society.[32] As a solution to this problem, Walzer urges that the projects of socialism, democracy, free enterprise, and nationalism all be relativized and brought together. Civil society is "the setting of settings: all are included, none is preferred."[33] Generally, for Walzer civil society is the incoherent and messy arena where groups "are necessarily fragmented and localized as they are incorporated. They become part of the world of family, friends, comrades, and colleagues, where people are made responsible for one another. Connected and responsible: without that, 'free and equal' is less attractive than we once thought it would be."[34] Although he admits that he has no magic formula for making such a world come into being,[35] Walzer's rhetoric suggests that the dominant way in which civil society can be made responsive to political authority is by being integrated into a larger order of unity, in his word, "incorporated." He suggests that civil society "requires many organizing strategies and new forms of state action. It requires new sensitivity for what is local, specific, contingent—and above all, a new recognition (to paraphrase a famous sentence) that the good life is in the details."[36]

How does incorporation operate? How are you and I connected to each other? What is the truth of our relationship when that relationship is mediated through the strategic organization (or "organizing strategies") of civil society? When I ask that question, I begin to worry because there seems to be an immediate effort entailed in such strategies to separate, to sort and fold, to stratify orders of connection between us. I worry about the slippage that occurs between the terms "fragment and localize" and "pluralize" from one version of Walzer's argument to the next.[37] It suggests an attempt to smooth over roughness, to deny the oppositional energy that animates civil society by suppressing the conflicts embedded in confrontations involving civil society's participants. It literalizes the "civility" of civil society, a move that is itself coercive to the extent that it smothers dissent.

Immediately upon hearing the word "incorporation" in this context, I worry about the poverty of the mechanisms that advance this liberal "quest for inclusion." How are the equal world of the voter and the unequal world of the earner connected and made responsive to each other? The policies of incorporation that organize and coordinate the local, contingent, and specific, that watch over the details of life, seem to foster neither freedom nor equality, regardless of what those who implement such policies might sincerely claim. Instead, when implemented, such policies predominantly (and unsurprisingly) administer and organize. Implementation shifts the focus of civil life from free interaction to an expansion of government, in a way that focuses on government's most insidious power, that of normalization and governmentality.[38]

For example: The right to vote is administered through elections. What effects do elections produce? Citizens have the right to vote in the United States, but they do not *exercise* that right in overwhelming numbers, as Shklar notes. The lack of participation in elections in the United States is a major wellspring of writing in American political science, as well as a more general source of concern among democratic theorists.[39] During the past decade that concern has been heightened by the dramatic expansion of the use of polling and mass-media advertising in elections with the attendant explosion in campaign expenses, an intensification of patterns of corporate involvement in electoral and legislative politics, and a rapid rise in levels of corruption among office holders. (It seems as though the primary factor that broke the hold of that corruption in the 1992 presidential election was the enthusiasm of a crank billionaire from Texas with millions of dollars to spare for an independent presidential candidacy.)

Several political scientists have argued persuasively that this "new" phenomenon is a contemporary expression of an older tension in the politics of representative democracies. Theodore Lowi has long argued that the modern liberal polity in the United States has been corrupted by the decline of pluralism into interest-group liberalism, a set of procedures which results in a state of "permanent receivership," whereby the distribution of goods is determined by processes of compromise rather than justice.[40] For Lowi participation follows the lines of a corrupted marketplace in which elites are systematically irresponsible.

More recently, Benjamin Ginsberg has delineated the relationship between mass opinion and the growth of the modern state.[41] For Ginsberg, the control of mass opinion has virtually been coterminous with the extension of suffrage.[42] From the perspective of those who rule, the sporadic participation by citizens in politics that is mandated by the most common electoral rules, even when there is electoral competition, operates to preserve a previously established distribution of power. "Rather than prevent mass electoral influence, democracies attempt typically to 'influence mass influence,' so that the electorate's decisions themselves will accord with and thus reinforce the power and wishes of those who rule."[43] The frequency, scope, and intensity of mass participation are limited by elections. The very development of the citizenry into a "mass" is encouraged by the lack of avenues for direct and substantive political involvement. Polls, originally designed to supplement involvement, now substitute for involvement,[44] and influence that residue of involvement which they have not yet replaced.

Ginsberg's cautionary message regarding elections and the channeling of consent is derived from Tocqueville.[45] If it were true that docility derived simply from democratic despotism, then our deepest concerns regarding the undermining of citizenship as standing could be relieved through appeals to principles of individualism and procedural fairness.[46] The resources of legal Constitutionalism would be sufficient, for instance, to enable effective resistance to the despotism that accrues from the creation and manipulation of mass opinion. But if instead of focusing attention on the principles of individualism and how they might be weakened, we concentrate on the practices of individuation that give sustained and ordinary meaning to that individualism, the picture becomes more complicated. Technical modes of gathering consent, cultivated outside the ken of Constitutional law, diverge from the lessons of procedural fairness in contributing to the moral psychology of civil society. Liberalism's commitments, embodied in law, are subverted by practices as banal as insurance and as mind-numbing as standardized school tests.[47]

Maybe we need to think further about the implications that flow from the organizing strategy of incorporation. One's place in a system where incorporation predominates is more or less fatally determined by attributes one shares with others. The elements of one's life are fixed on a continuum. Personhood is fragmented and localized, in a manner parallel to an "interest" in interest group politics, even as one's body may not be. Standing, in this dimension, has nothing to do with what one does, but neither does it have anything to do with who one is by dint of individual right.

To the extent that elections involve the construction and manipulation of mass opinion, the line between citizen and consumer becomes blurred. The standing of the citizen becomes uncertain. The materiality of a vote is the last sign of something beyond the abstract referent called the electorate. Thus civil society connects the equality of voting with the inequality of earning. Income distribution is less important for Shklar than is the dignity of being able to work. But the former largely determines the extent to which anyone has influence on those elected representatives who legislate, executives who execute, and bureaucrats who implement. Indeed, income distribution indirectly determines both the number and quality of employment opportunities.

Here is a connection between voting and earning that a major "setting" of civil society, namely, the institutions and policies of consumption designed and developed by corporate capitalism, has provided us. But to suggest only that the influence of corporations in this dimension of our life constitutes an abuse that should be checked is to misconstrue the distinguishing features of modern corporate power. Corporations in modern world civilization serve as a constitutive force for the integration of populations into sociopolitical orders.[48] "Checking" them, therefore, is not the issue. We might as soon set the clock back to the fifteenth century. But neither should we believe that incorporation operates to establish a sort of civil society in which differences are allowed to be.

For those of us who live in the rich centers of the world, the culture of the corporation is double-edged. It provides incredible wealth and impressive social disorientation at the same time. Our repeated retreats into privatism, the staggering material miseries afflicting so many of us as a consequence of the severely uneven distribution of goods, in the most general terms, the "growing disorganization [of civil society]— violence, homelessness, divorce, abandonment, alienation, and addiction,"[49] plausibly can be traced, at least in large part, to the power of this organizational form to condition, to allow and disallow, modern life. Yet most of us who think about this matter have so far evaded a confrontation with this forceful hypothesis.[50]

Tocqueville presented cautionary lessons concerning the danger of the business firm,[51] but the undermining of citizenship proceeds along lines that depart significantly from Tocqueville's diagnosis of democratic despotism, George Kateb succinctly summarizes Tocqueville's views on democratic despotism when he refers to the substitution of lenient for brutal regimentation, and a "therapeutic solicitude by those in power toward the many, who seem to crave it as solace for the rigors of an economically competitive life."[52] In his analysis of docility, Kateb appeals to that which escapes the grids of discipline and exercises of micropower, to that which may, within the operations of fabrication, create a greater depth to the subjects of power, allowing imagination and creativity to have some free play, and hence to contribute toward the reassertion of rights and the strengthening of freedom.[53] In doing so, he lays the ground for a possible response to the contemporary condition. But in its omissions, Kateb's argument evades the critique that applies precisely and directly to forces that shape and delimit docility at the level of the micropower, within the domains of everyday life where character is shaped. In Kateb's entire list of threats to freedom, he never mentions the corporation, which is a primary space of anti-individualistic docility in contemporary American society. This thoughtful individualist thinker remains silent concerning the organizational form that in combination with governmental power most thoroughly fulfills the quotidian enactments of discipline and normalization in our common life.[54] In his less reflective moments,[55] it is as though Kateb assumes that all of us are free to dabble in the enormous energies of popular culture and willingly accept the costs involved because we ourselves do not have to pay in boredom, fear of economic dislocation, and the blackmail of conditions. His admirable faith in the capacity of all of us in our own ways to participate in liberal democratic culture sometimes operates as a rhetoric for evading a confrontation with the most damaging conditions created and sustained by its corporate underpinnings.

Shklar, by contrast, highlights how corporate enterprise straddles the public/private distinction and how, as a result, the corporation becomes a central feature of civil society. But she still identifies the admittedly public character of corporations with all other forms of private property. "It should be remembered," she reminds us, "that the reasons we speak of property as private in many cases is that it is meant to be left to the discretion of individual owners as a matter of public policy and law, precisely because this is an indispensable and excellent way of limiting the long arm of government and of dividing social power, as well as of securing the independence of individuals."[56] But in her turn, Shklar ignores a primary feature of contemporary corporate power, namely, that in late capitalism ownership has been separated from control.[57] From her perspective it would not be possible to discern any techniques for contesting threats to freedom posed by corporate power.

Injustice and the Violence of Representation

Shklar identifies a major problem in the heart of civil society through her discussion of the heritage of chattel slavery. But her arguments concerning slavery underestimate the roles that discipline and normalization have played in the postslavery era. Moreover, she virtually ignores the role that cultural representations of freed slaves have played in the perpetuation of racism in civil society. For Shklar, as for other liberals, the emphasis is always on how ownership of slaves, and lack of self-ownership by slaves, persists as the primary cause of the suffering of African Americans, since alienation from property rights prevented the development of standing for liberated slaves. She does not discuss the violence of slavery, the physical beating and systematic degradation of slaves that was the norm of the slave experience.[58] Much of that violence *was* originally related to the peculiar relationship to ownership that slaves experienced and to the subsequent struggle they endured to achieve property rights. But that is hardly the whole story, even at the beginning of the period of liberation. Her focus on voters and earners means that Shklar does not examine the experience of liberated slaves. It is ironic that she thus fails to ask a question with which she presumably would be quite sympathetic: How could liberated slaves experience freedom when they continued to live in fear?[59]

The daily degradation of slaves, not only through their legal standing as chattel but also through the techniques of control used over them, has contributed greatly to the legacy of racism in the United States. It continues to be reflected in representations of African Americans. Jonathan Simon suggests that the abolition of slavery was accompanied by a confusion concerning how the newly freed slaves would be integrated into the legal order of not only rights but punishments as well.[60] Under slavery, explicit and ritual violence against slaves was ordinary. Branding, mutilation, the pillory, and most commonly whipping were used to maintain control over slaves.[61]

Accompanying the elevation of slaves to citizens were the first attempts to integrate them into civil society. But the focus was more on integration into a disciplinary order that would make freedmen suitable for the industrial enterprises of the United States than it was on social inclusion. The Freedmen's Bureau, established in 1865, had as its central concern the development of strategies to encourage the newly freed slaves to work. Simon emphasizes this passage in a report written in 1866: " 'Until they were emancipated, as a general rule the only stimulus to work was the fear of punishment. Faithful labor scarcely benefitted their physical condition, and, as a natural consequence, they were only industrious to the extent necessary to escape punishment for idleness.' "[62]

One way to discipline and integrate workers into the Jacksonian industrial order was the penitentiary system.[63] As Simon notes, the integration of freed slaves into the post–Civil War political order included the extension of this disciplinary form to them. The first section of the Civil Rights Act of April 9, 1866, included this language:

> All persons born in the United States and not subject to any foreign power, excluding Indians not taxed, are hereby declared citizens of the United States; and such citizens, of every race and color, without regard to any previous condition of slavery or involuntary servitude, except as a punishment for crime whereof the party shall have been duly convicted, shall have the same right, in every State and Territory . . . to full and equal benefit of all laws and proceedings for the security of persons and property, as is enjoyed by white citizens, and be subject to like punishment, pains, and penalties, and to none other, any law, statute, ordinance, regulation, or custom, to the contrary notwithstanding.[64]

The legally sanctioned use of whipping to punish white people had died out long before the Civil War, so the double intent of the legislation, to provide both equal rights *and punishments* to the freed slaves, is clear.

Simon contends that opponents of Reconstruction insisted that the integration of freed slaves into the disciplinary order of free labor was not working, and that they relentlessly attempted to use violence on the freedmen in order to exclude them from the disciplinary order.[65] The old form of punishment, beating and whipping, was suitable to those already too docile to labor diligently. The retreat from offering freed slaves assurance of their formal civil rights was accompanied by the establishment of the sharecropping system, the overseers of which used the old forms of terroristic control to keep freed slaves indentured.[66]

The immediate consequences of the end of Reconstruction are well known. But perhaps at a more covert level, defining the freedman's resistance to labor as laziness located the freed slave as the tain of the mirror in a new culture; they became the dull surface on which a more positive identity for unstable white workers might be projected.[67] The first to reflect a superior identity against this ground of black inferiority were poor white Southerners, who until the slaves were freed had suffered at the bottom of the order of free American beings.[68] The visibility African Americans achieved in this system was secondhand, in reference to the needs of those struggling to maintain a semblance of dignity in the cultural order of representation. Group after group was to follow. And yet a secondhand visibility, and primary invisibility, for those of African heritage persists.

The representation of the bodies of African American men, especially, by the time of the emergence of (the fictional) Coalhouse Walker, had undergone yet another shift in substance, while continuing to serve the same structural purpose of grounding the American norm of discipline. Michael Rogin has explored this shift in an essay on D. W. Griffith's *Birth of a Nation*.[69] He notes how racist discourse ceased to represent black male bodies as docile and placid and began to portray them as aggressive and violent. In cultural terms, one might argue that the slave had needed the whip to energize his labor, but the former slave needed the whip to restrain his appetites. The resolution of the Civil War in *The Birth of a Nation* is the reconciliation of Northern and Southern white men on the lynched bodies of black men. Through the use of film, a technology that, as Rogin argues, abolished interpretation in order to make representation a vehicle for replacing history,[70] Griffith transformed black men from lazy oafs into demons, insatiable monsters seeking conquest through the bodies of white (pre-sexual) women.[71] Lynching was the most spectacular form of violence done in the South to African American men during this time, but the more routine form of this violence was the continued use of predisciplinary forms in the southern penal system. The intense anxieties that white men had regarding women, who were leaving country for city and home for work, also came into play. The male fear of women energized the racist discourse of the era.[72] To be black meant being in constant danger, without any protection by the law if one was a woman, without any protection from the law if one was a man.

One might comprehend the difficulties that afflict African Americans stem from the discrimination in work, school, and voting that have damaged their life opportunities and from their continued lack of substantive representation in civil society a century and a quarter after their political rights were first protected by Federal law. If one took the polemical use of Willie Horton in the 1988 presidential election as an ordinary example, one would find the same motifs as are present in Griffith's *Birth of a Nation*.[73] What sort of pressure might the silence surrounding such representations create for those so represented? What happens when there is no protest from anyone other than those of us who are so demonized? And who are we in this case? How do I hold your attention when you are an African American woman, when you are an African American man, and I am a white guy sitting around theorizing? Who can I be to you?[74]

In *Ragtime* Doctorow poses the question of silence. Shklar seems not to have heard it. Coalhouse Walker's identity as a musician, far from distracting him from the political dimension of his terrorism, energized his sense of injustice in the first place. To be a ragtime pianist is to help shape one's cultural identity, not in conformity with the standards of an oppressive society, but in subtle resistance to it, using its forms to make a space for the creation of self.[75] Such a self is not merely autonomous, but communicates a sense of place and identification with other representatives in a democratic public culture.[76]

Coalhouse Walker, when invited into Father and Mother's parlor, behaves with dignity and self-confidence (which irritates Father, who later realized that what was puzzling about Walker was the fact that he "acted like a white man"). In performing "The Maple Leaf," he refers to its composer as "the great Scott Joplin." When asked by Father if he played "coon" songs, he explains that such songs are sung by white men in blackface, not by ragtime musicians.[77] A crucial source of his dignity is not simply earning or voting, but his expropriation and use of tools of representation. He is an artist, not as solitary creator, but as public performer. He is a popular artist.

Unlike Michael Kohlhaas, who sought relief from the abuse of social superiors within a stable social order in which he had standing, and then took to violence when his standing was denied, Walker created a new claim to standing through cultural appropriation. He fabulously (retrospectively) provoked the injustice that he suffered, and then used the standing that he had seized as a resources for responding (violently) to the injustice. "He was not unaware that in his dress and as the owner of a car he was a provocation to many white people. *He had created himself in the teeth of such feelings.*"[78] The racists who set upon him understood the usual ways of putting such people in their place. They attempted to degrade and humiliate him, they defecated on his belongings, they made him bow, they killed him. Yet Walker was not to be a victim; he was not to be hanged from a tree.

Death by a hail of bullets replaces lynching.

Walker's response to his degradation differs from Kohlhaas's, not because of the hopelessness of his cause, but because of his canny use of the popular press, popular celebrity (J. P. Morgan), and the mass-produced automobile to attract attention to the unjust suffering, because of his creative use of violence in a society where violence had long been used against him and virtually all members of his social milieu. By threatening to blow up J. P. Morgan's library (even though the seizure of the library was a happy error), Coalhouse Walker achieved his fictional fame. He holds hostage the image, and thus the person, of Morgan by taking hold of his collection.[79]

Walker dies at the end of *Ragtime*, just as Kohlhaas does at the end of

Kleist's tale. For Shklar, because racism persists, because there is no settling of balances, no closure, there is no justice for Walker. Indeed, he expects none. But if the struggle in which Walker and his followers were engaged was to construct identity in the face of hostile forces, then some measure of progress toward an imperfect justice was made. Progress in this situation does not result in greater conformity to the procedures of justice, to the courts of law, or to the pedagogic capacities provided by governmental institutions, where Shklar seeks them, but in the production of new possibilities of self-representation in popular culture. Such progress establishes politics beyond the limits of law and government. It also sets the stage to modify those forms. This is a substantive arena for liberal struggle in the postmodern scene.

In the final passage of *Ragtime*, Doctorow discusses an idea germinating in the mind of Tateh, the immigrant Jewish radical/laborer/artisan turned filmmaker. It is palpably recognizable to anyone who watches Saturday morning T.V. "He suddenly had an idea for a film. A bunch of children who were pals, white black, fat thin, rich poor, all kinds, mischievous little urchins who would have adventures in their own neighborhood, a society of ragamuffins, like all of us, a gang, getting into trouble and getting out again."[80] This inclusion may occur within the law, but it is not sufficiently produced by it; it is instead recognizable as Tateh's attempt to complete the reconciliation with the United States he had begun earlier in the novel, when, abandoning the great strike in Lawrence, Massachusetts, he started making moving books for a novelty company. Doctorow writes of this earlier moment,

> Thus did the artist point his life along the lines of flow of American energy. Workers would strike and die but in the streets of cities an entrepreneur could cook sweet potatoes in a bucket of hot coals and sell them for a penny or two. A smiling hurdy-gurdy man could fill his cup. Phil the Fiddler, undaunted by the snow, cut away the fingers of his gloves and played under the lighted windows of mansions. Frank the Cash Boy kept his eyes open for a runaway horse carrying the daughter of a Wall Street broker. All across the continent merchants pressed the large round keys of their registers. The value of the duplicable event was everywhere perceived.[81]

That this assertion of the trajectory of the artist's efforts immediately precedes a discussion of the Ford assembly line and the first Model T (a replica of which later was to be Walker's desecrated object) only heightens the irony of this story, and underscores the ambiguous political role of the popular artist in a mass democracy.

In *Ragtime*, civil society swarms with lives of violent representations and powerful signs through which meaning is communicated to all of those who will look and listen, through which those who look and listen become lookers and listeners.[82] People are rarely invited to be included in this society; much more often circumstances force them to make their way in it. Civil society is not only the realm of citizenship in the sense that Shklar and other liberals have emphasized. A time such as this, which in many aspects parallels the era of *Ragtime*, a time of high corruption and cynical jingoism, erodes belief in official modes of politics, while encouraging people to look elsewhere for affirmation.

But there are differences between then and now. Today the spaces for free play and for the manipulation of images, the terrain of the struggle to achieve an artistry that flows with the energy of America, is regulated and marked by the normalizing power of technological strategies to a greater extent than before. The power of an electronic information order to monitor people and their activities simultaneously extends the possibilities of domination by governmentality and opens new spaces for creative dissidence.[83] A realm never protected by any right other than the right of ownership, this dimension of civil society has been vitiated by the power of trademark and copyright even as it extends imagination into previously unexplored realms.[84] Cultural creativity is threatened anew by the imposition of uniformity in all cultures, but the techniques at hand in our corporate society present distinctive challenges now. We have both been shaped and smashed by this united state of freedom. Our challenge is at least to resist, and in resisting to create new possibilities, new free arrangements.[85] It may be that this challenge is most fully met in our popular culture by those who give expression to the terrors of our lives in common.

If today we have the visitation of ordinary terror on the citizenry, by the citizenry, and for the citizenry—the pessimistic response to Shklar's question concerning the justification for terrorism—this response may be a signal from those of us who have practiced terror from the bottom of society. But it is not, as a reaction, the *cause* of violence. Whose terror and to what end? Terror practiced by those on the bottom has rarely had the same consequences as terror practiced by those on top. And the gap between top and bottom yawns large in the last decade of this millennium. As those on top have corrupted the possibilities of a better public justice, those on the bottom seek new ways to make sense of their lives in civil society. For whom is it even useful to pretend that we are all together here? Must each of us choose a loyalty? I wonder.

Cruelty and Responsibility

There continue to be arbitrary and vicious expressions of violence in American civil society.[86] Indeed, a common currency in public debate is a fear of violence, expressed as a concern about crime. But if we fear violent crime, we also seem to conflate that fear with other fears, associated with our identities and our specific insecurities regarding those who challenge who we might be. Because so many demons are set loose by public arguments for the repression of violence, we might listen closely to the argument that current conditions call for a reinvigoration of the liberalism of fear. As Shklar puts the matter, "Unrestrained 'punishing' and denials of the most basic means of survival by governments, near and far from us, should incline us to look with critical attention to the practices of all agents of all governments and to the threats of war here and everywhere." It is not only war that she fears, because she notes various accounts of systematic government brutality "here and elsewhere." She suggests that it is in keeping with eighteenth-century reformers such as Caesare Beccaria to do so, and urges all theorists and citizens not to ignore them.[87]

But by framing the issue of brutality in eighteenth-century terms, Shklar can only understand dramatic rises in the levels of torture and repression to be the consequence of an increase in cruelty in the world. In this polity, such an explanation requires that we understand why the Bill of Rights has lost so much ground. Shklar does not provide such an explanation. But her failure only reflects our more general incapacity to address the ubiquitous role that government, especially in its police role, plays in civil society. The government uses imprisonment, for example, to pacify the citizenry by dividing it. Those with the lowest standing (the poor and minorities) are demonized and imprisoned. Those of higher standing, whose lives are relatively safe, are encouraged to fear violence from "others." All are thus (variously) encouraged to acquiesce to and cooperate with police rule.

The politics of these divisions intensify and extend patterns of violence against specific persons who lack access to the goods that Shklar believes would serve as a bulwark for them. As such, the cultural presence of violence obviates her hope for the securing of such rights. A greater understanding of how violence operates might help to understand how the liberal *telos* is thwarted. The violence that descends to the worst cruelty, torture, would seem to be most important to the agenda of the liberalism of fear. But, in a paradoxical sense, it isn't.

Shklar reveals the limits of the liberal critique of torture most clearly in her scathing review of Elaine Scarry's 1985 book, *The Body in Pain*.[88] "Although Scarry's intentions are palpably decent, her account is so wholly devoid of historical evidence and political information as to be worse than useless," she writes. Protesting Scarry's focus on the subjective feelings of victims of torture, Shklar sought to repoliticize the issue. In so doing, she set aside the "puzzle of the hangman," implicitly suggesting that inquiry into the psychological dimension of torture leads nowhere, and suggesting, as an alternative, that

> torture was long used in criminal trials to gather evidence and the confession had a significant place in the proceedings of the Inquisition as well as in those of the Moscow trials of the Thirties. Information is militarily extremely important in contemporary warfare, especially in ideological civil conflicts. . . . Torture takes place in the most primitive as well as in the most advanced societies. Above all, it cannot be understood as a phenomenon that takes place in a chamber between two people, a victim and a torturer. It is always a part of a judicial and political system.

Shklar suggests that Scarry misses the "real" world of torture by focusing on pain. "The real world of torturing regimes is a world of fear and lies, not of 'inexpressible' pain. The real task of Amnesty International is to force us to look at it and to do whatever we can, not to ruminate about 'objectification.'"

Shklar insists on the historical specificity of torture and then denies that torture might mutate historically. But when she claims that torture is always a part of a judicial and political system, she evades the same question that she criticizes Scarry for evading. That is, how does a liberal polity avoid making torture a part of its system? When does coercion become cruel? By the logic of the liberalism of fear, it will not do to disclaim the cruel acts of a government that one otherwise endorses.[89] The logic of the exception operates too easily as an excuse. We are to be held responsible for the pain that we cause. And if the systematic beating of arrestees, a court-sanctioned right to detain people without charges for forty-eight hours, the legal, systematic mistreatment of those imprisoned, and the increasingly common use of the death penalty constitute torture, then it would *seem* that liberalism is faced with a choice either to recognize its participation in torture or to oppose the system that permits such things to happen, rather than treat such incidents as exceptions to a system that sometimes goes astray. And the responsibility goes even deeper, for the liberalism of fear must address as well the ethos of violence that inhabits civil society, the failure of so many to be inspired by the procedures of Constitutional democracy when they take from its corruption in public life permission to brutalize others involuntarily.

A sympathetic reading of Scarry would suggest that a deeper appreciation of the extreme feeling that is involved when one is tortured, and thus has one's humanity effaced, might aid us in opposing torture. An even more sympathetic reading might affirm "ruminating about objectification"—especially since fearful liberals must, above all be ruminators as well. In fact, such ruminations might contribute to the ongoing evaluation of the extent to which citizenship as standing has been achieved or undermined.

But to admit that a torturer can destroy the humanity of a person would require Shklar to admit that the human subject is deeply situated in a politically salient way, which is to say that individualism is not rooted in natural right, but in history.[90] The effectiveness of torture in Shklar's "world" (as opposed to Scarry's, a world which Shklar derides) is that torturers can force people to become something other than they are, to act in ways that are inconsistent with what they would do as putatively free agents. Shklar insists on seeing only an unsituated agent as an individual; she does not address either that person's inner psychological states or the social forces that might render what he does non-volitional. But Scarry demonstrates that ordinary torturers often are not concerned with getting the tortured to *do* anything, for instance, to give up information. Indeed, often they don't even have the tortured as their audience. Their *function* is to efface the subjective status of the tortured, rendering the tortured less than human, while advancing their careers as police bureaucrats. If torture culminates in the disappearance of more of its victims, this is the consequence, not of less sophistication in the instruments of torture, but of a shift in its purpose, a shift that Shklar misses because of an ahistorical reading of the practice.[91]

Less interesting than the question of Scarry's success or failure is Shklar's opposition not only to Scarry's results but to Scarry's efforts as well. In shifting attention from the technique of the torturer to the ends of torture, Shklar once again shows herself to be influenced by eighteenth-century assumptions concerning such matters. But these assumptions disable recognition of the ordinary, prosaic, and powerful means by which torture operates in contemporary life. Indeed, an explanation of the resurgence of torture in the twentieth century would seem to require some understanding of a history of pain. Such a history would enable one to understand how contemporary subjects might be more vulnerable to torture than their predecessors, how the drama of torture might better inspire fear and deceit in societies where subjects are thoroughly shaped by the modulating forces of governmentality and the networks of pleasure that create a new range of needs for all who partake in it.

In fact, our fearful work must be to consider whether and how the degradation of civil society, the rearrangement of our united states, contributes to the emergence of a form of torture not yet recognized as such. To the extent that we cling to traditional visions of responsible agents engaged in the systematic imposition of cruelty, we fail to recognize the presence of torture in the banality of contemporary disciplinary practices. As most citizens find themselves between totally unsituated freedom and radically fixed positions, so does the implementation of violence proceed between the extremes of the sadism of evil men and the gray anonymity envisioned by Kafka. But recognizing the complex role that governmentality plays in the creation and sustenance of individuals, as both a pastoral and a torturous element of power, violates the spirit of a liberalism that seeks to advance the fiction of autonomy by insisting on condemning cruelty at the level of individuality, while effacing questions concerning the role that nonvolitional, individuating elements play in constituting the subject to be condemned.

Paradoxically, we can identify cruelty in the insistence that all acts of cruelty are agent-relative. The complex logic of agent effacement is at work in a little-noted 1991 Supreme Court ruling, *Wilson v. Seiter*. That case presents an ironic rejoinder to older liberal aspirations.[92] In it the Court ruled against the petitioner, who had filed suit seeking relief from degraded prison conditions. In ruling against the petitioner, the majority said that for the Eighth Amendment's prohibition of cruel and unusual punishment to apply the petitioner needed to demonstrate a wanton infliction of pain by a specific agent. This means that he first had to locate a specific agent who acted, and then demonstrate that the state of mind of that agent was such that he or she was deliberately inflicting pain on the prisoner. Chief Justice Rehnquist wrote,

> Petitioner . . . suggests that we should draw a distinction between "short term" or "one-time" conditions (in which a state of mind requirement would apply) and "continuing" or "systemic" conditions, where official state of mind would be irrelevant. We perceive neither a logical or practical

> basis for that distinction. . . . If the pain inflicted is not formally meted out
> as punishment by the statute or the sentencing judge, some mental ele-
> ment must be attributed to the inflicting officer before it can qualify.

The practical consequence of this ruling was to prevent prisoners from
seeking relief from the conditions under which they are imprisoned.[93]
Here the fact of imprisonment is separated from the conditions of
imprisonment, as Justice White notes in the dissent.

How does individual justice operate for us when large regions of our
experience are not shaped by *anyone's* deliberate intentions and when it
is in those regions of experience that most of the horrors of contemporary policing are committed? Depending on circumstances beyond
your control, you might be apprehended and then arrested by police
officers—*not* because they intend to arrest *you*, but because you match a
profile. Immediately you are propelled into the world of normalization.
One might argue that the goal is to achieve individual justice, that it is
wrong that there are such shortcomings, but that argument ignores the
theory and practice of contemporary crime prevention and criminal
administration, which now depends on analyses of risk to determine
how to control crime.[94] Such discriminations are made possible and
sustained by forces that the liberalism of fear does not address and,
given its eighteenth-century assumptions, cannot address.[95]

Wilson v. Seiter is an example of how rights discourse can disguise the
advance of disciplinary power.[96] Insisting on individual agency pro-
tects the "rights" of powerful institutions from small individual rights
claims and secures governmental power over subjects who are the
material embodiment of its most abstract ambitions, in this case, to
normalize those who are not so much convicted of crimes as they are
diagnosed as criminal. Against such power, the individual must, in
Foucault's terms, seek a *new* right, one not tied to the principle of
sovereignty.[97] I know that most American liberals sneer at that suggestion, but if we are to follow Shklar's advice to trace and condemn the
abuses of power that threaten the space of freedom,[98] we must resist her
way of closing discussion about cruelty and think of new ways to talk
about the relationship between rights and the bodies that bear them.

An Ethics of Fear

If I disagree with Shklar, it is because I worry that her common sense of
pain has led her students and admirers astray in ways that contribute

toward intensifying violence even as we seek to address the damage done to our polity through the years of right-wing rule. Moreover, if we decide to ignore those who would insist that we explore our world, the better to resist it, we risk extinguishing a very old but recently resurrected proposal that may help us more than some of us are willing to admit. Here is a formula for the care of the self that holds out the possibility of moving us backward, and perhaps forward as well.

> Just as the body must not let itself be carried away without the correlative of a desire in the soul, the latter must not go beyond what the body demands and what its needs dictate. But in the first case, what is involved is an illness, which remedies may be able to cure; in the second, what is involved above all is an ethical regimen, which ought to be applied to oneself. Rufus proposed a formula for this: "subdue the soul and make it obey the body."[99]

This proposal (re)appears when our bodies, apart and together, have been obeisant to the dictates of a singular soul whose ethics have subordinated bodies, denied them a proper place, for so long (two millennia now) that a bodily ethic sounds preposterous. Our liberalism, which has focused so closely on individuality, still lacks an ethic that locates individuals in bodies capable of reconciling and overcoming, or at least engaging, the dualism which is the awful heritage of Christianity.[100] Our liberalism, despite brave words from some of its adherents, has not yet departed from a philosophical tradition that subordinates freedom to the command of an infinitely demanding order.

Might it develop such an ethic? The bodies to which liberalism might turn are not of the same genre as those invoked by Rufus. Our modern bodies are even more complicated, constituted in the words of jurists, in the probes of medical technicians, in the disciplines of the eye, in the shafts of light that reveal partial and fragmented movements, in the silences and noises of multiple auralities, in the codes of cyberneticists, in the overwhelming presence of commodious living, in Bo Jackson's and Michael Jordan's Nike shoe ads . . . To the extent that liberal thinkers pretend that there is a unity to the self to which we can successfully appeal in measuring the good and evil of the world, liberalism fails to confront the difficulties of this time. For it willfully ignores the means by which the multiple selves it idealizes and unifies are fashioned into being. It risks ending up as just one more variation on the politics of mourning.

It is difficult to evade mourning, even if one has not yet lived long enough or experienced enough to become good at it. Nonetheless, there is something to be gained from an exercise in thought that thinks about the care of self, if out of a certain solitude emerge some uncertain guideposts concerning our united states.[101]

One might evoke the free spirit as a model for such a project. Richard Flathman writes,

> The free spirit goes beyond the self-discipline that prevents harmful or destructive conduct and forms and acts upon images and objectives that complicate and endanger, amplify, heighten and intensify her life. At once "prepared" and enabled, impaired and disabled by the culture in which she imagines, thinks and acts, she enacts and reenacts herself in part by availing herself of its accumulated capital, in part by contesting its prejudices and presuppositions, above all by descending into the dark waters of her impulses and inclination, ascending into the opaque mists of her visions and fantasies.[102]

Flathman praises individualist thinkers, liberal and otherwise, who risk the foolishness of being exemplars of other ways of living, especially those who do so by showing how there remains more than the ordinary in the ordinary. "The mystery, the singularity, the mutual inaccessibility that they esteem and promote reside within and among, are inconceivable apart from, the manifest, the ordinary, the shared, even the common elements of human experience."[103] This mystery is perhaps the most enduring attraction of our liberalism, and when I think of the extent of its availability to us, I am still thrilled, even as I am horrified at the accompanying costs.

Thrilled and horrified: perhaps that balances out to worried. I worry that the celebratory songs of liberalism too often smother the cries of the beggars outside the magnificent atriums of corporate power. To study the extraordinary as it resides within the ordinary, to follow the path of the free spirit in a time when the habitations of everyday life depend so heavily on the ordinal strategies of governmentality, suggests that political theorists attracted to the various conceptions of free individuality have not yet to come to terms with the state of emergency as a conditioning factor in contemporary politics.[104] The state of emergency in which we live compels free spirits, some of whom are liberals, to repudiate the notion that the cruelties of our age are somehow atavisms.[105]

Walter Benjamin suggested how one might heighten awareness of emergency in his endorsement of a materialism that would demand strategies of politics based upon the interpenetration of "body and image." In 1929, in a Germany on the verge, he wrote

Only when in technology body and image so interpenetrate that all revolutionary tension becomes bodily innervation, and all the bodily innervations of the collective become revolutionary discharge, has reality transcended itself to the extent demanded by the *Communist Manifesto*. For the moment, only the Surrealists have understood its present commands. They exchange, to a man, the play of human features for the face of an alarm clock that in each minute rings for sixty seconds. [106]

One might regard Benjamin's politicizing aesthetics as a deeply ironic (and prophetic) response to Nazism, and so perhaps, explain his hope for a Marxist transcendence as his answer to the limits against which he saw only the piled-up disaster of the twentieth century. Although rejecting any such messianic impulse, American free spirits might find it possible and necessary to engage in an art of alarm, to portray the dark vision that lurks in the shadows of everyday life, the latencies where body and image deeply interpenetrate. The angles of vision available to us in the closing years of the twentieth century as we attempt to unite in new ways might evoke surrealism's alarm.

What alarm do we sound? Our state has become the most dangerous one in the world.

This privileged angle of vision of individualism only partly extricates liberal political theory from its complicity with the worst that politics has become, because it allows liberals to get away with murder by reading with their eyes shut. The retreat from politics embraced by even the best of individualist thinkers seduces them into thinking that there is somehow a safe place outside politics where they might thrive, a pristine, Lockean state of nature recovered through the "noncoercive" space of civil society. That illusion, reflected in the premature celebration of the emergence of civil society in post-Communist Europe, reveals a deep idiocy on the part of individualist thinkers in identifying a perfect freedom with complete separation and alienation. But nobody's perfect.

Or, no body is perfect. To the extent that liberal theorists are capable of beginning to think through bodies that have become highly charged and interpenetrated, and to enunciate critical thoughts that do not for one moment forget the presence of governmental powers in the very energy that allows and disallows their criticism, then liberalism may aspire to the status of fear, turning toward the wild life that resides between the institutions of governance, rather than pretending to be above or outside them. To fear, as Shklar teaches, is to inhabit the interstices of the institutions that govern. It is to be between places, to hesitate on the threshold of comfort and security offered by those institutions in order to act as a surrogate for those whose visions have been blotted out by pain. An ethic of fear is a response to the fiction that effaces the cruelties of government by accepting them as exceptions. It recognizes how ordinary the emergency of the twentieth century is. Fear could yet be the ethic of a liberalism that would care for the present and permit those who aspire to a present more bearable than the one we currently imagine.

Enabling gestures might make more visible such an ethic of fear, which could be expressed in a cautious fidelity to the plurality of experiences encoded in the lives of our bodies or found in the messiness of our private lives. To advance such an ethic we should not seek allegiances to obsolete walls that act as enclosures, to boundaries that exclude in order to contain, but instead, we lovers of freedom should hope to cross the frontiers that shape our contemporary experience, to find a loving appreciation of bodily fluids carefully and kindly exchanged, to wage war against the fascism inside each of us, recognizing that cruelty is indeed the worst thing we can do to each other, and for that reason further exploring the multitudinous ways in which we are being cruel to each other in our united states. New paths of freedom will not be mapped by the certain voices of condemnation (a tenor of voice that is too clearly born of uncertainty, and which is itself a species of cruelty), but by voices appreciative of the liminal states of our bodies, such as they are.

But even such an appreciation, such a deferring gesture, if presented as conclusion, is itself . . . cruel. Is it possible to choose that cruelty, if it fails to evade one even greater?

Perhaps for this reason alone I should introduce you to my experiences cautiously, as useless as they might be. I know that I have not been tested. My body is, so far, unassaulted, protected, free and strong, white and privileged, encased in books. Mine eyes have seen too little, and those experiences I cherish are too often secondhand, derived from a reading of the lives of other, more visible representatives of our culture. You do what you can with what you got. Whose bodies, whose experiences, will help us learn more? Who will help us understand how to engage one another without spilling so much blood in the pursuit of united states?

We need to study our bodies, as they tremble in fear and radiate possibility, as they stand on thresholds of change, of metamorphosis. Where next? Well, even the president of the United States must stand naked . . .

CHAPTER THREE

George Bush, or
Sex in the Superior Position

I don't believe my family was an aberration; instead, I'm afraid it was an extreme example of a much overlooked American norm.

—Mikal Gilmore

"We Have Had Sex"

We spill a lot of blood to remain bloodless. Our blood is often shed in the service of a patriotism that dares not speak its name. We disguise this particular patriotism because it conflicts with our better sense, and if revealed would show an antidemocratic bias in the fidelity of many American men.[1] If the subordination of democracy flows from a need to keep certain secrets among men, the secrecy about this patriotism is the most open secret of contemporary politics in our united states.

The arrangements of power we find most appropriate in our united states are continuous with whom we love and how we love: our core love is for men in the superior position. If love is blind, then what we see and the focus of our fields of representation depend on the range of positions we can imagine being in, *together.* Not only what we say to each other with our mouths, but what we express through our other organs of culture as well, lie before us as a series of hallucinations.

What we think is visible is often buried by its very appearance. Because we so accept Freud, we may have succeeded in evading his most important insight, the idea that desire is itself a law. As John Rajchman puts it, "Law *is* our desire, is the imperious necessity of our desire."[2] To seek out and register instances in the history of our desire (our law) requires that we work through the constitution of the necessary in this psychoanalytic sense. Here and now, this imperative leads me to think about George Bush.

But George Bush is not who he seems to be, and neither are we. Consider the 1988 presidential campaign. That campaign had many strange moments, but strangest of all was a moment at Twin Falls, Idaho, in May. It appeared probable at this point that Bush would win the Republican nomination for the presidency, but it was not yet certain. In this speech, as in many others, he referred to Ronald Reagan in an attempt to associate himself with the popular president. But this time the speech misfired. It said,

> For seven and a half years, I have worked alongside him, and I am proud to be his partner. We have had triumphs, we have made mistakes, we have had sex . . ."
> There was a stunned silence in the audience, and Mr. Bush hastened to add, "We have had setbacks." After a roar of laughter, the Vice President observed: "I feel like the javelin thrower who won the coin toss and elected to receive."[3]

The report from the *New York Times* suggested that Bush misspoke. But another reading is available if we pursue the laws of desire that flow through the media of our political representatives. Perhaps Bush's slip exposed his wish to be fucked by Ronald Reagan. Can we assume a latency here, a little queerness lurking in the Bush? If so, what kind of latency? Why would Bush wish to have sex with the Great Communicator?

To study presidential politics by inquiring into the secret motives of presidential politicians leads us onto slippery terrain. I need to ask questions that are still taboo among most adult straight men. How do we men love each other in our united states? What private codes of desire inform our public policies? These questions become important when particular circumstances prevail, when the constitution of desire as a political field intensifies violence. The circumstance that does the most to intensify violence is the one in which desire is pervaded by secrecy. But when is that?

Do I betray my own attractions in this meditation I present concerning George Bush? Moreover, who am I to invade this private arena of consciousness and unconsciousness, of secrecy and exposure? What are my motives? And what am I not revealing about my own sadism here? Is it the case that my sadistic wish is continuous with the cruelty that I think we cannot avoid? Am I fulfilling a dark wish for revenge against my own father in seeking to expose George Bush? And what of Bush himself? Must I return his hatred with my own without also making the mistake of loving him, in our American tradition of entering united states? Virtually everything I know of Bush comes from the public record. Is the portrait that emerges true or false? All of these questions are undecidable, assuming as they do that there is a true Bush to which they might refer. But again, we choose to pretend that it is true and thus make it so.

I often wonder what my father thinks when he reads about these men and sees them on television, men who share a common formative experience in a great war, men who are like him in so many ways, and yet who seem to have betrayed the best part of their common ethos in the service of a brand of patriotism so different from his more modest faith and skepticism. The modesty of my father's life might explain in part his lack of interest in attaining an exclusive position of power over others. He never faced, nor did he seek, the choices that come with power. But unlike my father who never sought that position of choice, and unlike these other men, who did, can I come out of the closet as a straight man in a superior position who also fears power and wishes to do as little harm as he can?

It is necessary to try. Because so many Americans have been willing to discuss the most intimate details of our lives in public for therapeutic purposes, but the most important silences, those concerning our open secrets, have not been addressed politically. We enter therapy to be comfortable. And yet our collective ethos demands a more arduous search for truth than any therapeutic sensibility could provide. What I might say about my father and me is only one instance of what is true for many who belong in the same broad category as Bush and his sons.[4] Too much of our lives together have been circumscribed by our complicit silence concerning the appropriateness of our loneliness, together and apart. Most straight men in our culture have few friends. George Bush is no exception, unless you count his thousands of "contacts." When he reads this, will my father, now so firmly set in his ways, reconciled to his children in the winter of his life, not see too much of himself, his anger, his fears, in George Bush (a man who disgusts him, Bush with his upper-class hypocrisy, Bush whose manners disguise a basic indecency)? Will he not be startled by this confessional moment, resistant but captive to the generic search for absolution in our culture? Won't he, like so many men of his and Bush's generation, not find this passage to be one more example of the silliness of this thing called the "men's movement," probably best expressed in films about vicious business executives who must be shot in the head and suffer brain damage before they can find their "inner child"?[5] Perhaps the contempt my father and I share for Bush is tied up in our resistance to the mirror our presidents hold up to us, reflecting the men of united states, as presidents always do. In that mirror we straight men in the superior position see ourselves fucking, fucking each other, and other others. We experience the politics of the passive position to be the negative pole of straight male desire, and the passive position is the one most of us endure at work.

It is an ever renewable commonplace for Americans to note how sex and power are closely related, but too often we make a mistake concerning the relationship of sex to power. We understand sex as reward and punishment and resist thinking about how the achievement of our united states is an ongoing sexual accomplishment. We divorce personhood from the landscape of the desire we have invented. If, as more orthodox Freudian cultural analysts might argue, a return of the repressed *explains* the character of the persons involved in such systems of power,[6] then we have, paradoxically, failed to capture the meaning of that desire for our personal politics.

Our politics remain something that is predominantly between men. But there are men, and then there are men. Against those who besmirch the political innocence of gay men, Eve Kosofsky Sedgwick has sustained a distinction between the homosexual and the homosocial in contemporary life. Sedgwick issues this caution: "To assume that sex signifies power in a flat, unvarying relation of metaphor or synecdoche will always entail a blindness, not to the rhetorical and pyrotechnic, but to such historical categories as class and race."[7] She suggests that the connections between the homosocial (which she describes as the typically exclusive male realm of social relations where male bonding occurs) and the homosexual (in which men have sexual intercourse with other men) are bound to vary from one historical situation to another.

Sedgwick suggests that in American political culture the continuum between the homosocial and the homosexual is disrupted. "In fact," she argues, "for the Greeks, the continuum between 'men loving men' and 'men promoting the interest of other men' appears to have been quite seamless. It is as if, in our terms, there were no perceived discontinuity between the male bonds at the Continental Baths and the male bonds at the Bohemian Grove or the board room or the Senate cloakroom."[8] Indeed, in our society, homosociality is homophobic. She points out as well that homophobia directed against men is just about invariably directed against women too in the same way.[9] Agreeing with Gayle Rubin's argument concerning the traffic in women, she suggests that the construction of homosocial bonds constitutes the defeat of the feminine. This pattern seems as well to be an appropriate model for the pattern of relationships among straight American men: straight men are commonly in positions of superiority over women and gay people, so we feel compelled to construct a homosocial realm that must be homophobic and misogynist in order to allow us to maintain that position. The intense discontinuity between the homosocial and the homosexual is born of that desire for security through superiority.

Sedgwick presents an epistemology valuable for understanding straight men, but I doubt that the constructed gap between the homosocial and the homosexual is as wide as she claims. In fact, there are some strong linkages between homosocial and homosexual desire that operate in the corridors of straight male power, whether in board rooms or the Oval Office. These connections, neither essential to homosexual identity nor exhaustive as an explanation of the performances of political actors, nonetheless lead to disturbing questions concerning the politics of governance and the governance of representations.

The connections we commonly make between homosexuality and homosociality are retrograde. That is, they are usually confined to stereotypical discussions of black-booted Nazis and simpering weaklings, united in parodies of sadomasochism. In our obsession with national security, the theatricality of this construct less often carries Nazi than Communist Party associations. Yet those who have ferreted out communists (because communists possess a deviant desire to unite?), and who now ferret out terrorists (because of their deviant death wish?), are themselves reluctant to expose themselves. Why? Privacy devolves into secrecy, it seems, when it is necessary for men in power to pretend to have no desire for privacy. This pretense is most necessary when the private ways they express pleasure are associated with how they maintain their superior positions. To give away their secret is to make them vulnerable because part of the pleasure they hold out, especially voyeuristically, is the pleasure of a secret domination that is expressed only partly by being on top. Hence the male order in American politics depends on the maintenance of a secrecy about desire among men in power, a secrecy that complicates public discourse about politics and has enabled the associated secrecy of the national security state. The widespread sympathy expressed for Casper Weinberger's indictment for lying to Congress in the Iran-Contra affair by such luminaries as

Tom Foley and Les Aspin expresses more than the survival instinct of power brokers—it is the public shape that private desire takes in such circumstances. If political scandals of the late twentieth century have devolved around cover-ups and their exposure, then the politics of secrecy is associated most clearly with the intense violence of making our most representative bodies the sites of such hidden importance. Male secrecy is not the stuff of illicit conspiracy, usually, but neither is it easily capsulized within the ordinary categories of repression or false consciousness. Our secrecy is associated with longing, a hope on the part of friendless men to recover the boy they have lost by simulating friendship with other friendless men.

One might think about the therapeutic moves made by Bill Clinton in the early days of his presidency—his hugs, his expressions of affection, his orchestration of handshakes in the wake of other's diplomacy—but one can trace such simulated moves as well in George Bush's public life. For instance, the relationship of Bush to his most famous protagonist, Saddam Hussein, was forged in secrecy. They first encountered each other from a distance when one headed the CIA and the other the Iraqi secret police.[10] At the time, Hussein was, with the tacit approval of the U.S. State Department, repressing Kurdish Iraqis. General Noriega of Panama also enjoyed a secret relationship with the CIA. I mention this not to pursue a theory of conspiracy. Instead, I seek to understand how secrecy might operate as an indicator of the fraternity these leaders enjoyed. Having undergone virile rituals of manhood (having engaged in combat against contamination by external and internal elements), the relationships they enjoyed were based on a denigration of those outside, parallel to the relationships that predominate in college fraternities at "home."[11] The betrayal involved in the violation of the secret codes of fraternity lent a certain energy to Bush's indignation against Noriega and Hussein, both of whom he sought to humiliate personally (demanding, for instance, that Hussein make a personal statement of concession before ordering a cease-fire at the end of the war). That Hussein has survived him in office necessarily contributes to Bush's humiliation, a humiliation Bush has always invited.[12] This squabble continues even after the end of Bush's presidency, and now involves Clinton. The honor of America is threatened when an ex-president foolishly visits Kuwait to taunt his old nemesis, and his nemesis responds by trying to kill him.

To say that men are boys is nothing new. And to suggest that heads of states concentrate in themselves a broader ethos is an ancient observation. But the content of our ethos is too often presented as though through a filter that has somehow blocked out the impure elements that would cloud an otherwise clean picture. What *do* we straight men want? Exactly because feminists are now turning to that question, in an ironic parody of Freud,[13] it might make some sense to turn to him, not for his insights regarding the formation of sexual identity, but for the help he might provide in decoding the abundant clues that men give regarding our secret wants and needs. We need to let others in on the joke.

Jokes

In a key passage in *Jokes and Their Relations to the Unconscious*, Freud argues that jokes might be understood as elements in a symbolic economy of pleasure. The compression of language in punning, the reliance of the joke on the context in which it occurs, sometimes even the reduction of a joke to a simple gesture, all are evidence that the joke is a form that, by relying so strongly on a context created out of particularly situated language assumptions, is very economical in the production of pleasure. Jokes allow the subject to have pleasure in an otherwise unpleasant situation by presenting in words what cannot otherwise be experienced through the release of bodily energies. The sources of pleasure in tendentious jokes, as opposed to innocent jokes, are related to either obscenity or hostility. The purpose of the obscene joke, according to Freud, is exposure, that of the hostile joke aggression, satire, or defense.[14] But when one explores the specifics of obscenity in comparison to hostility, Freud's distinctions become more problematic, especially in light of most contemporary understandings of sexuality and power differentials between women and men. As always with Freud, though, even his problems are helpful and illuminating. His replication of the misogyny of the time illuminates the trap of a peculiar dynamic of straight male desire.

Freud develops his distinction between the two categories of such jokes first by examining obscene jokes because for him the purpose of the obscene joke is more obvious than the purpose of the hostile joke. He prefaces his discussion of the obscene joke proper with a discussion of smut, which is "the intentional bringing into prominence of sexual facts and relations by speech . . . [that] is directed at a particular person, by whom one is sexually excited and who, on hearing it, is expected to become aware of the speaker's excitement and as a result to become sexually excited."[15] In short, dirty talk made "public." Embarrassment by the person addressed is interpreted by Freud as simply a roundabout admission of that person's excitement. And a third person who laughs at smut is "laughing as though he were a spectator of an act of sexual aggression."[16]

For Freud the smut speech is close to the seduction speech. When a woman acts defensively in response to obscene speech, smut is the result. Freud writes:

> Since the sexual act is held up in advance of the act, it pauses at the evocation of the excitement and derives pleasure from the signs of it in the woman. In so doing, the aggressiveness is no doubt altering its character as well, just as any libidinal impulse will if it is met by an obstacle. It becomes positively hostile and cruel, and it thus summons to its help against the obstacle the sadistic components of the sexual instinct.[17]

Freud goes on to note a class distinction in the practice of smut, namely, that in peasant classes it begins when women appear on the scene, and in the bourgeois classes it begins when women disappear. In peasant classes the presence of women makes them both target and part of the audience, whereas in the bourgeois classes the male audience is more important. It is at this point, with the disappearance of the target in the middle class, that smut assumes the character of the tendentious joke.

Tendentious jokes, in Freud's reading, satisfy instincts (whether lustful or hostile) in the face of an obstacle that stands in the way of the instinct's satisfaction. They do so in a way that through the use of language, draws some sort of pleasure from an object that is otherwise unavailable. (This missed pleasure is due to considerations having primarily to do with repression of what Freud called instincts.) In the case of the obscene joke, the "object" is the woman of the bourgeois classes, and the obstacle to the satisfaction of the man's libidinal impulses is her modesty, which has increased as she has risen in class status. These libidinal impulses can no longer even be expressed in the language of smut, but must be contextualized even further in the form of the joke.

The obscene joke is distinguished from the hostile joke by Freud in the most minimal way. Where the obscene joke expresses sexual desire in the form of hostility, the hostile joke expresses hostility in the form of . . . hostility. "Since we have been obliged to renounce the expression of hostility by deeds—held back by the passionless third person, in whose interest it is that personal security be preserved—we have, just as in the case of sexual aggressiveness, developed a new technique of invective, which aims at enlisting this third person against our enemy."[18] The chief difference between the two kinds of jokes is that in the obscene joke the presence of the target of the joke depends on the class of the woman, but in the hostile joke the target is never present because the source of hostility lies in the more recognizable (and less "natural") social situation, in the domination of that person over the joke teller. This is the formal structure of hostility, a structure always brought to the fore in contexts of social domination, and more particularly in situations in which that domination is acted out.

Freud helps us understand a particular dimension of our cruel practices. If we update his insight by attending to the more general economy of language that he attributes to jokes, we might better realize the importance of the following joke. Norman Mailer records it in *The Executioner's Song*, the epic of the life and death of Gary Gilmore. It is told by Gilmore to his girlfriend Nicole Baker. The joke is important for several reasons, as I hope to make clear, but most of all because Nicole's laughter is culturally continuous with the political dynamic that drives George Bush to reveal his desire to have sex with Ronald Reagan.

The scene occurs in the narrative of *The Executioner's Song* when Gilmore had already started to shoplift with regularity, and it was making those who knew him nervous. They worried that he would be caught, among other things, and a violation of parole would have meant an immediate return to jail. They also worried that he was losing control, but they were more worried for him than about him.

One day he came home with water skis and that bothered Nicole. It just wasn't worth the risk. He was stealing something he probably couldn't sell for more than $25, yet the price tag was over $100. That meant they could get you for felony. Nicole hated such dumb habits. He would take a chance on all they had for twenty-five bucks. It came over her that this was the first time she ever disliked him.

As if he sensed it, he then told her the worst story she ever heard. It was supergross. Years ago, while still a kid, he pulled off a robbery with a guy who was a true sadist. The manager of the supermarket was there alone after closing and wouldn't give the combination to the safe. So his friend took the guy upstairs, heated a curling iron, and rammed it.

She couldn't help herself. She laughed. The story got way in. She had a picture of that fat supermarket manager trying to hold on to the money and the poker going up his ass. Her laughter reached to the place where she hated people who had a lot of things and acted hot shit about it.[19]

Freud would have called this a tendentious joke. It enlisted Nicole in Gary's resentment. Nicole has her own resentments against the rich, those people who have a lot of things. Both of them are very poor. Both know they have only each other. But Gary especially sees himself as dependent on Nicole emotionally. In this story, for instance, he depends on her to ratify his resentment against the bosses who run things.

Is this an obscene joke? The audience for the joke is a woman. Her participation is sought, and her approval seems to compensate for Gilmore's inability to ram the "true" objects of his hatred, those who run and have the world. When Nicole expresses her resentment at those who think they are "hot shit," she is both in solidarity with Gary, and expressing ambivalence. The supermarket manager's shit needed to be heated by the hot poker, but the joke got in to places where Nicole burned already, without need of a poker. Class resentment and Nicole's ambivalence about sodomy set the stage for her reception of the joke. The true object of the hatred then vacillates; Nicole resents the joke teller as well as its target.

What limit-experience is Mailer transcribing in his narrative? What does Mailer, the hipster, seek to understand by exploring criminality's meaning for our political culture? It is precisely the truth of the matter that is elusive in this text, a truth we must explore if we are to face ourselves, to face our love and hate for each other.

Gary himself may have wanted to sodomize that supermarket manager. Our first question might be to ask if Gilmore's story, whether "true" or "false," exemplifies the pornographic imagination. But to place Gilmore's story in the genre of pornography does nothing to resolve the problematic status of this joke. It instead complicates the picture enormously, despite what one might think of former attorney general Meese's attempt to enlist pornography as a clarifying *political* explanation concerning the status of the dangerous individual.[20] Indeed, Meese's own pornography problem (a problem he shares with Catharine MacKinnon) underlies the problematic status of the culturally determined "truth" of this matter.

William Connolly's observations concerning the marquis de Sade might help us understand how the pornographic is entangled in efforts to make politically "normal" situations true. In an analysis of *Philosophy in the Bedroom*, Connolly has suggested that "the pornographic dimension . . . advances as the text proceeds through the induction of Eugenie into the connections between pleasure and cruelty to the closing scene in which Eugenie takes revenge against her mother for being her mother.

Desire is now assimilated with revenge in a mixture which becomes . . . definitive of the pornographic."[21] For Connolly, the Sadeian text expresses that which is created by the codes of reason at the core of the modern political project. He writes, "The tightening and intensification of the affirmative standards of reason, order, virtue and responsibility creates a subordinate space within which pornography attacks this entire network of ordering concepts."[22] The problem of pornography is that the text of vengeance it acts out is always an incitement to further ordering by the agents of order. Under the old regime in France the marquis was confined in prison, and then under the revolutionary regime he was declared insane. In this manner the tactics of the pornographer mirror those of the order that the pornographer putatively opposes.[23]

We might note that the 1989 death-row confession of the mass murderer Ted Bundy, who claimed that reading pornography was the pivotal moment in his life's path, is consistent with the notion of pornography as a writing of the word. Bundy declared, before he died, that eventually he needed to satisfy his imagination by acting it out on the bodies of others. But when we acknowledge Bundy's claim, acknowledging the compulsion of deathboundness in his tortured voice, then we must also ask how the pornographic imagination varies from the normal. To ask that question is to answer it. The two are the same, which creates a problem that conservative ideologues like Meese and MacKinnon are unable to cope with.[24] The dissolution of the genre distinction between pornography and other writings, say for instance, this book, subverts both attempts to censor pornography and the liberating intent of pornography itself. The "issue" of pornography, when reduced to the issue of freedom of expression, shifts focus from the content of the writing to the degree of flexibility of the state in "allowing" certain liberties, whether they be based in community standards or in a broader, more abstract, but always, in the final analysis, limited polity.[25]

We typically try to reduce Gilmore to the margins of our experience, thereby separating him cleanly from the normal operations of politics. But if we juxtapose Connolly's understanding of the Sadeian pornographic strategy with Freud's interpretation of the joke as a compensation for frustrated desire, we begin to understand the complex frustrations faced by Gary Gilmore and, in so doing, begin to discern how he is our brother we love to hide. But that is only the start. Because if we want to understand the codes of desire by which Gilmore is inscribed as a subject and hence the manner in which the violence of justice was exercised on him, then we must also understand better how he saw himself as a criminal. Of course, our curiosity about that self-imagined criminality is not innocent, either.

There are many barriers to the successful negotiation of codes of criminality here. The degree of reflexivity inherent in the habits that constitute the modern person makes even the most simple of observations tendentious, even before we try to sort out how we are violent in special ways. To take a relevant example, in attempting to comprehend more fully the politics of fascism, Klaus Theweleit shows how the rank and file of the German Nazi party were motivated by a hatred of women. But he also cautions against categorizing this misogyny as "latent homosexuality." Citing the prejudices shared by such left "kulturcritiks" as Theodor Adorno and Bertolt Brecht in regard to homosexuality, citing in particular a passage from Adorno's *Minima Moralia*, in which Adorno equates totalistic views of reality and homosexuality,[26] Theweleit writes,

> Within the context of Adorno's own system of values, this assertion can be seen to amount to an annihilation of those who were the victims of this totalitarian disease. To direct an accusation of this kind against Adorno appears particularly justifiable in relation to a proviso of his own insertion, in which his masculine allegiances come to light. For him, the "tough guys," despite their alleged hatred of effeminacy, are "in the end . . . the true effeminates." Are we then dealing with competition among men to determine who is the "real man"? Is effeminacy the worst imaginable shame?[27]

Is it a contest about who is the real man? This question introduces the issue of male gender identification in a complex way. The truth of masculinity here becomes a subcategory of the question, what is the truth of sex?[28] The construction of the dominant male gendered body as an artifice[29] seems to be at stake in the development of fascism. But how?

Theweleit does not pursue Adorno far enough. If Adorno naturalizes this question at one level, at another he describes with great clarity the acts of violence that are required for the formation of masculine identity. Adorno suggested in that aphorism (in the English translation, "Tough Baby") that there is a particular kind of violence at work in the creation of the tough guy. His model is cinematic, quite possibly Humphrey Bogart, or even more likely, given the bourgeois patina he places on it, Cary Grant (especially in his role in Alfred Hitchcock's *North by*

Northwest, this model would seem to be borne out). The objects with which such men surround themselves are those of "smoke, leather, shaving cream." "The pleasures of such men," Adorno wrote, ". . . have about them a latent violence. This violence

> seems a threat directed against others, of whom such a one, sprawling in his easy chair, has long since ceased to have a need. In fact it is past violence against himself. If all pleasure has, preserved within it, earlier pain, then here pain, as pride in bearing it, is raised directly, untrans-formed, as a stereotype, to pleasure: unlike wine, each glass of whiskey, each inhalation of smoke, still recalls the repugnance that it cost the organism to become attuned to such strong stimuli, and this alone is registered as pleasure. [30]

By applying dialectical logic to the habitual experience of pleasure and pain, by elevating the hedonistic calculus to the psychodynamic of a "named" neurosis, sadomasochism, Adorno succeeds in naturalizing the phenomenon he describes, suggesting that the "he-man" is the "true" effeminate. [31] But we need not follow Adorno to his conclusion. Instead, we can think, as Theweleit does with other pieces of evidence, about the description itself.

That description places a male body at risk in the continual reinscription of a code of desire through small acts of violence. The strong stimulation of whiskey (an "acquired taste") is but one example of the damage done to the body to construct a particular range of pleasures in resistance to the organism. So although Adorno suggests that "he-men are thus, in their own constitution, what film plots usually present them to be, masochists," [32] that masochism can be read as such only if one ignores the ambiguity of the term "constitution." That the constitution of masochism is culturally specific is suggested by Adorno's construction of his aphorism as a joke.

The title of Adorno's aphorism on the he-man is "Tough Baby," even in the original German edition of *Minima Moralia*. The ironic inversion that Adorno enacts here is summed up in two American words of slang, juxtaposed. A "tough baby" is a contradiction in terms. But "tough" takes on many meanings in American English—for instance as unfortunate or unlucky—and so does "baby," referring to a sexy woman who is subordinated to a man, to fellow men in African American English (Hey, baby), so there can be a register of meaning, ranging from the most masculine man to the most feminine woman, depending on how the reader negotiates the juxtaposition of the two words.

Adorno's assertion of the "truth" of the constitution of masochism and homosexuality's relationship to totalitarianism belies a *political* problem underlying his joke title. Adorno must have recourse to some truth that will enable him both to understand the problem of a totalitarianism he despises (and yet which he replicates in his worst moments) and a homosexuality that he explicitly loathes (and yet might aspire to). His reliance on dialectical logic enables him to be less responsible for his politics than he otherwise would be. Rather than inhabit the bifurcation of men into intellectuals and tough guys, he encompasses both sides to throw both away, the tough baby with the bathwater. By shifting poles just when we would expect him to embrace a conclusion (totalitarianism as an aggressive principle gives way, in the final analysis, to a "feminine" passivity and the intellectual becomes the "real" man, not unlike Clark Kent/Superman), he succeeds, at least to his own satisfaction, in escaping a fixed judgment concerning homosexuality. Homosexual desire becomes subsumed under the more tragic problem of fascism, it becomes fascism's mere shadow. Thus Adorno embraces the conventions of "normal" sexual desire, tragically following a path of least resistance.

If Adorno's joke falters when confronted by the specter of homosexual desire, what might be a better way to laugh when confronted with the problem of fascism and its relationship to homosocial hatred? Jacques Lacan provides another key in his famous essay on the mirror stage, in which he introduces the idea of the body-in-pieces.[33] The fantasy of the body-in-pieces is an anxiety retrofitted onto the child's assumption of his completeness, a completeness achieved when he first recognizes himself in a mirror. The child identifies his ego, or "Ideal-I," with his body. The subject thus anticipates a wholeness and completion that is not available through subjective experience. For Lacan, this infantile assumption presents a primary paradox for the adult subject. He writes,

> This *Gestalt*—whose pregnancy should be regarded as bound up with the species, though its motor style remains scarcely recognizable—by these two aspects of its appearance, symbolizes the mental permanence of the *I*, at the same time as it prefigures its alienating destination; it is still pregnant with the correspondences that unite the *I* with the statue in which man projects himself, with the phantasms that dominate him, or with the automaton in which, in an ambiguous relation, the world of his own making tends to find completion.[34]

Reflecting on the relationship of the body-in-pieces to Hitler's fascism, Susan Buck-Morss emphasizes its connection to war trauma.[35]

She notes that the mirror stage's importance lies in its retroactive apprehension. That is, it is triggered in the memory of an adult by contemporary experiences. She suggests, "Thus the significance of Lacan's theory emerges only in the historical context of modernity as precisely the experience of the fragile body and the dangers to it of fragmentation that replicates the trauma of the original infantile event (the fantasy of the *corpes morcelè*)."[36] The experience of this fragile body, which Buck-Morss situates in Germany, is of course not limited to German culture. It haunts our contemporary united states and poses a "choice," of sorts. Can we or will we be able to break through the fear that tempts us to remain narcissists, can we seek a third term through which we might break the reflexive relationship of a state of security?

If we are to make use of this Lacanian insight, we must more fully understand the joke that summarizes our anxiety. We must explore the political space of the tough baby. Rather than abandon that space, Norman Mailer inhabits it.[37] In *The Executioner's Song*, Mailer pursues the sexual ambivalence of Gary Gilmore unto death. In a variety of artful ways he suggests how it was that Gilmore came to be invested in some sort of evil having to do with sexual deviance. First, in his relationship with Nicole there is the fact that he wanted her to shave her pubis; when she complied he was more easily aroused.[38] He seemed to prefer anal intercourse with her,[39] and he often called her "pardner" after making love.[40]

Second, there is the larger context of the seasoned convict, in which power is equated with rape. Mailer quotes one of Gilmore's letters to Nicole:

August 20

What a bunch of punks. I'll bet I could take any one of them posse punks and fuck him in the ass and then make him lick my dick clean.

I was interviewed by a couple of psychiatrists today. They wanted lurid details . . .[41]

Gilmore juxtaposes an image of violent domination with an observation about the pornographic interest of the health professionals assigned to his case. He understands that the inmate code radiates beyond prison walls. The universal language of violent domination in American culture is that of sexual domination. "Fuck you." "He really fucked him over." "We got screwed." "Asshole." "Prick!" These colloquialisms function as the smutty compensation in language for the frustration of a desire, as Freud knew. To understand Gilmore's joke, a joke that is not so rare, requires that we admit that he openly transgresses boundaries most straight men deny transgressing, even though we transgress them every day.

Gilmore recognized that the psychiatrists "wanted the lurid details." Why wouldn't they? In Western societies the need to know who a criminal is has replaced as the determining factor in punishment the question of what acts a criminal may have committed. The specific entry of psychiatry into the question of criminality was occasioned precisely by a desire by the authorities to understand and control violence. This process, which Foucault has called "the psychiatrization of criminal danger," is invested in a series of concerns about the development of laboring and dangerous classes of people.[42] The role that psychiatry plays in this process is less that of establishing an imperialism over determinations of guilt and innocence than of securing a modality of power, a power that as long as it remains mysterious to the social order, threatens security. By demonstrating the existence of something called a "homicidal mania," psychiatrists intervene in the juridical process to prevent juridical administration at one level, because penalty is suspended in the case of insanity. But at another level, they operate to validate justice, because in the purest form, homicidal mania presents the citizenry with "proof" that there does indeed exist something that might be called purely criminal behavior, or as Foucault put it, "that in some of its pure, extreme, intense manifestations, insanity is entirely crime, nothing but crime."[43]

The pure criminality of Gilmore incited the impure psychiatrists to press for lurid details. They were attracted to his purity. But Gilmore's letter is very ambiguous. What did the psychiatrists seek details of? Gilmore's murderous acts or his sexual desires? His tendentiousness or his obscenity? Mailer suggests that Gilmore operated on the edge of a criminality worse than that of the homicidal maniac. The problem, it seems, is that of man/boy love.

In our united states, pedophilia is considered to be the worst case of homicidal mania, in that the pedophile commits a harm that is, peculiarly, imaginably worse than death. The pedophile is the invisible criminal, the criminal who most thoroughly characterizes the infinite deviousness of the criminal act and hence the ubiquitous horror of a potentially infinite harm that can underlie a criminal act. The social construction of this monster is the result of the enabling of a particular term, one that appears in French law under the rubric *attentat sans violence*, and which perhaps in English is best characterized by such terms as "child molestation" and "sexual harassment." Foucault notes a peculiar characteristic of sexual legislation of the nineteenth century, that

> it was characterized by the odd fact that it was never capable of saying exactly what it was punishing. *Attentats* (attacks) were punished; an *attentat* was never defined. *Outrages* (outrageous acts) were punished; nobody ever said what an outrage was. The law was intended to defend *pudeur* (decency); nobody knew what *pudeur* was. In practice, whenever a legislative intervention into the sphere of sexuality had to be justified, the law of *pudeur* was always invoked.[44]

At stake in the laws of sexual morality is the construction of what might be called "vulnerable populations." The establishment of children as such a group is the first step in a process by which this political strategy might be enacted. An intervention to protect children will work better than any other criminal commission because the vagueness of the offense is matched by the vulnerability of the object. This offense is dangerous to "society" itself.

(How dare you even look at my darling child!, I think, as I fall into this cold and neutral tone, this distance from the warmth of home. How dare we make our children into victims so as to better manipulate them, I think, on second thought. How do we dare to set aside our beloved children, knowing that we cannot spare them the knowledge, yet putting off their initiation into life a little bit longer, a deferring gesture, a limit-experience if ever there was one?[45] We dare to do this as part of our desire for points of stability, while secretly seeking these violent experiences. Our children! How do we straight men care for them, anyway, other than as things to be protected? That our sexuality is constructed to enable this sort of violence motivated Foucault in his investigations into ancient and alternative erotic ethics, just as I suspect it motivated Mailer in his study of Gary Gilmore.)

In one of his letters to Nicole, Gilmore mentioned his attraction to a thirteen-year-old boy.

> He was real pretty, like a girl, but I never gave him much thought until it became apparent that he really liked me. . . . One time he . . . asked if he could read this Playboy I had. I said sure, for a kiss. . . . He was one of the most beautiful people I had ever seen, and I don't think I've ever seen a

prettier butt. Anyhow, I used to kiss him now and then, and we got to be pretty good friends. I was just struck by his youth, beauty and naivete.[46]

In a powerful moment of empathy for Gilmore, Mailer recreates the thought of a writer, Barry Farrell, as Farrell dwelled on the meaning of this letter.[47] Farrell's character, knowing about Gilmore's taste in child pornography, is made to think,

> Could it be that Gilmore's love for Nicole oft depended on how childlike she could seem? That elf with knee-length socks, so conveniently shorn— by Gilmore—of her pubic locks. . . . You could about say it added up. There was nobody in or out of prison whom hardcore convicts despised more than child molesters. The very bottom of the pecking order. What if Gilmore, so soon as he was deprived of Nicole, so soon as he had to live a week without her, began to feel impulses that were wholly unacceptable? What if his unendurable tension (of which he had given testimony to any psychiatrist who would listen) had something to do with little urges? Nothing might have been more intolerable to Gilmore's idea of himself. Why the man would have done anything, even murder, before he'd commit that other kind of transgression.[48]

So the joke is on Gilmore, because the play of vengeance in which he was involved implicated him far deeper in the role of the pederast than he could tolerate. Gilmore's attempts to deny his attractions comes too late. He goes down in Mailer's book, on the basis of the presentation of evidence, as a pornographer. His pornographic imagination led him to his death.

Death or pedophilia, these are the alternative scripts to our united states.

One of our favorite political clichés is that issued by sexual libertines in polemical responses to movie censorship. They argue that explicit violence is less harshly censored than sex. They argue that the priorities of American society are out of kilter when sex is considered to be "worse" than violence. The joke is on them, as well as on us.

Love and Marriage

One could write an entire book about the role of sodomy in Mailer's art. Some have. The less sympathetic readings of Mailer declare him a misogynist and a homophobe who is "actually" a repressed homosexual, a classic woman hater. That is one reading, one Mailer himself undertook in his story "The Time of Her Time," and which he meditated on and complicated enormously by the time he wrote *Harlot's Ghost*.[49] But if Mailer is a misogynist, his misogyny is anything but simple. We might alternatively read Mailer as someone who gives expression to codes of desire that *explain* rather than merely embody the torturous path of male love in our united states. Then, perhaps, Mailer's understanding of the politics of prison and its constitutional connection to the politics of our experience can be seen as a theory concerning the operations of power and justice in the political culture of the superior position.

We can learn much of this theory from Mailer's correspondence with Jack Henry Abbott, who achieved a brief fame following his release from prison, the publication of his prison letters, and his subsequent conviction of manslaughter for killing Richard Adan, an aspiring actor and night manager at the Bini-Bon restaurant in New York City. Mailer and Abbott began a correspondence when Abbott discovered that Mailer was writing about Gilmore. Abbott offered information on what life was like in maximum security prisons in the United States. *In the Belly of the Beast* was the result. Mailer contributed a preface to that book. The preface introduces, not the thought of Abbott, but the code of desire that Mailer understands to fuel our justice.

Mailer writes, "Prison, whatever its nightmares, was not a dream whose roots would lead you to eternity, but an infernal machine of destruction, a design for the Dispos-All anus of a prodigiously diseased society."[50] This is how Mailer characterizes Abbott's understanding of the prison and what must be overcome to think intelligently while in it. The belly of the beast has an infernal anus. The paradox of the prison is that it submits to torture the best of the young as well as the worst. "It is that not only the worst of the young are sent to prison, but the best— that is, the proudest, the bravest, the most daring, the most enterprising, and the most undefeated of the poor.'[51]

Another, perhaps more remarkable metaphor sustains Mailer's equation of violence with bravery and nonviolence with cowardice.

The timid become punks and snitches, the brave turn cruel. For when bold and timid people are forced to live together, courage turns to brutality and timidity to treachery. A marriage between a brave man and a fearful woman may be exceeded in matrimonial misery only by a union of a brave woman and a fearful man. Prison systems perpetuate such relations.

Abbott doesn't let us forget why. I cannot think, offhand, of any

American writer who has detailed for us in equal ongoing analysis how prison is designed to gut and corrupt the timid, and break or brutalize the brave. No system of punishment that asks a brave human being to surrender his or her bravery can ever work for the common good. It violates the universal stuff of the soul out of which great civilizations are built.[52]

Mailer uses marriage, a civil relationship that is made not between a man and a woman but between them and the law, which is a contract mediated by the state, to underline his concern for the common good. Mailer's benchmark of justice is our common good and its harsh requirements. For Mailer our common good requires the preservation of the universal stuff of the soul. He thus replicates the debate concerning justice that has dominated political theory in the United States and Britain in recent years, the argument between liberals and communitarians about the fate of the souls of men. Siding with liberals, he insists the common good can only be achieved when individual freedom is maximized. But he goes further than John Rawls.[53] To constrain those poorly matched to a particular station is to exercise violence over them. Justice must recognize the circumstances of its coming into being. Justice fails that fails to adjust its judgments to radical differences in circumstance.

For Mailer, such uniformity contributes to the blandness that is currently overwhelming our culture. He sees prison as the great leveler that forces us to accept as our national anthem "the laugh of the hyena" that reverberates through every TV set.[54] Mailer does not resolve this problem of leveling noted since Tocqueville. He merely delineates it as the context from which Abbott's writing proceeds. As a brave man turned cruel, as an observant intellectual of the brutal, Abbott tells us about the justice we make.

Abbott's understanding of the prison radically separates reason from punishment and punishment from correction.

A system of justice that does not instruct by *reason*, that does not rationally demonstrate to a man the error of his ways, accomplishes the opposite ends of justice: oppression.

No one in any prison in this country has ever been shown the error of his ways by the law. It is an annoyance no one involved in the administration of justice wants to be bothered with.

So it is relegated to the prison regimes.[55]

Abbott's faith in reason during this period of his life (prior to his post-fame parole) is expressed through his Marxism, though after his return to prison he turns to the Torah for its reasonable truths to qualify the cold dialectic of Marx and Engels.[56] But Abbott places his faith in the very justice that damaged him, the very reason expressed in the violence of justice, the very repression that promises the liberation he doubts. He still believes in sex in the superior position.

Only the brave or foolhardy attempt to think about how violence is inherent in justice. It isn't easy. Robert Cover, a powerful legal theorist, recognizes Abbott's plea while trying to press beyond it. "Between the idea and reality of common meaning falls the shadow of the violence of law, itself," he writes.[57] Although Cover hopes to recover a law that would somehow be a privileged space of violence, that would, as he understands it, establish a style of adjudication that separates legal interpretation from all other fields of interpretation by virtue of its monopoly on violence, he is still mistaken in the same way that Jack Abbott is mistaken. Enlightenment itself has forced those of us who address current strategies of justice to abandon the counterstrategy of confrontation and concentration, because that counterstrategy participates in the sadism that is its inherent teleology. It is mistaken for the same reasons that the marquis de Sade's pornography is mistaken. The pressures each places on the contemporary encodings of power generate responses that implicate those resisting it into the directives of power itself. Privileged transcendencies of all stripes bring us, as subjects of desire, to a common threshold. Once we cross over, those of us who resist violence suffer more damage than we can possibly inflict on the structure of violence itself.

But there is an alternative path that might enable us to understand better the degrees of violence and possible paths of remedy in established codes of our justice. If we follow Jack Abbott to where he has thought more painfully and thoroughly than have most of us—to the area of gender relations and gender oppression—then some tentative steps toward a tactical opposition to the violence of justice might appear. Abbott takes us to the door that Bush, Mailer, and others open, but refuse to walk through.

A key passage in *In the Belly of the Beast* is Abbott's discussion of the relationship between sex and violence.

> . . . It is an absurd contradiction that in (at least) American society for a man to see the sexual penetration of his wife (or female companion) as a consecration and expression of love—and then to see this *same* act of penetration, but of another male, as just the opposite: a *desecration* and expression of the deepest contempt. It is because of this contradiction that sexuality is so profoundly and deeply wed to violence.

One of the first things that takes place in a prison riot is this: guards are sexually dominated, usually sodomized. I'm not pretending I do not "understand" this; we all do. I disagree on several counts that this is "natural" and that all overt acts of sexual aggression fit the concept of *violence*, because violence is *destructive*. There are those who entertain such acts out of *love*. But what is clear is that when a man sodomizes another to express his *contempt*, it demonstrates only his contempt for woman, not man. The normal attitude among men in society is that it is a great shame and dishonor to have experienced what it feels like to be a woman. I think such a radical attitude reflects *strong* feelings on the matter.[58]

Abbott understands the violence against women implied in the forcible sodomization of a man. He shows political acumen by focusing on the moment of decision, when the motive of the act informs its execution. His assertion that the decision has been made, time after time, in favor of the degradation of women flows not from his identification with women but from his negative experience of manhood. Make no mistake: he does not suggest that it is for the sake of women that a man must choose to love rather than rape. It is because the decision to rape is already implicated in the normal structure of power that the political criminal might oppose the code of desire the penitentiary inscribes in inmates and a masculine culture inscribes in power. A transgressive politics of manhood will renounce sex in the superior position. It will rewrite the linkages inscribed in contemporary life.

The violence Abbott suffers in prison is the type that insists on making a man of him. (Similarly, Wilbert Rideau, an inmate at Angola Prison in Louisiana, discovers that manhood is at stake in prison rape. He writes, "Within that peculiar societal context, an exaggerated emphasis is placed on the status of 'man,' and the pursuit of power assumes overriding importance because power translates into security, prestige, physical and emotional gratification, wealth—survival.")[59] As a state-raised convict, like Gary Gilmore, what is at stake for Abbott is the retention of manhood. But like Mailer, it is also the soul that Abbott wishes to preserve. In an exchange with Mailer, Abbott writes,

The most fragile and delicate of all ideas are those that reflect the fact that within human beings, there is an impenetrable area that *no one* can enter and defile: a heart of human tenderness so tenacious, so all-suffering and accepting, calm and *resilient to* human response, to love, that no force on earth can ever defeat it. It is the idea of the soul—and there are many of them; they are born "fragile and delicate" and have to survive each day and be re-created each day under the most difficult of conditions.[60]

The prisoner we are asked to free is already the effect of a subjection much more profound than himself. "A 'soul' inhabits him and brings him into existence," Foucault writes, "which is itself a factor in the mastery that power exercises over the body. The soul is the effect and instrument of a political anatomy; the soul is the prison of the body."[61] Abbott seeks the soul that already inhabits him. He seeks to be strong, so that his manhood, his humanity, will not be taken from him.

The irony is that his humanity is what has already subjected him to that special torture suffered by the penal subject. Abbott's most open plea for sympathy, a plea he has since silenced in himself, asks men in search of the child inside, to imagine as he does.

> Can you imagine how I feel—to be treated as a boy and not as a man? And when I was a little boy, I was treated as a man—and can you imagine what that does to a boy? (I keep waiting for the years to give me a sense of humor, but so far that has evaded me completely)
>
> So. A guard frowns at me and says: "Why are you not at work?" Or: "Tuck in your shirttail!" Do this and do that. The way a little boy is spoken to. This is something I have had to deal with not for a year or two—not even ten years—but for, so far, eighteen years. And when I explode, then I have burnt myself by behaving like a contrite and unruly little boy. So I have, in order to avoid that deeper humiliation, developed a method of reversing the whole situation—and I become the man chastising the little boy. (Poor kid!) It has cost me dearly, and not just in terms of years in prison or in the hole.[62]

Abbott has come to believe, like most metaphysicians of justice, that he must overcome his subjectivity because it is only possible to face himself through the lens of the punishing power of that soul of his, a soul that he knows, despite its fragility, is far too hard on the little boy it chastises. He identifies that poor kid as an orphan, parentless, but he could say more, he could mention that the boy is motherless, not because of a primal identification that he has missed, not out of the nonresolution of an Oedipal drama, but because he has been raised by the state.[63] Abbott desires to become a political subject, yet he also seeks the common ground that he identifies, from a distance, as being the normal experience of the depoliticized citizen of our united states.

If we straight men might be said to be *pained* into becoming *persons* by virtue of submission to the law, if indeed the peculiar subjectivity of straight men in the superior position is tied to the specifics of our legal project, then the question of desire becomes more important than most studies of power and politics have ever acknowledged. But even those of us who have faced this issue still flinch in the face of the full ramifications of its meaning. The problem, in its essence, is that we are caught in a reflexive relationship with law. We come to want that which we seem to repudiate, the terms of legitimate personhood as sanctified by the just and the good that always lies slightly beyond the powers that force us into being. Like the ideal pornographer, we can only find identity by taking seriously that which threatens to destroy us precisely to the extent that we take such matters seriously.

Abbott claims to have no sense of humor. Jokes appear to be a defeat for all, a compensation that the criminal political theorist cannot allow himself. That lack afflicts not only Abbott but all theorists who think that there are appropriate and inappropriate moments for laughter, and that the business of power is exclusively a serious one. Perhaps only those who are power's casualties can laugh from the belly these days? The casual brutality of Gary Gilmore's joke and the desperate laughter it produced in Nicole Baker might be explained then, not so much by reference to the compensatory function of the tendentious joke as by reference to the economic condensation of a language that represents the condition of power as it ceases to be mediated by ordinary politics. Mailer suggests that Gilmore "believed that he could find no happiness this side of death," but that Abbott, in contrast, was "a potential leader."[64]

The Trial(s) of the Century

If our prisoners are self-conscious about sex, what about our politicians? Bush is at the end of long line of political actors who stumble over the terms of sexual discourse. If the claims I have been making here, however, are sensible, then he stumbles as a consequence of his experience of the violence we conceal. When Bush suggests that we might be able to overcome AIDS by changing our behavior, he expresses as well his own bad faith regarding sex in the superior position. His politics, the politics of an operator more than an ideologue, suggest less a right-wing dream of purity than the gendered male in the superior position lusting for whatever he might grab.

Political operatives, professional fixers, those identified as reactionary in their views and shallow in their political commitments, inhabit the middle ground of this political culture. They rule through connections and exclusions. Take Roy Cohn . . . please. Cohn is the exemplar of the contemporary political operator.

When Cohn died of AIDS in 1986 a minor furor erupted. He had built his reputation accusing others of harboring secret desires against the government of the United States. And whereas Cohn's work as legal counsel to Joe McCarthy focused primarily on exposing people as members of the Communist Party, he also focused efforts on exposing the "problem" of homosexuals in government. Despite his own sexual relations with men, he maintained a lifelong public posture against homosexuality and gay rights. His relationship with another member of McCarthy's staff in the early 1950s, David Shine, was the subject of rumor and speculation.[65] In the years that followed his mother's death, Cohn became less "discreet" about his sexuality; but even then he claimed not to be homosexual.[66] Cohn circulated in the highest circles of New York and national politics on the assumption that he was part of a homosocial, as distinct from homosexual, network of "power play-ers."[67]

Cohn was a remarkably disingenuous political actor, chronically under indictment for shady legal practices, often under investigation by the Internal Revenue Service for failure to pay taxes, branded for life by his association with McCarthy, known as a "mob" lawyer. But he also enjoyed the respect of "inside" politicians for his ability to "fix" things, that is, to trade favors with those in positions of power. The game of politics, it seemed, was his primary source of sexual pleasure. Cohn articulated the relationship between sexual desire and American politics in the following description of how he did his homework as a boy.

> "I'd get done in an hour what other kids needed three or four hours to do," Roy said and then, "I'd stay in bed and think. When I finished my homework I would lie in bed without any clothes on and I would just think. I would think about politics. I had already met Roosevelt. I would think about the law, because sometimes later in the evening I would go down to my father's chambers or I would sit in court and I would think. . . . Sometimes I'd jerk off."[68]

Or, while describing a social evening.

> At his parties he'd haul people to their feet to sing "God Bless America," evidently his favorite song, and though he was a life-long opera-goer, Roy's idea of a good time was to a close a piano bar in Provincetown after having spent the hours to last call with the gang singing patriotic ditties. A

friend recalled going home early one summer evening, and inquiring the next morning how the rest of the night had gone, being told that, "We all stood around the piano. Roy sang three choruses of 'God Bless America,' got a hard-on, and went home to bed."[69]

Why not find the very *idea* of American politics sexually stimulating? After all, politics for him, as a man in the superior position, is no more and no less than the exercise of desire. It finds its most salient expression in the play of exchange, in one hand washing the other, in the winning and losing that occurs between men. Cohn operated under a code that Sidney Zion, his authorized biographer, describes as favors given and favors received.[70]

Within the matrix of that game, one seeks protectors as well as protagonists. Although Joe McCarthy was a major sponsor, Cohn's protector was someone of much greater importance to twentieth-century political culture. Behind Cohn stood J. Edgar Hoover. Although McCarthy gave his name to the era, Hoover was the person responsible for its most enduring heritage of fear. Hoover guided Cohn through his earliest incursions into the world of Communists, providing him with information and advice during the course of Cohn's prosecution of the Rosenbergs. Hoover protected Cohn from his enemies, giving him inside knowledge that helped him escape conviction after he was indicted.[71] Hoover did so in exchange for a particular kind of fealty, the willingness of Cohn to adopt an obsequious attitude. Cohn was adept at this posturing toward older men. Moreover, Cohn shared a common enemy with Hoover in Robert Kennedy, whose own hatred of Cohn led him to abuse the office of attorney general of the United States in order to violate him. Hoover aided Cohn and attempted to damage Kennedy, because the Kennedy brothers, John but especially Robert, represented, in their commitment to civil rights and their compulsory (and compulsive) heterosexuality, commitments that both Cohn and Hoover feared and loathed.

The career of J. Edgar Hoover has repeatedly been told, but not too many of us have seemed to appreciate how exemplary his story is. Adopting the techniques of the organizers of Bible schools to the bureaucracy of justice,[72] understanding the importance of the development of the cult of personality and using it to his fullest advantage,[73] absolute in his moral fervor, yet never moving beyond the sanctioned approval of those presidents whom he hated (absolute in fervor, but when the crunch came, always willing to compromise), Hoover developed the "Americanism" that informed right and wrong in the prosecution and punishment of law offenders for half a century. He insisted that people like Jack Henry Abbott were animals. He developed the policing policies that would ensure that they were treated as such.

Richard Powers writes that Hoover started talking like a "tough guy" after 1935, when his image as a superhero had been solidified by his ceaseless efforts to achieve a Hollywood-hero image.[74] His rhetoric concerning the "nature" of the criminal began to resound with the passion of the purist. And yet there was also another edge to it. For instance, in a speech to the Hi-Y clubs of America in 1936, Hoover said, "John Dillinger was nothing but a beer-drinking plug-ugly, who bought his way from hideout to hideout, being brave only when he had a machine-gun trained upon a victim and the victim was at his mercy. When Dillinger finally was brought to bay, he was not a romantic motion picture figure but only a coward who did not know how to shoot, except from ambush."[75] These comments harbor the experienced knowledge of a fellow undercover operator. Dillinger could not shoot, except from ambush—he needed to sneak up on people in order to discharge his weapon. Against the filthiness and the hidden dangers presented by such criminal aspirations, Hoover counterposed a world of decency.

> There is no romance in crime and there is no romance in criminals. We have passed through an era in which ill-advised persons and sentimental sob-sisters have attempted to paint the desperate law violators of America as men and women of romance. They are the absolute opposite. They are rats, vermin, regurgitating their filth to despoil the clean picture of American manhood and womanhood. They sink deeper and deeper into a mire of viciousness which inevitably leads to filth in mind, filth in living, filth in morals and bodily health. They travel steadily downward until at last they are no more than craven beasts.[76]

The opposition between clean and dirty governs Hoover's moral discourse. Moral filth is closely associated with bodily filth, and the filthy are linked to the romance of "sob-sisters." It is an old discourse, predating our Revolution (see, for instance, Benjamin Franklin's *Poor Richard's Almanac*), but Hoover's moral hygiene had its roots in more contemporary and more personal circumstances as well. If in fact Hoover had sex with men while despising homsexuality, his drive to degrade the criminal and ridicule the sob-sisters who refused to do so becomes understandable as more than a police practice. When one realizes that Hoover had a special personal relationship with one of his agents, Clyde Tolson, that lasted from 1928 until Hoover's death in 1972, his moralistic fervor, bodily metaphors, absolutist rectitude, and gendered discourse begin to fit together.

Hoover believed that his absolute duty was to protect us against social change. Change from the status quo of his parochial Washington, D.C., upbringing, whether it had to do with race relations and shifts in the extent of rights enjoyed by people, the evolution of family structure, or even the appearance of organized crime, were disturbances that cluttered up the world of right and wrong. The incoherence he perceived in the very idea of civil disobedience allowed him to understand the civil rights movement to be, in some ways, worse than communism, in that it presented a challenge to law that was explicit and graphically enacted. The sexual peccadilloes of Martin Luther King became for him the most salient reflection of the general moral degeneracy of the entire civil rights movement, because they represented someone who was more than willing to live out ambivalent desires. Such inconsistency was for Hoover a simple sign of filth.

Hoover's persona fits the political profile of the narcissistic fascist characterized in Buck-Morss's reading of Lacan. A primary expression of such anxiety is fear of contamination. In Michael Rogin's study of American demonology, he notes the obsession of Richard Nixon and the Nixon administration with metaphors of dirt and cleansing. Rogin suggests that such a use of metaphor reflects fears that will never be resolved because they are based on personality complexes that are, by definition, unresolvable at any level other than that of exorcism.[77] Theweleit's *Male Fantasies* suggests an even more troubling, though perhaps also more remediable, link.

For Theweleit the link between homosocial culture and misogyny in Weimar culture was rooted in the fear of dirt, and that fear was associated in a variety of ways with bodily fluids.

> At some point, his bodily fluids must have been negativized to such an extent that they became the physical manifestations of all that was terrifying. Included in this category were all of the hybrid substances that were produced by the body and flowed on, in, over, and out of the body: the floods and stickiness of sucking kisses; the swamps of the vagina, with their slime and mire; the pap and slime of male semen; the film of sweat that settles on the stomach, thighs and anal crevice, and that turns two pelvic

regions into a subtropical landscape; the slimy stream of menstruation; the damp spots wherever bodies touch; the warmth that dissolves physical boundaries (meaning not that it makes *one* body out of a man and woman, but that it transgresses boundaries; the infinite body; the body as flow). Also the floods of orgasm: the streams of semen, the streams of relaxation flowing through the musculature, the streams of blood from bitten lips, the sticky sweatiness of hair soaked with sweat. And all the flowing delights of infancy: the warm piss-stream running down naked legs; the mire and pulp of fresh shit in the infant's diapers, the fragrant warmth that lets the body expand, the milk-stream from the mother's breast, the smacking of lips on the comforter, the sweet pap that spreads over hands and face, the sucking on a never-ending thumb, the good-tasting stream of snot running from the nose into the mouth, not to mention the liberating stream of hot tears that turns a mask into a pulp and then a face again.[78]

Theweleit notes that during the Weimar period, boys were raised to cut off these flows.

One thing is certain: as part of the boys' very early training to be sol-dier males (and what Wilhelmine bourgeois—or, indeed, what social-democratic—education didn't have that as its goal?), harsh punishments were meted out if any of the wet substances in question turned up other than in its specifically designated place or situation. One after another, the streams were cut off or banished to the back of beyond. A social dam and drainage system captured every stream—even beer-laden streams of vomit, which had to vanish into a particular basin of the clubhouse before any of the "old boys" caught sight of them. As far as I can see, only three streams were permissible: streams of sweat; streams of speech; and the inexhaustible streams of alcohol. Under specific conditions (toward which the entire system steered), a fourth stream was added: the stream of blood from murdered victims, or the stream of your own "raging blood."[79]

This frantic concern with corruption, particularly linked with female bodies and flows, the regimentation, suppression, and control of flows as a sign of masculine control of the body, this terror constituted the hatred and anger of the German *Freikorps*. But what does it have to do with the campaigns of Hoover?

Powers makes note of the connections in his biography of Hoover.

In both Europe and the United States, veterans who felt threatened by revolutionary ideology organized themselves to defend against the revolu-tion. The most violent was the German *Freicorps*, which put down the

German revolution and killed Karl Liebnecht and Rosa Luxemburg. In the U.S., the leaders and members of the wartime American Protective League, disbanded after the armistice by order of the Justice Department, begged to be allowed to regroup to oppose bolshevism and, in isolated instances, this offer was informally accepted. In an uncomfortably close parallel to the *Freicorps*, the American Legion was founded on May 15, 1919. In November 1919, there was a pitched battle between members of the IWW and the American Legion in Centralia, Washington, in which one of the IWW members, Wesley Everest, himself a World War I veteran, was castrated, hanged, and shot to death by a mob of Legionnaires.[80]

Powers notes that Hoover had to concern himself with the excessive enthusiasm of the Legion, because its members too often went beyond the law in their campaigns. But the existence of such a group marked an American constituency similar to these German men, a constituency that shared a common concern. The morass, the muck, the swamp, or as Hoover put it, the filth that would "despoil the clean picture of American manhood and womanhood," had to be destroyed in order to keep things clean, to keep America pure.

A recent biography of Hoover by Anthony Summers enables us to understand how the struggle for purity shapes the closeted operative's identity.[81] Summers documents charges that Hoover engaged in cross-dressing as a prelude to group sex with younger men. At least once he dressed in a fluffy black dress and stockings, and another time wore a red dress. He would wear makeup. Summers's informant notes that he didn't participate in anal intercourse. Quoting his source, Susan Rosenthiel, who was at the time married to one of Hoover's sexual partners, Summers writes, "Hoover had a Bible. He wanted one of the boys to read from the Bible. And he read, I forget which passage, and the other boy played with him, wearing the rubber gloves. And then Hoover grabbed the Bible, threw it down and told the second boy to join in the sex."[82] Hoover allowed himself to be played with, but he avoided that dirty orifice. Hoover found having the Bible read to him to be arousing.[83] Rosenthiel also suggests that Hoover made no attempt to disguise who he was, remaining obviously the FBI Director dressed as a woman.[84]

One could say that Hoover seemed unable to introduce a third term that would break the infinite regression of the duality of the mirror.[85] Rather than blurring boundaries between a male self and female other to break with his narcissism and enter a symbolic order, cross-dressing seems to have operated as a gesture of absolute appropriation of the female other into the misogynist, narcissistic male. Hoover's hatred of women, particularly women who he thought denied the role of the traditional mother, might speculatively be connected to narcissistic cross-dressing through the case of Ethel Rosenberg.

The incidents of cross-dressing Summers reports occurred in 1958, about five years after the Rosenberg electrocutions. Hoover despised Ethel Rosenberg, not least because when in prison, Ethel Rosenberg refused to see her mother (who took the side of Ethel's brother and urged her to betray her husband Julius).[86] Rosenberg's rejection of her mother was unimaginable to Hoover. As Virginia Carmichael suggests, "Hoover's relationship to his own mother served a defensive function in his obsession with the enemy within."[87] The threat Ethel Rosenberg posed was that of overturning the man in the superior position, dominating him by evading her natural function as a mother. As one report on Ethel and Julius's relationship suggested, "Julius is the slave, and his wife, Ethel, is the master."[88] Ethel was sentenced to death in an attempt to get Julius to confess to his crimes; that he never did became for Hoover retroactive evidence of the disorder of their relationship.

Five years later, Hoover put on a red dress. Roy Cohn introduced him as "Mary" to Susan Rosenthiel: perhaps this is but a reflection of the commonplace name given to older homosexual men.[89] But "Mary" was also the name of the mother of Christ, who was killed by the Jews only to rise again. Hoover, as Mary, Mother of God, donned the garb of the unnatural daughter and obliterated the unacceptable third term, represented externally by Ethel Rosenberg, a woman who refused even to be a good criminal. Thus Hoover armored himself against his fear of the body-in-pieces.

The celebration of flows, the desire for and celebration of ambiguity, the readiness to open oneself up emotionally, physically, and politically, the experimental cast to one's bodily arrangements that characterizes gay culture, contrasts strongly with the terrors of corruption and fear of flows underlying the cultural discourse of the superior position cover-up. The prevention of infection that has been made controversial again because of the rise of AIDS has not loosened its grip on our collective imagination and has in fact been used by those who would demonize queer culture. Being a man in the superior position in this culture means to define oneself against queerness, as anyone following our recent national debate concerning homosexuality and military service knows. But we men in the superior position cannot stop sharing in queerness. It is our compulsion, and hence we must purify our selves to avoid its debilitating effects, its threat to our power. How much more effort will it take to purify our selves, what political bargains are we men willing to make as the epidemic spreads? What repressions will we tolerate and condone? The queer politics of AIDS is thus confronted with the united state of national security.

"Take My Vice-President, Please!"

The irony of the national security state must be that it leads its protectors into temptation to violate its secrets. The temptation to confess as well as to seek vengeance are parts of this structure, parts of this struggle. One might think that George Bush's Freudian slip is indicative of his wish to reveal the resentment of the vice-president, the second banana, the potential leader, so to speak. The vice-presidency, as once described by a holder of the office, "isn't worth a warm bucket of shit." To generalize; as the excremental office, the vice-presidency is the perfect office from which to gain a perspective on the operations of justice in an age of decline.[90]

Bush, as the potential leader, holding the vice office, performed a rite of self-abnegation in pursuit of ideal office not dissimilar to that undertaken by Jack Abbott in his pursuit of ideal justice. Bush did not resist the terms of his apprenticeship, he declared undying fealty to a man he previously held in contempt (recall his statement about "voo-doo economics"). Bush becomes the man punishing the boy for wanting approval from a father who is never there when he needs him and is always judging him when he doesn't need judgment. Bush's father, in this case, is someone who Bush could never satisfy—first because his first father, the senator, was someone whom Bush superseded in stature only with his own rise to the presidency itself—second because his second father, Richard Nixon, who taught him the ways of secrecy and made him head of the CIA, betrayed him at every step of his advancement, constantly holding out yet another potential reward but always withholding it in the end[91]—and finally, because the third father, Reagan the movie-star president, is a man whose own defense against the primary source of pain in his life (his own drunken father, which makes Reagan fatherless) was to withdraw from all potentially painful relationships. (Reagan is like Clinton, who provided Bush with yet another fatherly rebuke in the second 1992 presidential debate by reminding Bush of Prescott Bush's condemnation of McCarthyism.) Reagan's strength as a politician is that he learned early in life not to care too deeply. Bush's response to Reagan is not unlike that of Reagan's oldest son, Michael, who has written an entire book about his father's lack of affection for him and his absence from Michael's life in the wake of Reagan's painful divorce from Jane Wyman.[92]

The estate of the desperate debtor, Thomas Hobbes suggests, is a dangerous state of being. It engenders deep resentments, which reflect the tensions of those who know that beneath a patina of civilization, tenuously held in check by the sword of an authority, every man must lock his door at night and his strongbox all the time. Hobbes's description of this estate makes no distinction between public and private: such a distinction is perpetuated in the wake of the establishment of authority and must always be guarded against, at best cautiously employed. We all know that Bush could never express his hostility to Ronald Reagan, but an entertaining element of our political spectacles has been precisely in the artifice of civility that always threatened to slip away in his public moments. The civility of public discourse is always at risk in situations where it is possible for candidates to slip. When Bush jokes, exposure is always possible. Because the joke operates precisely to make accessible resentments and desires in a form that is acceptable, it makes allowable what otherwise is not. So, appropriately, Bush directs the force of his joke in Idaho, not at Reagan, but at himself. As the winner of the coin toss who elects to receive the javelin, he truly fucks himself.

Of course, he does so only in the interest of power. And he chooses a pretty young man, a fellow Deke, to be *his* vice-president. Throughout his ritual hazing Dan Quayle showed that he too had neither dignity nor pride. Frustrated by the handlers who insisted on keeping him away from Bush after the series of embarrassments concerning his record and style, Quayle had no choice but to submit. Yet when he first appeared in front of the American public acting like a hyperactive child, punching the air, hugging Bush, who visibly flinched, one also could recall the hyperactive Bush himself, playing eighteen holes of golf in an hour, running from one event to the next.

Bush does not want to be exposed. But true to the logic of secrecy, he insists on it. Shortly after the presidential election, he returned to his ancestral home at Kennebunkport, Maine, and announced that his father (the senator) would have been proud of "his little boy."[93] With that statement, the parallel between criminal and president is complete.

Gary Gilmore and George Bush are brothers under the skin. Both were, in a sense, raised by the state. Both sought out father figures throughout their lives to guide them. Both suffered abusive childhoods, experienced abandonment, were institutionalized in their teens. Both drifted away from home. Both eventually became killers. Both ran continuously from their most secret impulses while creating codes of desire that enabled them, like the pornographer, to enjoy vicariously the pleasure otherwise unallowable. We might protest that Bush enjoyed a privileged life, that Andover is not a prison, that wealth surely made up for the chiding of a father, that going to Texas to invest family money is not being a drifter, that fighting for one's country, serving in Congress, defending Richard Nixon, directing the CIA, and being vice-president are radically different than holding up gas stations, murdering young men, and being condemned to death (although it appears Bush is under death sentence by Saddam Hussein). And of course they are, after a fashion, but to establish those differences requires that we expose their common link in the same code of desire. Even before thinking about the position of the bodies of young black men in this matrix of power, we might note that Bush never would be in his position were it not for the superior position he had enjoyed since birth. All of his life, he has enjoyed the privilege that can make one overlook the damage one does, that allows one to keep the secret of sex in the superior position secure.

We are witnessing a moment in the history of power when the codes of desire that channel and regulate politics are undergoing mutation as a consequence of becoming more and more transparent. The compulsory homosociality of the Reagan and Bush years is to be superseded, it seems, by the compulsory heterosociality of the Clintons. The focus on strategy and tactic that informs electoral politics is only indicative of the transparency of these codes. Most of us know that hostility hides desire, that whom one loves and why one loves are closely tied to what one wants, and that what we want is determined by advertisements, music, and drugs. We know that the prison furlough advertisements featuring Willy Horton in the 1988 presidential campaign were racist (as Lee Atwater's deathbed confession makes clear) and that the war in the Persian Gulf was not fought to secure freedom but wealth. No one but Jack Abbott and a few political theorists believes in justice anymore, because the rest of us have learned to repress our knowledge of the brutality that shapes desire, and then to be concerned only with the damage that our repression has done to us. All of us are concerned with taking care of ourselves, at this point all of us seek the appropriate twelve-step programs to relieve our guilt and to stabilize ourselves, all of us are hopelessly indebted to others for whatever measure of security and prosperity we might enjoy, and no one knows what to do next.

We made Bill Clinton our president to succeed George Bush, but did we repudiate Bush-ism to do it?

In the final 1988 presidential debate, Michael Dukakis disparaged as meaningless Bush's employment of the phrase "a thousand points of light," thus threatening, if only briefly, to disrupt the Bush campaign juggernaut. The "points of light" rhetoric was the cover for the open secret of racial fear that energized Bush's campaign. But Dukakis's attempt to reveal the code, and thus to scramble it, encountered a formidable obstacle. Under one cover was another. Willy Horton inverted the accusation of meaninglessness, and made the tough baby invulnerable to attack.

As the moderator of the second presidential debate of 1988, Bernard Shaw took upon himself the responsibility of asking the first questions to the candidates.[94] He asked Dukakis, "Governor, if Kitty Dukakis were raped and murdered would you favor an irrevocable death penalty for the killer?" Some say Dukakis lost the election when he failed to show himself as a man in the superior position. He said,

> No, I don't Bernard, and I think you know I have opposed the death penalty during all of my life. I don't see any evidence that it is a deterrent, and I think there are better, more effective ways to deal with violent crime. We've done so in my own state and it's one of the reasons why we have had the biggest drop in crime of any industrial state in America and why we have the lowest murder rate of any industrial state in America.

That Dukakis responded to a question phrased in the present conditional ("*would* you") with an answer in the indicative (I *don't*) indicates that he had scripted an answer to the question in advance. That is not unusual in itself. But more damning, intent on making a clear policy statement, he failed to defend his wife. He didn't seem to realize that responsible policy is beside the point when vicious rapists and murderers are at the doorstep (even though he would insist that they aren't). He was a weakling, or in J. Edgar Hoover's phrase, "a sentimental sob-sister."

It might be worthwhile to reexamine Dukakis's moment of failure. Bernard Shaw is the first African American anchorman for a network, in this case of the Cable News Network (unlike his predecessor, Max Robinson of ABC, who at his peak was a coanchor), and was the only black man to participate in the presidential debates. His question was all the more damning for Dukakis, in two senses. First, that an African American man asked this question underlined the concern with crime that is shared by minorities, who suffer most severely from violent street crime and the systematic crimes perpetuated by corporate violators of law. But at a second level, Shaw was standing in for Willy Horton. His initial question to Dukakis was a figurative mugging. The question implicitly questioned Dukakis's "manhood," and Dukakis's answer demonstrated his impotence.[95] Had Dukakis attacked Shaw, he might have repaired the breach, but that action would have undermined his image in minority communities. His retreat to legalism gave Bush victory.

Bush throughout the campaign had placed the "legal" under the sign of weakness. Legal strictures such as the Boland amendment had "tied the hands of the President" in the fight against Communism; and the Bill of Rights had tied his hands in "the fight against crime" and in the fight against drugs. National security, foreign and domestic, could be guaranteed only by a tough baby. Dukakis appealed to legality, but legality did not appeal to a frightened and uncertain electorate.

In attempting to provide balance, Shaw asked a similarly difficult question to Bush. It did not concern Barbara Bush, but Dan Quayle and Bush's wisdom in choosing Quayle as his running mate, as a potential president. Bush responded in tough baby mode, suggesting that no one had been attacked as viciously as had Quayle during the campaign and that Quayle had demonstrated his manhood by "taking it."

(In 1992 Governor Clinton, at the height of his campaign, went back to Arkansas to execute a man so brain-damaged that he saved the dessert of his last meal, thinking he would eat it after returning to his cell following the execution. Clinton learned a lesson in how to be a tough baby from Dukakis's failure and Bush's success.)

Bush knew that "taking it" is how one gains respect in a homosocial order such as ours. In that order, undergirding the official set of categories is another having to do with the fears of the swamp, the terrors of flows, the worries about the piss and the shit that constitute a large part of the quotidian dimension of life. That life has been segregated to the spheres of women and children. In the indeterminate mix of roles available to people once they unshackle themselves from the naturalizing discourse of J. Edgar Hoover's "clean picture of American manhood and womanhood," perhaps lie some answers to the troubles that afflict this culture.

But there are always those who insist that the proper course of action is to keep things clean. As evidence of this desire, we need only look at the "humorous" sidebar that accompanied a report from the felony trial of Oliver North in 1989. During cross-examination, the prosecutor, John Keker, asked North about some code words that he had used to describe CIA contacts. North conceded that one of the words he used was "fool." But it was another word that Keker wanted North to admit having used.

> Keker asked if there was another code word and handed North a document obtained from his files.
> "It was a profanity I would prefer not to use in the presence of ladies," North said, bowing his head in a courtly manner. "It was male language, used among friends. If you want to use it in this courtroom, you may, Mr. Keker."
> "Does it start with an 'a'?" Keker asked with a smile.
> "Yes," said North.
> "Does that describe what you thought of them?" Keker continued.
> "At the time, yes," the retired Marine replied.[96]

What does it mean to say that "asshole" is "male language?" And why are women to be excluded from such a discussion? Is it not because to penetrate a bodily hole is also thought by these men to subordinate the one penetrated? Is it because the men who engage in such talk in such a way are also afraid of the flows that emanate from assholes? Why are those who refuse these stringent codes to be called scum?

Perhaps by understanding our jokes according to how they are codes of these desires, we might even get a better sense of what they express and permit. The rehabilitation of Dan Quayle reached full swell in the national media during the 1992 campaign. He became a "player" by chairing a presidential review commission intervening on behalf of businessmen against government regulators. He fought Senator Gore to a draw in the vice-presidential debates. He is now a hopeful for the Republican Party presidential nomination in 1996. The beginning of Quayle's rehabilitation can be traced to reports in 1989 about how Quayle jokes were becoming "kinder." One report quotes a man named Robert Lichter who was director of the Center for Media and Public Affairs (a right-wing institute that generally fulminates against the press).

"Quayle humor has become almost a genre," Lichter said. "Dan Quayle, the lovable lunkhead." Most important, Quayle himself was telling jokes about himself. Echoing the ambivalence that Bush had let slip in his references to Reagan, Quayle told the following joke at the 1989 annual Gridiron dinner: "The President has been very supportive of me. The other day he called me into the Oval Office and said, 'I know you've had some rough times, and I want to do something that will show the nation what faith I have in you, in your maturity and sense of responsibility. . . . Would you like a puppy?'"[97] Quayle the lovable lunkhead child is to receive one of Milly's puppies from father-knows-best George Bush. The trivialization of Quayle was part of his rehabilitation, but one might note that the joke also trivializes Bush. This is the safest route to political rehabilitation in present-day America.

In 1951, Adorno thought he was witness to the ultimate degradation of a form of civilization in the wake of Auschwitz. He subtitled *Minima Moralia, Reflections from Damaged Life*, and concluded that study with an observation on the task of thought: "Perspectives must be fashioned that displace and estrange the world, reveal it to be, with its rifts and crevices, as indigent and distorted as it will appear one day in the messianic light. To gain such perspectives without velleity or violence, entirely from the felt contact with its objects—this alone is the task of thought."[98] The violence Adorno sought to escape through the thought of redemption, despite his denial that the reality or unreality of redemption is at stake in this impossible exercise, lies implicit in the very force of the thought itself. But the felt contact with objects requires a move that is inevitably violent. And yet what is at work here, for us who inhabit the superior positions, is a willingness to ignore the violence we do to remain innocent, tough *babies*. We men in charge proceed in opposites, countering the clean to the filthy, the hetero to the homo, the white to the black, the man to the woman; in each instance we make sex in the superior position the norm.

But in a democratic culture there are other forces at work. Democratizing processes might still inspire movement away from these codes of desire. In other words, it might be possible to think through these bodily tensions which afflict our possible futures in united states. Indeed, one future concerning the problematic of homosociability might be found in the ongoing response of women in the United States to the fact that their rape has nothing to do with them at the same time that it has everything to do with them.

The vicious character of our representative politics continues to disguise the violence of the desires of its puritan practitioners. We rely on sordid subordinations, ultimately boring sexual arrangements—but boredom can be a form of cruelty as well—in order to achieve identity, coherence, order, and security. Our leaders speak a language of love in the commission of death. We bury thousands of Iraqi teenagers alive, conscripts who merely wanted to survive. Our arrangements won't do. The American century reveals that these pretenses are killing us. Bush, our symbolic leader, is an obscene figure. But he is not alone. He is us men in the superior position, magnified.

CHAPTER FOUR

Rodney King, or
The New Enclosures

There's a black person up our street and we say "Hi," like he's a normal person.
—Resident of Simi Valley, May 1992

Loving the Monster

What do men in the superior position fear, what do we know of our other selves? Our fear wears many masks. Masks hiding masks: often we have told ourselves that our most dangerous masks are those which best conceal our selves from ourselves. The masks fit so well that we forget we are wearing them. And then, if all is going well for us, when we remember, we forget again. Remembering to forget—this is our endless task.

If resistance to domination takes infinite effort, so does the construction of what is to be resisted. The claims we make concerning populations of people, the categories of others who are diminished in the sight of official discourse, whose pain is ignored (in part, because it is too painful), who are not to be considered except within the exciting and ephemeral moments of violent appearance, these others suffer the consequences of our masking. They are forced to remain dependent on our symbolic codes, even in their resistance. Their lives are diminished by the predominance of secondhand maskings in their lives. Their struggles for masks they might better control and recognize as their own seem to parallel, in a diminished way, our own resolute self-concealment.

And yet it is foolish to think that we might remove our masks and stand exposed before one another. In so doing, we would be putting on yet another mask, the mask of authenticity. I am convinced that it would be better, which is to say less damaging to the others who complement and complete ourselves, to evaluate the quality of the performance, the beauty or ugliness of the masks we make and wear, and then to question how and why we force others to wear our masks, and how much of their experience is found in the masks we wear. Such a task is not simple, of course, but it proceeds, as Slavoj Žižek reminds us, from the recognition that "The mask is not simply hiding the real state of things; the ideological distortion is written into its very essence."[1]

This thought concerning masks is a preface to a question: What does it mean to be a young black man in the face of the power of this unified denial? Men in the superior position live with a mythology about gangs and gang members, but when I was in East Los Angeles these deadly gang-bangers, these demons of the *L.A. Times* and every tabloid television show, turned out to be children. We would sentimentalize them differently were they not living where they are, in our open-air carcerals.[2] Here is a gap to consider, between their experience and their existence, a gap covered over by a series of masks.

They are not only the children of their natural parents, but the monstrous progeny of our love and hate. One of the most potent masks men in the superior position wear is that of the loving *pater familias*. But that mask easily turns into one composed of hate. To the extent that others seem to share in our identity, we need to find grounds to reject them. Our hatred intensifies to the degree that we sentimentalize our officially recognized children, because when we do so we are giving masked expression of our hatred and resentment for them. Conversely, a powerful attraction is at work when we demonize our monstrous progeny, the denizens of state institutions and mean streets. Our overt condemnations hide a secret pride in their accomplishments. They are our lesser children, but they are our children nevertheless. They are produced. The tension that we feel regarding them is a consequence of the scandalous emotions they evoke in us. We will repress our love for them. It is not seemly.

Our love and our hate are close together, but we wish for them to be far apart. Missionaries who work in the slum neighborhoods of American cities, who engage in a form of urban triage based on a sense about those who most lack love, seem deceived by how we keep these children at arm's length. They seem to think we do not care. But the truth is more complicated. They do not recognize our horrible ardent passion. It seems as though they too are busy arranging their own masks, missionary masks.

The prophet Cornel West calls for love, but his call also seems to misapprehend the passion that burns among men in the superior position. He seeks to build a similar love relationship for the downtrodden and oppressed. "Nihilism," he writes, "is not overcome by arguments and analysis; it is tamed by love and care." He continues: "Self-love and love of others are both modes toward increasing self-evaluation and encouraging political resistance in one's community. These modes of valuation and resistance are rooted in subversive memory—the best of one's past without romantic nostalgia—and guided by a universal love ethic."[3] Care of self coupled to a democratic ethos might stand in opposition to the sort of love we men in the superior position advocate. But West also attempts to conjure up a universal love. In this he seems closely in step with the love of the man in the superior position, the love of the father. Whether in Christian theology or in the person of our president, this is a love that damages, giving us a way to distribute benevolence and to avoid dirtying ourselves with the particulars of the lives of those who receive our largesse. The mask of the profession of Christian love is its generality, which covers the nihilistic void of particular lovelessness.

But perhaps I beg the most important question. How might we negotiate our way through these masks? In a different context Marie-Hélène Huet has suggested, "What resemblance conceals, the monster unmasks."[4] I take her aphorism as a guide, a reminder of how to understand this complex hatred and love of our monstrous progeny. Who are the Original Gangsters? In the mythology of the Crips and Bloods in Los Angeles, OGs are members of gangs who have been jumped in for a long time (rarely is an OG still in his teens), and who have developed a mythical reputation for courage and viciousness.[5] There is another, paradoxical element of "originality" concerning the mythical status of OGs which concerns the effacement of memory. Not only gangsters, but almost all of the minority children of American cities suffer a routinized erasure of collective memory. One result of that erasure has been that many of them simply seek to reconstruct meaning in life on the basis of the materials that remain available to them in the wake of repression.[6] But even prior to that, if we are to have any hope of shedding some light on the situation that has given rise to these children, we must explore our crime of neglect and intervention. We men in the superior position are the original gangsters; the mythology of the monstrous criminal is the negative out of which our image appears.

Michael Rogin uses the term "demonology" to explain the matrices of the repression of "others"—Indians, African Americans, women, Communists—through the course of American history. He joins public history "to the familial patterns and psychologically charged images of private life."[7] In linking the personal to the political, Rogin raises three issues, addressing in turn the status of the idea of the personal, the importance of family, and the significance of the woman question in the creation of demonology. The structure of our political institutions and ideology has guaranteed a special place for women in the history of demonology. "Manifestly they have been made into victims whose persecution justifies revenge and into the guardians of civilized virtue who stand against aggression and anarchy," he writes. "But women have also been cast, implicitly and explicitly, as monsters."[8]

To dig into the elements that have framed women in this way, Rogin uses Freud, mediated by Melanie Klein, who embodies a feminist resistance to Freud.

> The male organ, for Freud, was a sign of the power of the father. Feminist psychoanalysis in one of its versions sees phallocentrism as a response to the power of the mother. Castration anxiety at the pre-oedipal stage signals the fear of being absorbed by the mother. At the oedipal stage it signals desire to have her. In the one case danger comes from the mother, in the other case from the father. When the father's law ultimately establishes itself in the resolution of the oedipal complex, it does so against a (fantasized) prior maternal threat.[9]

The image of the preoedipal mother haunts men in the superior position. Anxiety about boundary breakdown and the accompanying fantasy of a devouring enemy form a "disturbed ideology," as he puts it, which provides psychological protection for men in the superior position. "Protection," of course, is a suitably strange word choice here, echoing the idea of maternal defensiveness in an inverted way.

Rogin demonstrates how such a dynamic operates along the dimension of race in his study of D. W. Griffith's *Birth of a Nation*. He analyzes the symbolic role of the castrating sword of the KKK in restoring "white manhood" to a place of dignity and power, after it had been challenged by a sexual conspiracy between white women and black men. In *The Birth of a Nation*, the phantasmic connection between white women and black men operates as an urtext by which to understand demonological representation.

Consider the issue of casting in Griffith's movies. Originally, the role of Elsie, the innocent white woman, was to be played by Blanche Sweet, but Griffith decided that Sweet projected too much sexuality and replaced her with Lilian Gish. Rogin writes:

> When Griffith replaced Sweet with Gish he was shifting sexuality from the white woman to the black man. The regression to the presexual virgin and the invention of the black demon went hand in hand. White supremacists invented the black rapist to keep white women in their place. That strategy, counterposing the black man to the white woman, hid a deep fear of union. Griffith wanted what one viewer called the "contrast between black villainy and white innocence" to undo the association of his unconscious, which had merged women and blacks.[10]

This attempt to make the African American man the repository of (evil) sexuality and to make the white woman asexual and innocent covers up the initial violence in miscegenation, the rape of black slave women by white male slaveowners. It also covers the guilt, the endless echo of the original sins of slavery, turning the victim of evil into an evil object.

This transposition of guilt to the innocent is not symmetric, by any means, even at the symbolic level—black women, as slaves and as women slaves, were not, and could not by definition be in any sense agents against black men; lacking agency on two fronts, they were the most invisible of the invisible.[11] Yet an opposition between African American men and women in regard to the character of their sexual relations with whites has been a ghostly source of friction and division, especially in times when there are increasingly intense racist pressures at work in response to other fears held within the dominant culture.[12] When Flavor Flav of the rap group Public Enemy speaks about how ordinary it is for him to beat "his woman," his misogyny also reflects this resentment.[13] It is in tune with the worldview of some of Clarence Thomas's supporters. How dare Anita Hill "misinterpret" the ordinary codes of male-female interaction in the African American community, was the barely implied question that commentators such as Orlando Patterson asked shortly after the Thomas hearings concluded.[14] In fact, we can see this secret unveiled in the video of Public Enemy's song "Can't Truss It," from *Apocalypse, '91: The Empire Strikes Black*.[15] In that video, slave/owner relationships are juxtaposed to contemporary white-collar/blue-collar issues, blended with scenes of rape and the sexual harassment of African American women. Women are presented as objects of possession and exchange between two competing male forces.

This division between African American men and African American women, created in the crucible of their oppression through the residual institutions of chattel slavery, helps to obscure the interdependent roles racism and sexism play in demonology.[16] Then men in the superior position are free to discuss such notions as the pathology of the black family.[17] But a particular confusion remains, especially when we transpose the demonological model from the context of early twentieth-century political culture to our time. That confusion results from the uneven reception of the two major liberation movements in the United States, one racial and the other sexual.

Moms and Dads

In thinking through the problem of racism, Rogin suggests that in male demonology, women, perhaps even more than black people, are cast as monsters. But this formula does not quite add up. Even excepting the erasure of black women as an important category, in Rogin's demonological formulation the representation of women as evil is a consequence of their primal relationship with the newborn (male) progeny. The primary anxiety of the baby (concerning the withdrawal of the breast) is at the root of subsequent identity with the powerful phallus, and the recasting of blame on women for the failures of sons in the postoedipal politics of the family is a result of the powerful metaphorical (and oppositional) connection between the fear of being reabsorbed by the mother and the narcissistic desire to absorb the world. Mom as monster is a devourer.

Yet there is another element of the politics of the family that plays directly into the creation of monsters—the (until quite recently) definitive uncertainty of fatherhood. Huet highlights the more general role that patrilineal uncertainty has played in demonizing mothers in the West in her discussion of the emergence of a modern science of embryology in the era of French classicism. She traces how mothers have been assigned responsibility for the creation of monstrous progeny. Several features attributable to monsters are relevant to this discussion. First, monsters violate the first law of obedience, namely, that children should resemble their parents. Second, by resembling other creatures, monsters disrupt the natural order of things. The problem of resemblance is of great importance, because the determination of fatherhood depends on an adequate likeness in the child. Moreover, because resemblance has been an issue of aesthetic consideration as much as of generative origin, attention has been focused on the role that imagination plays in producing monstrous progeny.

Huet traces as far back as to Empedocles (fifth century B.C.) the connection of mother to monster and shows how it was asserted as one of imaginative sensitivity, a communicating link between the musing mind and the body. "Following Empedocles' theory, it was long believed that monsters were the result of a mother's fevered and passionate consideration of images; monsters were the result of an imagination that imprinted on its progeny a deformed, misshapen resemblance to an image—that is, to an object that did not participate in their creation." [18] During the French Enlightenment the debate that raged between imaginationists and their opponents concerned the power of women; those who opposed the imaginationist thesis did so because they felt that women were too passive to be able to have such an impact on the children they carried. [19] As late as 1788 a major and thoroughly scholarly study was finished by Benjamin Bablot titled *Dissertation on the Power of the Imagination of Pregnant Women*. [20]

Determining the role of the mother in the creation of monstrous progeny had a practical aspect, as Huet demonstrates in her account of an inheritance suit in which the question of the paternity of a deformed child was at issue. The law determined that a monstrous child is still a child (taking a stricter position at the time than did the Catholic Church). The mother's imagination shapes only the exterior of a child's body. But rather than diminish the role of the mother, this understanding intensifies its importance. First, it places her work outside nature, and in the realm of reproductive art (copying, or *eikastiken*, in Plato's sense, devoid of interpretive qualities that would render the reproduction beautiful by selection of the best parts). Second, it attributes to her the power to erase the father's image in the appearance of the child. This aspect of the mother's power makes her an agent of monstrosity, a monstrous mother; she reminds everyone of the horrible truth, that paternity could never really be proven, "that if nothing is more undeniable than maternity, paternity, until very recently, could never be verifiable or physically ascertained." [21]

Huet shows how a mobilization of knowledge against this imaginative power of the woman was to inform the development of modern sciences of embryology. If the power of women was a result of the power of their imagination, then it would seem that the force of imagination in the shaping of materiality must be discounted. The notion of progeny needing to have *exact* resemblance to parents was discounted. Eventually, resemblance is discredited as the final arbitrator of progeny. The role of resemblance in the securing of identity becomes discounted because to maintain it is to acknowledge the terror of the monstrous. Imagination is thus decoupled from material meaning. She concludes:

> As the role and importance of resemblance disappear from the medical discourse on procreation, so does the mother's haunting power over her progeny's features. In fact, the mother's privileged role in procreation is slowly dismantled as the history of generation now enters the field of embryology. The scientist alone will create monsters in the controlled space of his laboratory, the modern womb. The stage is set for the single father, for the monstrous father. The stage is set for *Frankenstein*.[22]

In France, then, the role of women is reduced and denigrated as the stability of the bourgeois household is carefully sustained, first by class warfare, which provided the overwhelming explanation for understanding disorder in the social sphere, and second by the wholesale state intervention into the conditions of family life, which would defuse the possibility for the creation of the kind of intense oppositions of responsibility between men and women among poor and repressed groups.[23]

In our united states, where class divisions are obscured and responsibility is framed in familial terms, the stage is set for a repetitive theme in demonological strategy, the justification of dehumanizing policy on the basis of a true, scientific knowledge of the meaning of resemblance. From the typologies of Zebulon Brockway, founder of the Elmira Reformatory, to those of Richard Herrnstein and James Q. Wilson, contemporary purveyors of racial theories of criminality, we men in the superior position have portrayed ourselves as the fathers who can understand, and hence control, the monstrous progeny of wayward women. A precondition of white male dominance in this country is the ability to assume a distinction between ourselves and such monsters, to cast them outside the sphere of acceptability. We call such monsters criminals. And because men in the superior position have been the pioneers in criminology, we have succeeded in assessing blame for monstrosity squarely on the bodies of young black men.

The thing about Frankenstein is that science gone wrong produced his monster. But we act as though we know better, as though we know that it is the sleep of reason, not a practice of reason, that produces monsters. The linkage of law, science, and morality is a powerful source of monstrous production in the history of the United States, dating back at least as far as Benjamin Rush's participation in the construction of the first American penitentiary.[24] That Rush's invention is now primarily the habitat for young black men is perhaps a historical irony. Rush worked as well to ameliorate the condition of African Americans, and in doing so unintentionally helped establish their status as monsters. We might be able to fathom this historical irony better if we examine certain aspects of a case involving a young black man, one in which the victim of lawless police, Rodney King, is avenged by the lawless rage of monstrous children.

Representing a Riot

The uprising in Los Angeles following the verdict in the trial of the men who beat Rodney King has been treated by many commentators as just another urban riot. A special series of reports in the *Los Angeles Times*, for instance, compared the 1992 riots with Watts in 1965.[25] It emphasized a similar circumstance of poverty, a similar situation of overt brutality by police forces, and a similar despair over the future of the children of the city. The series noted as well the pleas for harmony and peace at both times, and even mentioned earlier commission reports and studies on how to solve the core economic and social problems at the roots of the uprising. Conservatives repeated their usual charges as well, decrying the lack of respect for law, calling for tougher prosecution of those who would loot and burn.

But this time there is one major difference. It can be put in the form of a question: Why does the entire country know the name of Rodney King, whereas no one remembers the young man (Marcus Frye) whose arrest on 11 August 1965 for speeding and reckless driving was the catalyst for the Watts riots?

That the video representation of Rodney King in March of 1991 led to the uprising at the end of April 1992 is uncontested. But what was the power of that image? Why did it have the capacity to shock? We have seen beatings before, and the eventual rationale that the jury developed was available to all of us. The problem is that it was an image that could not be evaded. "Look! Look!" television anchors seemed to say as they ran and reran the video clip.

We were prepared for the message of the King video by a deeper disillusion with the mythologies of the 1980s. George Bush lay bare our secrets for us. His representation of morning in America was unpersuasive; we were coming to "know" that the eighties were over, and were looking for a new "truth" for the nineties. During the period leading to the L.A. riots, several highly publicized books and media discussions concerning gangs, the intensification of racism during the Reagan era, the possibility of its "permanent" quality, and bleak characterizations of the generally desperate conditions of the urban "underclass" primed the country for a reassessment of the plight of urban minorities.[26] The misery of minorities receives its most "clear" verification through the image of King.

Then came the verdict and the riots. We were to spend the second half of 1992 studiously (and desperately) trying to ignore the conflagration of our largest urban area as represented to us in the first half.[27] There are many ways to ignore such matters. Perhaps the most insidious is to acknowledge the painful consequences of our privilege and to then pretend that their presence is not a matter of consequence. In the field of representation a cynical but common rhetorical move is involved. William E. Connolly has demonstrated one way to enact such a procedure through the construction of a "subtext of realism." Analyzing a passage in Michael Walzer's famous study *Spheres of Justice*, Connolly points out how Walzer builds a "grammatical wall" between the "shared standards" concerning the treatment of criminals confined in prison and a subliminal acceptance of precisely the violations of those limits. First Walzer lists the standards straightforwardly and clearly. A comment is thrown in as a rhetorical aside: "I am sure those limits are often violated." The two sentences together give Walzer a plausible deniability for the actions of the very agencies of justice he endorses. Connolly suggests that such rhetorical protections serve a triple function: "They protect us from offenders; they organize our ambivalence about crime and punishment into a psychically tolerable structure; and they offer us deniability during those rare moments when prison violence becomes too visible to ignore."[28]

If one were to transfer Walzer's understanding concerning the operation of the prison to the open-air carceral of South Central Los Angeles, it might read like this: "Our understanding of the good society allows there to be no discrimination in the distribution of social opportunity, and uniform application of laws designed to protect citizens from the savageries of slumlords and bigots. I am sure those standards are often violated."

Connolly proposes one way to cut through this apologetic nonsense.

I think there is another way to proceed, one compatible with Connolly's sympathies, but which starts by evoking a different sensibility concerning the historical shifts in the truth of American experience and its representations. To discuss the power of the image in the case of our contemporary situation necessarily implicates the events concerning the King beating in an unarticulated crisis in the politics of representation in our united states. I believe that the image of King developed out of three interrelated perspectives, each of which contributed to a racist mode of understanding King's circumstance, each of which connected the example of King to a more general category of criminal "type." The first strategy is that of scientific racism. Scientific racism, deployed by some academics, implicitly informed the primary representation of Rodney King. This racism fits neatly into the second perspective that still operates; older disciplines of observation convey scientific racism and are associated with contemporary monitoring techniques, not only in our united states, but in those of most European-influenced societies. Finally, a strategy of normalization operates to encourage the internment of black minorities. The strategy of normalization could not have emerged had it not the correlational use of "scientific" racism and monitoring. Together they sustained an ensemble of forces that allowed the beating of King to occur and provided the jurors with a roadmap to its *post hoc* justification. These forces operate not only in Los Angeles, but in other urban areas of the United States. Each has a history, yet their coming together in Los Angeles is perhaps a new event in the political history of the United States. If it is not totally new, it is at least the most developed instance of these forces operating together. If so, Los Angeles may be the first city to experience in full measure the political crisis brought about by the establishment of lines of representational power likely to predominate through the remainder of this decade. And if that is the case, then the body of Rodney King is only an early representative of that tortured body to be ignored by normal people.

A Racist Science of Similitude

How did the members of the jury in Simi Valley reach their verdict to acquit the Los Angeles police officers? An old answer might suffice. They did by succumbing to the racial fears they suffer. The jurors simply wished to see Rodney King beaten, and they wished to send a message to the world that the police must be allowed to beat black men who act suspiciously, especially outside their own neighborhoods. It's simple, you see. They are nothing more or less than bigots. ✸

That explanation is too comfortable. It is part and parcel of what might be called Walzerism. Generally speaking, in this view racism can be easily comprehended as an atavism, a simple hatred of others based upon the fear of what is unknown. The background chatter on the LAPD Mobile Data Terminals (MDTs), which referred to African Americans as "gorillas in the mist" and "mo fos," which casually mentioned beatings ("I obviously didn't beat this guy enough") and the presumed lack of pain felt by people with black skin, can all be assimilated to this simple racism.[29] Alternative explanations advanced by the police for these communications, appealing to irony, "black" humor, and the siege mentality that afflicts police in dangerous situations could, from this perspective, be explained as elements in a cynical cover for racial hatred. The jurors who voted to acquit could be understood as racist sympathizers from a fearful community ignorant of minority experience.

There is something to be said for such an explanation. It is undoubtedly true that raw hatred is still endemic to American culture. The relevant question concerning such an explanation, however, is how much does this overt racism explain? Might there be more than a conspiracy of racial hatred at work in the Simi Valley verdict? If all of the jurors voted simply out of a fear of a black planet, then the only problem with their verdict would be that it was motivated by racism in what we presume is an era of racial enlightenment. Indeed, it is possible that if evidence of such racism were concealed by the prosecutors, then the verdict itself might be thrown out on grounds of fraud. Moreover, if only this form of racism were at work, a more careful screening process, better education concerning difference and similarity, and more vigorous enforcement of laws forbidding racial discrimination would eventually marginalize such atavistic behavior.

But this explanation is nonetheless not sufficient. Contemporary racism is not simply a stupid hatred. Or, to be more accurate, it is not stupid in a simple sense. Most stupidities are not. Racism may be based on ignorance, but it also depends on a form of knowledge. That knowledge, sometimes wittingly, sometimes unwittingly, operates to reinforce fear and hatred by providing rationales for hierarchizing differences. ✸

This hierarchizing became especially intense in the late nineteenth century after the emergence of <u>Darwinian evolutionary theory</u> led to its application to different human groups under the guise of social Darwinism.[30] One might trace "scientific" racism back to the American Enlightenment. An early and instructive instance of "scientific" racism can be located in the theory of race advanced by Benjamin Rush. Rush, a leading figure in the American Enlightenment of the late eighteenth century, posited that the color of the skin of black people was a form of leprosy.[31] He rooted his theory in his desire to *ameliorate* the condition of African Americans. He suggested that if the leprosy that made skin dark and hair wooly were to be cured (through purges, bleeding, sexual abstinence, psychological shock cures, and chemical bleaching), the prejudice against those suffering the condition of black skin would no longer hold. He suggested that even black people who thought they liked being black really would prefer to be white. Finally, Rush suggested: "We shall render the belief of the whole human race being descended from one pair, easy, and universal, and thereby not only add weight to the Christian revelation, but remove a material obstacle to the exercise of that universal benevolence which is inculcated by it."[32]

Rush's universalism obliterated difference in the name of benevolence. His theory is a <u>utopian fantasy of peace achieved through</u> "sameness." It predated malevolent theories that would insist on the preservation of difference in the name of the superiority of one group over another. It also anticipated the general trajectory American social policy has since taken.

With the emergence of both evolutionary theory and the science of genetics in the nineteenth century, biological theories of race with their specious logic of genetic inferiority came to the fore and dominated "scientific" discussions of racial difference. The credence that such theories enjoyed in the sciences, however, ended after the Second World War, when they were decisively disproved.[33] Since then, theories of biological inferiority have migrated to the social sciences, where statistical probability tests are used to validate claims concerning inferiority. In these theories, deep explanations based on the mechanisms of genetics have been displaced by arguments concerning the representations of racialized characteristics of appearance. The work of earlier geneticists who employed cranial measures to try to infer genetic characteristics is now used for a different end. Physical characteristics are freed from arguments about essential racial inferiority and are simply associated with whatever behavior the racist wishes to attribute to the other, whether it be passivity and laziness or violent hyperactivity.

"Race," in this newer sense, becomes a marker tied to a series of associated social phenomena. Its attachments to the body are not connected through a logic of strict causality, but an alternative logic of statistically valid correlation. Race becomes a normalizing category that uses a shorthand of visible markers to communicate its separations.[34]

• This is the strategic imperative underlying the work of James Q. Wilson and Richard Herrnstein.[35] Their studies of criminality are the epitome of contemporary scientific racism, a racism that can strategically deny the power of its categorizations. Like most theories of crime, theirs ignores most crime that doesn't involve immediate violence and then, focusing on racial variations in violent crime rates, suggests that people of color are more likely to be violent than whites. Indeed, by characterizing criminal proclivities in terms of pathology, Wilson and Herrnstein follow the lead of (or perhaps they themselves lead) mainstream modern criminology, dividing populations into the normal and the pathological, reinforcing views of the "abnormality" of minorities, and intensifying a general interpretive frame for criminalizing "otherness." Their book attempts to justify the police beating of Rodney King by suggesting that such a response might be reasonable in the face of statistical verification that people fitting Rodney King's profile have violent proclivities. ✦

Wilson and Herrnstein offer a variety of explanations of the etiology of criminal behavior, but their most notable contribution is their explanation of how physical shape and appearance contribute to criminal behavior. In a section titled "Anatomical Correlates of Crime," they suggest that "character" is shaped by physical characteristics. Although they conceed that the "constitutional traits" associated with criminal behavor cannot ultimately predict what any one person will do every time, they suggest that "constitutional criminal predispositions"[36] make it likely that someone will behave in a particular way, thus moving the focus of study from accountability for specific acts to response to predictable populations. Historically revising the work of the nineteenth-century physician Cesare Lombroso, they suggest that there exist strong genetic correlates of crime:

The average offender tends to be constitutionally distinctive, though not extremely or abnormally so. The biological factors whose traces we see in faces, physiques, and correlations with the behavior of parents and siblings are predispositions toward crime that are expressed as psychological traits and activated by circumstances. . . . The existence of biological predispositions means that circumstances that activate criminal behavior in one person will not do so in another, that social forces cannot deter criminal behavior in 100 percent of a population, and that the distributions of crime within and across societies may, to some extent, reflect underlying distributions of constitutional factors.[37]

Wilson and Herrnstein argue here in a biological mode. But they constantly try to escape the charge of biological determinism by associating a biological feature with a cultural danger. They suggest, for instance, that low intelligence makes one less aware of the dangerous consequences of law-breaking.

But it is their understanding of the connections between visible features and underlying biological traits that makes Wilson and Herrnstein's work so powerful and dangerous. In outlining the constitutional factors that contribute to criminal behavior, they emphasize the use of "somatotyping" as a way to measure a propensity for criminal behavior. A somatotype is a description of a person's physique according to endomorphy (roundness, or chubbiness), mesomorphy (muscularity, or heavy-bonedness), and ectomorphy (linearity, or thinness). Referring to the work of W. H. Sheldon in the mid-1950s, which established seven-point scales on each of these measures, Wilson and Herrnstein suggest that it might be possible to measure according to physique for criminal "traits." According to them, those more likely to be criminals are those who are "mostly mesomorphs deficient in ectomorphy" (that is, heavily muscled people who are not thin and tall), and who have a characteristic called "andromorphy," which they explain is having "such masculine traits as a broad chest flaring toward the shoulders, low waist, relatively large arms, prominent muscle relief, large bones and joints, fat distributed throughout the body, etc."[38]

This formula articulates race at the level of sign and signified. We are able to render conclusive judgments concerning the character of a person on the basis of that person's bodily appearance. The body is a sign to be read for its truth, once the code of its representations is cracked. For Wilson and Herrnstein, those people who flinch when they see a bulky young black man approaching them are not conditioned in prejudice, but are only performing a streetwise reading of the body. They intuit what Wilson and Herrnstein systematize. From this perspective an aggressive response to the Rodney Kings of the world is only sensible, not bigoted. Size, shape, and skin color become signs of a genetic code to be read in a system of cultural representation.

When summarizing their explanation of crime, Wilson and Herrnstein write the following sentence: "An impulsive person can be taught
greater self-control, a low-IQ individual can engage in satisfying learning experiences, and extroverted mesomorphs with slow autonomic
nervous system response rates may earn honest money in the National
Football League instead of dishonest money robbing banks."[39] One
might apply this racist understanding to Rodney King. Rodney King,
an "endomorphic mesomorph" of a size and shape and skin color *corre-
lated* with a propensity to behave violently, probably impervious to
pain, not likely to be very intelligent, has in all likelihood followed the
path that leads to robbing banks, unless he were recruited as a professional football player instead. Vicious consequences follow from this
logic. Because Wilson and Herrnstein predict only the probability of
King's behavior, there remains an element of volition or choice. The
degree of freedom associated with any statistical correlation, holds King
(at least partly) responsible, responsible enough to be imprisoned, and
dangerous enough to be beaten, should he remain free to roam the
streets.

King's responsibility extends not only to what he does, but to who he
is. His body informed on him to the police. Even in its inability to be
perfectly still, King's body showed the police that he was dangerous.[40]
But finally, and most insidiously, even though his body made manifest
his criminal propensity, he nonetheless has a meaningful choice in his
behavior. He could have played football in the NFL. This is the double-
bind of free will and determinism imposed by Wilson and Herrnstein.

Wilson and Herrnstein drop the Walzerian veil of liberal compassion.
They do not seek to advance a standard beyond their hard-core condemnations of those damaged by privileges they enjoy. "Realists" in the
rhetorical sense outlined by Connolly, they are tough babies in the
sense outlined by Adorno.[41]

When they develop this sort of racist representational schema, contemporary criminologists move the categorization of the dangerous
individual to a new level. Even if the criminal does not speak on his own
behalf, even if his motives are not explained by investigation and
confession, the body of the criminal itself speaks the "truth" of the
criminal's character. Such a strategic move returns the relationship of
criminal and sovereign power to an earlier moment in the history of
crime, when the role of the spectacle of public punishment was crucial
to determining the meaning of crime and its punishment.[42] But there is
one difference. Now, instead of a liturgy of punishment in front of an

assembled crowd, the representation of the body of the least condemned person is conveyed through television, reinforced by television's repetitions, its slowing down of imagery, and its use of stereotypes to convey the reassurance of serial continuity.[43]

Wilson and Herrnstein do not hate Rodney King any more than they
hate the unfortunate person who possesses a body of the "wrong"
somatotype. Scientific racism is not about hate. But in its concern to
establish certainty about the distinctions that might be made among
categories of people and to render secure judgments concerning the
social capacities of people on the basis of those distinctions, it plays into
the code of politics in the superior position.

From Surveillance to Monitor

A common theme in the post-trial interviews of jurors from the King
beating trial was the insistence that "King was in control" that night:
"'He refused to get out of the car,' said one juror who was interviewed
by the *Times*. 'His two companions got out of the car and complied with
the orders and he just continued to fight. So the Police Department had
no alternative. He was obviously a dangerous person. . . . Mr. King was
controlling the whole show with his actions.'"[44] This understanding of
King's conduct was received with astonishment by many, who saw it as
clear evidence of racist hatred at work. A simple and disingenuous
excuse was created for blaming the victim and excusing the victimizers.
However true that might be, the evocation of *movement* as a synonym
for control shifts the terms of understanding from the level of King's
body to its place in a larger system of representation. Wilson and
Herrnstein characterize dangerous criminals as hyperactive, which reflects a deep historical concern about movement and control recapitulated symbolically in the concern about King's unwillingness to be still.

What motivates the fear of men such as Wilson and Herrnstein?
These are honored and secure intellectuals, part of what we once called
the power elite. What are they so afraid of? One might translate this
into a more general question. How is anyone to achieve a secure place
under the circumstances that govern movement in an era when movement itself is not secured? This question reaches the heart of the issue
concerning King's movement. It has its historical precedent in the great
Enclosures of the seventeenth century in Europe, when various attempts were made by those in power to control the movement of
"masterless men" by establishing poor laws to criminalize vagabon-

dage.[45] For masterless men, freedom was deeply associated with mobility and the accompanying lack of legal accountability to a superior. In the sixteenth and seventeenth centuries, peasants who were thrown off the land as a consequence of the Enclosures flocked to the cities in search of anonymity.[46] The response of political authorities to the growth of these populations was to establish poorhouses and the first gaol-houses, predecessors to modern penitentiaries.[47] Masterless men came to be understood as dangerous to political order, especially as the shift to market values made property more important and as they engaged in crimes against property to sustain themselves. As Foucault put it, "The illegality of rights, which often meant the survival of the most deprived, tended, with the new status of property, to become an illegality of property."[48]

For the jurors from Simi Valley, Rodney King was "obviously a dangerous person." Why? Because his movement was an indicator of his masterlessness. King was mobile. He was stopped in the Valley, in the neighborhood of Lake View Terrace, not in South Central Los Angeles. Allegedly, he was driving his car (an inexpensive Hyundai) at an excessive speed. His presence on the freeways of Los Angeles signified the free circulation available to poorer residents of Los Angeles, a city that relies first and foremost on the automobile as its mode of transportation. King was but one more acolyte in one of the most potent cults of twentieth-century America—the cult of the automobile. Los Angeles has always been the headquarters of this cult. But that cult is generally not perceived to include big African American men. Indeed, one of the nightmares of white suburbanites is the migration of drive-by shootings by gangbangers in South Central to prosperous (white) peripheral neighborhoods. This nightmare came true in December of 1987 when a young white woman was caught in the cross fire of a gang drive-by shooting in the posh neighborhood of Westwood, on the edge of UCLA, close to Santa Monica.[49] That shooting contributed mightily to the creation of Operation Hammer, Police Chief Daryl Gates's major gang-intervention program, which used the model of war to round up young people in South Central. Rodney King's mobility, then, his movement on the streets of suburban Los Angeles as a dangerous young black man carried enormous demonological significance.[50] A desire to control the mobility of this archetype was thus transferred from the movement of his automobile to the movement of his body. This mediation of his body is yet another twist on the old theological figure of the "King's" two bodies.[51]

Michael Stone, counsel for Laurence Russell, the policeman who delivered the most blows to King's body, stated his defense strategy after the verdict: "We got the jurors to look at the case not from the eye of the camera or the eye of a video cameraman, but from the eyes of the officers who were out there that night."[52] In moving from the singular "eye" to the plural "eyes," Stone perhaps unconsciously was implying a move from the singular vision of panopticism, with its idea of an objective vision of control through visibility, to the stereoscopic vision of more pluralistic techniques of observation that have emerged in the twentieth century. These techniques of the observer suggest that perspective can be multiple.[53] The defense relied on resetting the video footage of the beating in a larger temporal frame (providing descriptions of what might have been happening prior to the time that the camera was turned on), slowing down the speed of the video (inuring the jurors to the force of so many blows occurring in "real" time), freezing different moments of it (giving plausible alternative interpretations of the special relations and the movements of the various viewed persons), and repeating the video during the course of the trial (habituating the jurors to the use of force). All of these tactics were techniques for disciplining the viewing of the jurors so that they could "see from the eyes of the officers." Issued as an invitation, Stone deployed a sophisticated notion of envisioning. In short, he confronted the notion of objective truth (and guilt) with perspectivism (and reasonable doubt).

It is likely that the jurors might have been inclined to accept this invitation as a result of their social sympathies with the police. But for that invitation to be accepted, it first had to be received. The attempt to position the jurors as stereoscopic viewers presupposes a widespread shift in the "viewing habits" of modern subjects. From a way of seeing largely based on the ubiquitousness of *surveillance*, there has been, through this century, a shift to a way of seeing based on the *monitor*. It is not as though surveillance has ended.[54] But the modern connection of surveillance with the idea of perfect visibility, the idea that there can be an objective visibility that discloses the subjective status of the individual, no longer exercises the same hegemony over observation. The more modest task of the monitor is to provide partial coverage of dangerous spaces, not to make surveillance perfect, but to ensure that in protected zones defensive actions against invasions might succeed.[55] Jonathan Crary suggests that the observing subject, one who has the skills to "de-objectify" the power of surveillance, begins to come into its own in the nineteenth century through new disciplines of vision. Thus he suggests that the opposition between surveillance and spectacle is no longer clear. The objectification of the viewed subject is the product of a _discipline_ of observation that has its own history.[56]

The move from surveillance to monitoring is consistent with the reemergence of the spectacle in the twentieth century.[57] The politics of the contemporary spectacle, as opposed to the classical spectacle of the scaffold, is mediated by cinematic and electronic technologies of representation. Because of the expenses and the organizational powers entailed in the proliferation of these technologies, state institutions and corporate powers usually act as gateways for the appearance of things that otherwise would not rise to the level of visibility. They do so not simply as censors, but by producing the contexts of visibility through which images are observed. The underlying scandal of the entire King affair is that it emerged on TV as a spectacle uncontrolled by these powers. The privately shot video is a new phenomenon, not yet subject to the scrutiny of the regularized editorial judgments to which such videos are likely to be subjected in the future. In the proper order of things, the police would monitor public spaces with their helicopters, patrol cars, video cameras, reports, and court appearances. The surfacing of a video, monitoring the monitors, provides a latter-day instance of the Carnivale of the European Middle Ages.

Like the crowds toward the end of the classical age of public punishment, the video spectators of the King beating became unruly and threatened the sovereign power on display. The highly publicized investigation and findings of the Independent Commission on the Los Angeles Police Department (popularly called the Christopher Commission), and the trial of the police officers (given impressive coverage by the news affiliate of the maverick Los Angeles Fox Network) became exercises in damage control by officials who realized that their authoritative interpretation of events had been superseded by the mob. The government and its corporate sponsors were obliged to recuperate the prevailing discourse of political subjectivity by reasserting their power in the venues of commission and court.

The Normalized Community

This process of readjusting the techniques of the observer is not unusual. It can instead be considered an inevitable part of the history of the disciplines of the eye. That the King affair played itself out on the streets of Los Angeles only underscores, through the irony of a historical coincidence, the shift in American power from East to West, from the representative forms of description to those of film and video. I suggest that the current readjustment is part of larger process through which American society is becoming more reliant on observational techniques of monitoring and less reliant on surveillance as the primary channel of power. As policymakers in the United States deploy techniques of social control free from individuating disciplines, the disallowance of the perspective of the victim of police violence suggests not simply corruption, but a frightening transformation in the activity of policing. The techniques of surveillance that gave rise to modern police forces were designed to individuate even as they normalized. They accompanied a regime of rights within discipline. When policing moves from surveillance to monitoring, a shift in priority is made from the correction of individuals to the control of populations. When policing moves from surveillance to monitoring, rights become anachronisms.

There are powerful ambiguities at work in such a process that make the move to monitoring potentially explosive politically. First, the continued reliance on a discourse of personal responsibility (King could have chosen to be a football player), when coupled with the withdrawal of the individuating discipline of surveillance, puts unbearable pressure on those who are designated as marginal. They are first damned, and then damned for being damned. Second, the technique of monitoring, which substitutes a passive control over protected space for a corrective and interventionist surveillance of individuals, forces the development of public policies to handle what could be called the waste products of social control, the ever growing numbers of people who cannot be integrated into the "normal" social order.[58]

Of course, the other side of this process of "normalization" is the development of new modes of inclusion, in this case the development of communities of consumption. In such communities, television monitors are used extensively to observe the ingress and egress of persons who live in private housing developments. Mike Davis reports on one such community in Los Angeles, Forest City Enterprises. "As a spokeswoman for the owners observed, 'it's a trend in general to have enclosed communities.'"[59] These communities privatize what would once have been considered public spaces by erecting gates of entry and departure to provide security for those who can afford to live within them. Monitors provide a continuous flow of information showing who has entered and who has departed, who is in and who is out. Those within constitute communities of consumption. As Davis suggests,

> The designers of malls and pseudo-public space attack the crowd by homogenizing it. They set up architectural and semiotic barriers to filter out "undesirables." They enclose the mass that remains, directing its circulation with behaviorist ferocity. . . . This Skinnerian orchestration, if well conducted, produces a veritable commercial symphony of swarming, consuming monads moving from one cash point to another.[60]

Or, as Arend Collen, a manager of a MacDonald's in Simi Valley put it, "It's one of the few communities left where you can go shopping and not get hit up by people wanting money."[61]

Normalization through the social organization of consumption is consistent with key elements in the Marxist critique of consumer capitalism.[62] But normalization proceeds through techniques governing the allowance and disallowance of activities beyond consumption as well. François Ewald, among others, has noted some of the techniques by which populations are constituted in relation to risk and insurance. These are norms which allow and disallow not only consumption, but activities of production as well.[63] Normalization, at its most general level, is a technique that permits withdrawal from the special interventions of individual discipline by manipulating populations at large. Through the establishment of norms, people become parts of systems of equivalence that substitute, for an equality based on particularity, an inequality based on comparison to a standard based on an average. No single person is ever average, and hence no one is ever completely normal. One's place in such a system is determined by the attributes one shares with others. Each attribute places a dimension of one's life on a specific continuum. Personhood itself is fragmented, and elements of it become signs of one's place in reference to a norm.

In Simi Valley, the expression of normative values is closely associated with the practices of normalization. The mayor, for instance, is quick to note, "There is no question, in this community, that somebody out of the ordinary sticks out quickly. And people are very quick to report anything suspicious, very quick to call the police, and expect them to be there."[64] In the minds of its residents, Simi Valley is a lifestyle that separates those who live in the suburbs from urban others. Those who are different are perceived as dangerous.

> Residents insist that what binds them is not their common race or ethnicity, but a shared middle-class life style. "We like living in a place with educated people, people who believe as we do," said Brian Arkin. . . . "But I don't believe skin color is a criteria."

"There's a black person up our street and we say 'Hi' like he's a normal person," Mr. Arkin continued. "This isn't about race. It's about whether you let your property run down."

"Or whether you sell drugs out of your house," his wife, Valerie, interjected.[65]

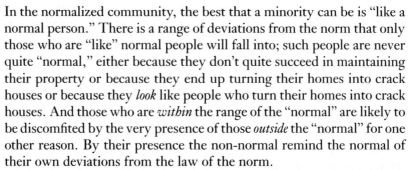

In the normalized community, the best that a minority can be is "like a normal person." There is a range of deviations from the norm that only those who are "like" normal people will fall into; such people are never quite "normal," either because they don't quite succeed in maintaining their property or because they end up turning their homes into crack houses or because they *look* like people who turn their homes into crack houses. And those who are *within* the range of the "normal" are likely to be discomfited by the very presence of those *outside* the "normal" for one other reason. By their presence the non-normal remind the normal of their own deviations from the law of the norm.

The normalized community is itself an enclosed space, as Davis notes, with sharply delineated points of entry and exit. Simi Valley is described as a very safe place, in part because of its plan: "The geographic configuration of the 12-mile long valley, and its carefully planned street grid, makes a safe place safer. Just as each subdivision in Simi Valley is a self-contained web of cul-de-sacs, so the whole city can, in effect, be cordoned off simply by blocking four highway exits."[66]

Such a system of streets encloses Simi Valley from the dangerous people of the outside world. People feel safe because they are surrounded with a familiar sameness. Those who are different are far away, spatially. Those who invade will be contained and removed.

What happens to those who are cast out of these enclosed communities? The non-normal face of normalization is that of the deviant. If it is true that techniques of normalization are becoming less discipline-centered than ever before, then those who are considered deviant from norms are not left to their own devices. Instead, they are threatened with a loss of the standing they may still enjoy as citizens.[67] In the end they remain subject to the recently rejuvenated, repressive power of the juridical apparatuses of the United States.

In the American version of normalized society, the least normal (and most despised) group are young African American men. From 1980 to 1990, the prison and jail population of the United States exploded (from 350,000 to 1,200,000). Young African American men are highly over-represented among those in the arms of the law. A Sentencing Project

Report, using U.S. Department of Justice and Census Bureau data, has shown that as of 1990, 23 percent of African American men between the ages of 18 and 30 in the United States were in prison, jail, on probation or parole, versus 6 percent of white men in the same age category. The report noted, "The number of *young* black men under the control of the criminal justice system—609,690—is greater than the *total* number of black men of *all ages* enrolled in college—436,000 as of 1986. For white males, the comparable figures are 4,600,000 total in higher education and 1,054,508 age 20–29 in the criminal justice system."[68] A second study conducted by the National Center on Institutions and Alternatives found that 42 percent of the African American men in Washington, D.C., between the ages of 18 and 35 were in jail, on probation or parole, or awaiting trial or sentencing. The study noted that as many as 70 percent of the African American men in the city have been arrested by the time they turn 35, and as many as 85 percent face arrest at some time in their lives.[69]

The dramatic shift in the scale of punishment has turned prisons into internment centers. There is less effort than ever to engage in the discipline of an earlier era, in what was once called "rehabilitation." Since the middle of the 1970s, what Leon Radzinowitz labeled the "neo-classical revival" in punishment has gained ground in the United States.[70] It was in 1975, in the conclusion of *Thinking about Crime*, that James Q. Wilson suggested the path that would be followed in subsequent decades. He wrote, I suppose with the objectivity of the social scientist, that "wicked people exist. Nothing avails except to set them apart from innocent people."[71]

Set them apart. Wilson's ideas for determining what constitutes wickedness and innocence are inextricably linked to the latest techniques of normalization. The categories that determine dangerousness versus harmlessness, based as they are in the racial sciences, which make being an African American male a criminal proclivity, can be seen to contribute to the arrangements that result in 85 percent of the African American men of Washington, D.C., facing arrest in their lifetimes. Once such a theological category as wickedness is reintroduced to provide a justification for the infliction of punishment on "abnormal others," the normalized community has moved into an ominous zone, where lives might collectively be condemned and eventually be taken, in the name of justice. When "scientific" racists such as James Q. Wilson turn into moralists, people like Rodney King become new bearers of the mark of Cain. We seem to need such marks to assure us.

Belief in natural evil (as opposed to the more difficult kind, the evil produced by the effects of cultural fears, resentments, and drives to dogmatize identities) relieves the powerful of the need to examine how we construct our demons. Expelling our demons does no good. No positive good can be said to have ever come from retribution, only a reordering of the moral universe by enactment of the evil that one sought to remove in the first place.

The New Enclosures

After the rioting began, Rodney King went on television to plead with his fellow citizens. He asked, "Can't we get along?" Then he added, "We can all get along. We've just got to, just got to. *We're all stuck here for awhile.*"[72] King recognized the finitude of the space of Los Angeles. He resisted the temptation to separate, to enclose, to substitute for the messy and open qualities of heterogeneous urban spaces the closed and deadened spaces of the suburbs. In making his plea he implicitly endorsed an ill-defined notion of toleration and plurality. He gave us a moment to reflect on the possibility of a democratic existentialism. The world is worlding. The forces of normalization operate to constrain, to separate, to exclude, and to intern. Our hope is precisely phrased. We're all stuck here for awhile.

The melodrama of the Rodney King story is quintessentially American. His broken body cracked an icon that had been built with care for decades, the icon of the monstrous young black man. For a moment we were able to see the hurt in the eyes, just as Boris Karloff once gave us a pathetic rendering of the monster in the film version of *Frankenstein.* Does it matter that the children of Los Angeles bear little resemblance to the pathetic and monstrous images we have received? In both cases, the body of a black man is meant to do work for whites, to reestablish a moral order over a disorder that grows deeper with each failure of American political culture to confront the paradoxes that grow out its whiteness.[73]

Can we replace our masks? Or better, perhaps, can we construct new masks? The representation of the normalized community that I have presented here is white, suburban, middle-class, male, straight, and law-abiding. But each of the norms is a mask. Each flows along a specified dimension of existence. The threat of a normalized society does not rest with the existence of norms, but in how the norms coalesce into operations of enclosure and internment. The vision of enclosed space—tightly controlled, perfectly monitored—has long been the beau ideal of Los Angeles, home of Disneyland. In a meditation about Los Angeles, the urban geographer Edward Soja notes this, and also notes that "when all that is seen is so fragmented and filled with whimsy and pastiche, the hard edges of the capitalist, racist, and patriarchal landscape seem to disappear, melt into air."[74] Just so. And yet it is also important to avoid the sorts of reductions that would make those hard edges blunt through overuse. Contemporary racism in the United States has several dimensions. Class cannot substitute for race, even when the two overlap, and the visions of politics associated with the new Enclosures are not reducible to the analysis of the distribution of goods, any more than they can be the result of a pseudo-theological explanation based on the growth of evil in the hearts of criminal beings.

The new Enclosures can not endure if a democratic style of united states is to remain a possibility. Their continued presence indicates a decline in democratic wonder. Although suburban life is not necessarily an oxymoron, it becomes one when those who do not live in suburbs are excluded from the peace they produce. That alternative future is upon us, the macrovision of united states achieved through exclusion. That vision will result in replications of the Los Angeles riot. But at the same time, that vision contains its opposite as a positive alternative. It is possible that there will be the emergence of a politics of deterritorialization and reconnection, a politics in which arguments over space—its enclosures, exclusions, and internments—become the subjects of debate and the inspiration for new practices. The initiation of such a politics is a short step in the long journey to beginning the process of ameliorating the current problem. Can we who have run west so long to secure our united states, to maintain our innocence, can we, for so long lacking a need to think about space, begin to think in spatial terms? Can we begin to act upon those thoughts with our bodies?

Some have already begun to do so. Yet the labor is only beginning, and it is not without its pain and piety as well. Deterritorialization is an awkward word, but the deterritorialization of the body is something we can probably learn best, not merely from the body of the condemned man, but from the everyday experiences of women as we look upon them, and as they begin to look back.

CHAPTER FIVE

Barbara Kruger, or "You Really Crack Me Up"

Is it possible to construct a way of looking which welcomes the presence of pleasure and escapes the deceptions of desire?

—Barbara Kruger

Intercourse

Straight men in the superior position have few friends, but those of us who are women, whatever form our desires take, seem to have, or at least to seek, more friends. Why is that? Carol Gilligan tells stories about nurturing and the desire to remedy that informs womanly experience. But women in our united states too often seem attached to men who damage. Men in the superior position are estranged from the women who try to connect with them, if not as lovers, at least as the authority figures these men want to be. For men in the superior position, women achieve a place at their side by inciting the repulsions they feel, shaping their hurts and hopes.

But women, Gilligan suggests, are not first inclined to think in terms of condemnation. They proceed from sympathy to try to maintain connection and to ask that an ethic of care be a primary consideration in living our lives.[1] An axiom of the politics of care-ful life might be: Do not seek to mete out justice, but think instead about how justice might be made part of a way of life that does not take so seriously the concerns of a male-dominated context.

In seeking united states with other men, men in the superior position kill women. Women link men to men through the abject desire men seem to discover anew in each generation. The locus of this male desire and dread finds its most stupefied expression in the hole that leads back to birth. Do I put this too crudely, too stupidly? Every murder, I know, is as unique as a snowflake. And yet the messiness against which we measure ourselves every day, the beatings, the humiliations, the multiple abandonments, the brutish facts about how men treat women, *is* a crude and stupid thing.

Such a mess inspires a wish that the genitalia of women no longer serve as the sites and symbols of engendered power. But tough babies wonder. On what reconfiguration of politics would the fulfillment of that particular wish depend? Or, from the perspective of the paranoid (failed) tough baby, radio commentator Rush Limbaugh, why is it that feminists are so ugly? What gendered pleasures must be abandoned if we are to attain peace, and what new ones invented? And what must we do about our memory fetishes? How are we to move beyond the fascism of everyday life organized around the myth of a singular woman's body, good only for one thing?

I pause. Caught inside myself, again, I know that I must ask the other question, because these are the wrong ones. What would it mean to efface the history of masculine sexuality, rather than to learn to work through it? Why this fantasy of disappearance associated with the wish to abandon gendered pleasure? In disappearing myself, don't I also want to make women disappear as well? What is the lack motivating my desire to ventriloquize a womanly concern? Can we break from the repetitions within which we are caught, expose the narcissism we suffer, and avoid the ridicule that accompanies the attention we seek?

Judith Butler suggests the repetitions themselves are a key to understanding gender as an effect. She offers an exposé of gender that might not condemn it:

> To expose the contingent acts that create the appearance of a naturalistic necessity, a move which has been a part of cultural critique at least since Marx, is a task that now takes on the added burden of showing how the very notion of the subject, intelligible only through its appearance as gendered, admits of possibilities that have been forcibly foreclosed by the various reifications of gender that have constituted its contingent ontologies. [2]

This is a risky business. A contingent ontology is a philosophical bastard. Where is the body under all that performance? one might ask. Whose body? More generally, what limits have we imposed on embodiment? Or should I mean to say, "imposed *by* embodiment?" I would not

want to suggest that we must seek to transcend our bodies. To attempt
that move is only to return to the grand Christian tradition of body-
bashing. And I won't pretend to be disembodied. That idea is one of the
worst errors liberals make.[3] In fact, because the idea of the malleable
subject seems to echo the liberal notion of disembodiment, some feminist political theorists have committed what I think is yet another
mistake by suggesting that the unveiling of the history of sexuality is a
strategy by misogynist men trying to make women disappear. Who are
we men to take away the idea of a grounded subject endowed with
rights just as women are becoming autonomous subjects themselves?[4]

Unfortunately, that question doesn't make much sense for us. On the
primal scene of our united states, the politics of the superior position
has invariably unfolded from and relied on a strategic essentialism.[5] In
every sphere of life, essentialist polemicists work to recapture existence
by forcing their version of the real over all who would transgress it.
Diana Fuss issues an appropriate caution. She suggests that to proceed
as though it is possible to identify an essence is a reactionary construction that plays into the game of those who enforce power through
essentialist reductions.[6] But too many subalterns too quickly endorse
the strategies of those who project essentialist versions of the real. "This
time," they insist, "we'll get it right."

That recapitulation is a mistake. In the struggle over power, it only
reasserts the old real. It settles things, rather than moves them. It
ignores at its own risk Butler's repetitions, the parodies that politicize
the practices through which the contingent ontology of gender is asserted. The gender genealogist goes down with Butler, with a rueful
laugh appreciative of the hot iron(ie)s that go way in.[7] Where powerful
representations are enforced through resort to essential categories we
can counter with a strategic inessentialism expressing the complexity of
our constructions of truth, resisting the allure of right.[8] What might
help us in that work is some examination of the styles of representation
that hold the mirror of Bush up to Bush. We seek to circumscribe,
rather than to describe, to impose a less intrusive violence of examination against the more intense violence of the gaze as a technique of
knowing. Might I present a silhouette, or perhaps a tracing? Can I take
on the guise of a sensitive man, alert to the circumstances that inform
some of the ordinary operations of violence in the united states of
intercourse? The superior position always already threatens to reassert
itself.

That Hole

Perhaps it is an easily recognizable horror that we face. This passage is from Andrea Dworkin's *Intercourse*.

> Sometimes, the skin comes off in sex. The people merge, skinless. The body loses its boundaries. . . . The skin is a line of demarcation, a periphery, the fence, the form, the first clue to identity in a society (for instance, color in a racist society), and in purely physical terms, the precondition for being human. It is a thin veil of matter separating outside from inside. It is what one sees and what one covers up; it shows and it conceals; it hides what is inside. The skin is separation, individuality, the basis for corporeal privacy and also the point of contact for everything outside the self.[9]

Dworkin has the audacity to be apocalyptic about sexual intercourse, making its facticity scream at us not merely as a practical matter but as an ontological principle. One might dismiss her claims by effacing them, by suggesting that she makes women more vulnerable than ever by failing to explore the terrain of gender in ways that emphasize its performative elements, by emphasizing how she makes women into victims and then seeks the aid of the most reactionary elements of state power to advance their protection as victims. For Dworkin there is no getting around male construction sites.

For instance, the question of the violation of boundary is a legal one, whether the law be one of intimacy or of international relations. We might consider this passage, one continuous with Dworkin's understanding of boundary, taken from Catharine MacKinnon's *Feminism Unmodified*: "To consider 'no more rape' as only a negative, no more than an absence, shows a real failure of imagination. Why does 'out now' contain a sufficiently positive vision of the future for Vietnam and Nicaragua but not for women? Is it perhaps because Vietnam and Nicaragua exist, can be imagined without incursions, while women are unimaginable without the violation and validation of the male touch?"[10] We could ignore the fact that those slogans *were* insufficient. MacKinnon's major point is that an outer boundary is transposed to an inner space. The politics of violation is a politics of boundaries violated. The folding within becomes folded back, the speculum reveals, as usual, nothing, an empty space.

In our united states we have always been flexible when it comes to boundaries. We draw them, invade them, configure them according to our urges toward manifest destiny; we try not to be too serious about respecting them. It is interesting that the idea of the boundary line has not loomed large in most critiques of Dworkin and MacKinnon's analysis of male violence. Because so much controversy has attended their political intervention into the law by way of their advocacy of anti-pornography ordinances in several midwestern cities, much of our conversation about their radical feminism has centered around questions concerning the behavioral relationship between "violence" *and* "representations." Ordinary sexual libertarians, those who separate sex and violence, take MacKinnon and Dworkin to task for their refusal to leave sexual expression alone, whereas defenders of the antipornography movement point toward pornography as a form of speech not deserving of protection. But another objection, developed most fully by feminists like Susie Bright of the lesbian porn magazine *On Our Backs*, and theorists such as Butler, is that the closures such structures present for those who would want to play with the idea of sadomasochistic pleasure and other curious experiments with our bodies are themselves cruel restrictions on our humanity. To insist on a singular sexuality that is exclusively male in orientation today while presenting women as struggling to achieve a yet to be realized species-being evokes a sterile utopianism over and above the possibilities of living in the world as it is. Such utopianism resists resistance and ignores the lives of those who have broken with what Butler calls the "heterosexual matrix."[11] Joan of Arc might be kinky enough in some circles, but ultimately this virginal purity depends on a lack of imagination, not a fulfillment.[12]

But then MacKinnon's point is to insist that we stop visualizing each other and instead interact in unmediated ways to overcome the horrors of representation by destroying the possibility of representation. Her understanding of pornography is that it is "not fantasy or simulation or catharsis but sexual reality: the level of reality on which sex itself operates."[13] Her model is one in which Marx meets barefoot empiricism. All representation, all imagination, is outlawed. MacKinnon's wish, then, seems to be for an antinomian state before our fall into knowledge, an edenic site where there is no temptation through representation itself.

This is the wish of the antipornography crusader. But one predicament of pornography, as we have already seen in the case of George Bush, is that it can only be subordinate to the order it challenges.[14] And even that is not the only difficulty. Susan Stewart also calls attention to the relationship between desire and representational practices that leads to another predicament for pornography, "the impossibility of describing desire without generating desire; the impossibility of separating form and content within the process of sublimation; and most important, the impossibility of constructing a metadiscourse of pornography once we recognize the interested character of all discursive practices. We cannot transcend the pornography debate for we are in it."[15] Even more directly to the political point, Stewart notes, while examining the homeopathic similarities of the Meese Commission Report and the marquis de Sade's pornographic epic *120 Days of Sodom*, that for both "representation always preempts sexuality, just as the Meese Commission, in its search for a sexuality freed from representation, had feared."[16] Stewart thus suggests that pornographic strategies of representation are designed to create a total world by way of an articulation of space, the positioning of actors in that space, and "the invention of the social," as she puts it.[17] This closed world is controllable by the pornographer, in fact, it is a world of control. It gives rise to opposition strategies that replicate the pornographic discourse itself.

Within the site of the pornographic enactment might be a clue to the imprisoning reaction that Dworkin and MacKinnon seek in response to what they understand the pornographic to be. We might read both MacKinnon's essays and Dworkin's studies of rape *as* pornography.[18]

Several years ago, I heard and watched MacKinnon speak to an overflow audience in Johnson Chapel at Amherst College.[19] It was a scene that might have been staged by the marquis de Sade himself. Johnson Chapel is a minor site of male power in American higher education, a room lined with large oil paintings of powerful men from the past century and a half, former presidents of the college, a former president of the United States (silent Cal Coolidge), a former chief justice of the Supreme Court, and no women. In that sacred space of men in the superior position, MacKinnon defied and defiled the sanctity of their order. As she emphasized the violence in pornography, she slowed her speech and became especially dramatic. She made explicit references, emphasizing especially the connections between the erotics of porn and the degradation of women. As she urged her audience to cease to think in images when thinking about sex, to censor their imagination, she incited us to picture the most violent pornographic pleasures. Indeed, she insisted that to visualize sex acts at all was to engage in an act of violence, showing how we are imprisoned in the pornographic imagination at every level. She exemplified Stewart's cautionary message. MacKinnon's was a *masterful* performance, the creation of an ideal Sadeian space within which nothing (everything) was to be permitted. Her intervention was a spectacular instantiation of the pornographic through the medium of critique.

But MacKinnon need not worry that she is engaged in a transgression. The pornographer is always refuted at the moment that a radical break is possible, because the structure of transgression, one of revenge in his reading, employs weapons that are going to be too close for comfort to those of the adversary.[20] Dependent on the structure of power that it assaults, pornography will always fall short of its putative goal. This paradox is the monkey trap of the pornography debate, in which the subject is captured by desire and needs to let go of the bait in order to be free.

Of course, we might claim that the severe dissociation needed to set the pornographer free has been visited upon us. But if that is the case, the suppression of skin magazines is the least of our problems. In these days when we hang sex offenders, there is little reason to think that there is a problem to be solved by voiding the pornographic *imagination*.

The paradox of pornography does not go unnoticed by Dworkin. She expresses an ambivalence and pain at the core of her enterprise that admits of the ambiguity of our common life. Even at the heart of "Intercourse in a Man-Made World," when discussing the stigma of sex, Dworkin does not simply condemn men, but suggests that women are stigmatized by sex under conditions where a rich inner life is not appreciated. Dworkin gives us room to admit that it is only an empathic capacity for pain that enables men and women to distinguish, for example, tenderness from mere fucking. But it is when the transgressive pain of extreme circumstance is transformed into the ordinary condition of our lives that our lives become unnecessarily miserable.

Dworkin writes, "Being stigmatized by sex is being marked by its meaning in a human life of loneliness and imperfection, where some pain is indelible."[21] She identifies an "indelibility," a mark in pain that constitutes the boundary condition of human being for a category of people who are to be defined by a less-than-human, stigmatized, status. Pain elevates us to human status. But the stigma is also a mark of an extrahuman quality for her, and the realization of this extrahumanness is achieved through intercourse. Nonetheless, for her such respite from the intercourse wars is only available when considering the human condition of women. That human condition is what is always and everywhere contested by the normal world of men in the superior position. When the specific condition of women as humans is contrasted with that of the male remainder of humanity, women assume an inferior status.

But precisely because her understanding of boundaries relies on the epistemology of the men she opposes, Dworkin's description of intercourse, one that MacKinnon picks up on, is that of an occupying army. She writes, "He has to push in past boundaries. There is the outline of a body, distinct, separate, its integrity an illusion, a tragic deception, because unseen there is a slit between the legs, and he has to push into it. There is never any real privacy of the body that can coexist with intercourse: with being entered."[22] The vaginal opening is essential to the human condition of women. "She is defined by how she is made, that hole, which is synonymous with entry; and intercourse, the act fundamental to existence, has consequences for her being that may be intrinsic, not socially imposed." Rejecting the anus, which she claims is not "exclusively" for entrance, Dworkin thus posits a metaphysics of womanhood.

But the vagina is not exclusively for entrance either. On special occasions—birth—it becomes an exit. It is the terror of birth that one might counterpoise to Dworkin, the fear of death as an exit asymmetrical to birth. In effacing the vagina as a point of exit, then, Dworkin participates in phallocentric metaphysics; she seeks to avoid death by avoiding birth. It is a metaphysics of powerlessness and of a fearful respect for law.

How can I object to this metaphysics, based as it is on the terror of powerlessness? I can do so because possession endures as the discourse of power, especially in American culture and, dispossession is no more than the mirror of that power. If we are to move between the danger provided by self-possession and the terror of its opposite, to be possessed by another, we must be prepared to move more fearfully than most of us have yet to imagine possible. I want to pose objections to this metaphysics of the powerless, to look for people who are less willing to reverse the gaze and more intent on shattering the mirror.

Breaking Gazes

Barbara Kruger addresses me. Or is it me she addresses? Who am I to her? How might I be constructed by her address? Moreover, how does

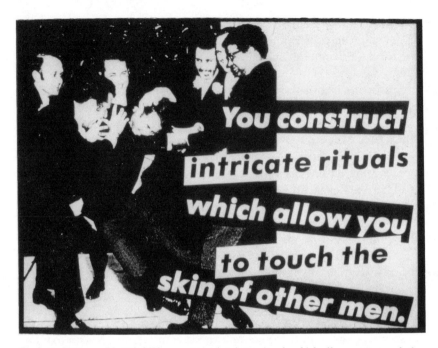

Barbara Kruger, *Untitled (You construct intricate rituals which allow you to touch the skin of other men)*, 1980. Photograph, 37 in. × 50 in. Museum of Fine Arts, Boston, Massachusetts. Courtesy Mary Boone Gallery, New York.

her address, located at a vaguely mapped, but nonetheless distinctive crossroad of representational power, operate in relation to the power it seems to critique? Is *she* caught up in the pornography of representation? Or is something else occurring here? Her address is only as complicated as I make it out to be. Surely I can decide, one way or another, what I will do with this picture she has sent me. Surely.

But if I am caught looking, her picture has trapped me. I am marked by her enactment of a set of complex strategies. She has employed certain techniques by which I am reduced and managed, and no dismissal on my part will forestall or prevent her address from reaching me, reducing me, and managing me. I am pinned down by a gaze that challenges me as a man in the superior position, by a gaze that does not originate from behind the screen of authority but from that indefinite fissure which opens between the vision of the eye and its supportive text.

First of all she makes me laugh, a disarming laughter. Like so many of her other pictures, this one is outlined by a thin red frame, which contains both text and photograph. In this picture the text consists of five strips, half in and half out of the photographic image. The strips draw visual attention toward the man in the middle of a group of men. All are formally dressed. Perhaps they are at a wedding. He is laughing, they are all laughing. He must be the groom. Perhaps they are tickling him. He is laughing hard, he is losing his breath, maybe that's a grimace on his face. He might be in pain. They might be hurting him. Maybe he is being assaulted. Maybe that's a grimace of pain. Maybe not. Maybe he's having the time of his life. Maybe.

We've seen this sort of ambiguity before. The comedy short "The Idle Class" presents a scene in which Charlie Chaplin, having just been informed by his wife that she is leaving him because of his drinking, is left alone. He turns his back to the camera. His shoulders hunch together. He begins to shake, his body seems racked by sobs. He turns around, his countenance calm and concentrated. The audience sees that he has been mixing a drink in a cocktail shaker.[23] Chaplin's performance anticipates themes Kruger investigates. The everyday ambiguity in Chaplin's body language is replicated in the postures of the men in Kruger's photograph. A mistaken representation of action leads to a surprise that results in laughter. Out of that laughter we find a moment of democratic play in Chaplin, as well as in Kruger.

Kruger is famous for working the imagery of advertising, having come to know certain archetypical body images through years of exposure to the repeated postures and the rehearsed body positions of models in photographs. But her discernment is even more catholic than the world of advertising. She has seen the photojournalism of the world, and has abused it, distorted and fractured its consumptive purposes in order to make images of men and women resonant with the ironic slogans of postmodern deferrals. The configuration of these men thus has a source of familiarity different from that which might be provided by other men who might be found in similar clothes. Clothes make us men, but clothing also goes down to our bodies and extends out from us. If we were to replace the morning suits of the men surrounding the groom with the uniform of police (nightstick at side, revolver, khaki pants, perhaps even cavalry hats, like the State Police), replace the morning suit of the groom with the uniform of the male student (blue jeans, long hair, plain shirt, sneakers), the same group setting and text could remain unchanged. Let us imagine other combinations, Klansmen and lynch victim; Lee Harvey Oswald doubled over, surrounded by police, while Jack Ruby tickles him with a pistol; Pope John Paul II and Mehmet Ali Agca; British football hooligans and an opposing fan; Secret Service agents and John Hinckley; the members of the National Security Council and Ronald Reagan (George Bush behind him); the winning Super Bowl team and their coach; gang-bangers and the kid they are jumping in; Gary Gilmore being raped in prison. The image remains the same. Is the point too polemical? Or is the polemic not the polemic it seems to be?

In advertising, we use the personal pronoun to make specific floating and impersonal messages.[24] Designed to include, the rhetoric of direct address is a form of persuasion often used by politicians and editorial writers. It also informs my rhetoric here, an attempt to make of myself and the readers of this book an interpretive community. There is always a cost to this rhetoric, usually borne by the reader, who is seduced by an invitation to be part of the world of whatever he or she is reading. In the case of this study, he or she is shaped as a special person indeed by virtue of being here, of reading these words on this page. I can only hope that unveiling the rhetoric mitigates its effects. It always remains for you to gauge the extent to which I am concealing my effects by pointing them out.

But when Kruger writes "you" in a text within a photographic picture, the strategy of the gaze is different. The focus and hence the intent of the address shifts. Instead of being seduced, I am *accused*. I am presented with the absurdity of my self, I am shown to be a foreigner, a weird being, out of touch in both figurative and physical ways. Within the frame of the picture, pinned by the terms of address that allows no honest escape, I have no choice but to think ruefully about certain weapons of my gender which I have casually used, had once succeeded in convincing myself were not weapons at all. Now I remember. Now those weapons (what weapons?) are being turned on me. From Kruger I learn that every time I look at a woman's body she knows that I am looking, and in that knowledge she may also know how to resist the presumption of my gaze. The terms of Kruger's direct address move me from my superior position to one of equality with the person who presents this image to me. In advertising, this democratic move is designed to prepare me to receive a commodity. But here, the moment of relaxation disarms me to receive . . . a message, one that will make me uncomfortable in my passivity, will make me see something I do not want to see. The principle of visibility that has served me is inverted.

I have two choices then. First, I can lie to Kruger and to myself concerning the impact that her gaze has on me. But my lie, my refusal to accept the truth of her terms, is born of my belief that I can still be an invisible observer. The broader history of modernity, in its contemporary bureaucratic expression, has disciplined me. Discipline itself depends on a trap of visibility that has "feminized" me, that has moved most men to a sort of inferior position similar to that inhabited by women.[25] Kruger pins me down to a place in a cultural order that assumes my masculinity to be expressed in terms of my work uniform. Moreover, my invisibility is diametrically opposed to the visibility of an African American man. Rodney King's uniform is his skin.

If I refuse the first tactic, can I live with the consequences of the question I must then ask? My question makes explicit my unaccustomed position as the inferior. The question I want to ask is that of the loser, the bully on whom the tables have been turned. I move to the position of the pervert.[26] I try to suspend "the libidinal and psychic constancy that [the pleasure principle] supports."[27] My question: Is Kruger's democratic gesture only another spectacular ruse,[28] one designed simply to reverse a hold that we men have had on women for so long? The answer: Yes and no. To uncover the politics of vision that inform Kruger's visual works requires investigating the contemporary sites where vision is contested. It is to engage in that least neutral political study of the histories of the modern gaze.

Kruger's work is schooled, not only in the visual skills of commercial art and copyediting but in the history of the disciplined eye. That history has been the subject of much attention in critical circles in recent years, in part because of the popular reception of Foucault's expropriation of Jeremy Bentham's principle of panopticism.[29] Yet the focus on panopticism has distracted attention from a more complex and variegated comprehension of the relationships between vision and power that inform Foucault's work.[30] Kruger seems fully cognizant of the complexities of vision that inform this analytic of visual power. Not limited to a study of the diagram of power as it operates as an exemplary technique,[31] not attendant only to the question of visibility, and finally connected not to a pessimism that emerges in identity politics and leads to complicity with power so much as a hyperpessimism that emerges from the genealogy of power and leads to the exhilaration of a reactivated politics, her work operates to incite thought about the dynamic politics of vision in specific settings.

The Visible Body

Whose body is this? Where did it come from? What is the touch that informs its every movement? How did it come to be that one hand touches itself and comes to know what Merleau-Ponty once called fleshiness?[32] The fleshiness of what we touch, the solidity of embodiment, contrasts with the body as a visual field opened for inspection and dissection. If we can shift perspective, we can also come to a better understanding of the fragmentary, partial constructions that fundamentally inform how we unite. We might also come to understand better how the varying fields of human understanding touch on the visual, even those which seem to be independent of visual references. It's a funny notion, kindred to the urgent advice given by the character Annie Savoy to Nuke, the young pitching protegy in the movie *Bull Durham*, on how to gain control on the mound. "You've got to learn to breathe through your eyes," she insists. Her advice (to which she adds the suggestion that Nuke wear a black garterbelt with tassles under his uniform), coupled with the veteran catcher Crash Davis's mantra ("Don't think too much!"), points toward the relaxed focus needed to open our bodies and minds simultaneously.

The idea of reimagining the body to incorporate its "representativeness" into a reconfigured sense of the self is not novel. But it is one of the presumptions of poststructuralist criticism to reinvigorate the interrogation of especially those separations of body and mind predicated on an autonomous visuality. John Rajchman, citing Gilles Deleuze, has claimed that "the territory of the visual spans knowledge, art, ethics, and politics, and so it illustrates why Foucault had no difficulties in dealing with 'the relations of science and literature, or the imaginary and the scientific, or the known and the lived.'"[33] Given the possibility that the construction of a particular kind of "reality" is what is being contested politically when we look at anything in a particular way, an exploration of the construction of a particular kind of vision, its enclosures and disclosures, its objects, and its subjects, might be understood in a radically historicized context.

Ambiguous Bodies, Lonely Men

Foucault's documentary of the French hermaphrodite, Adelaide (Alexina) Herculine Barbin, is an illustration of the historical body as a battleground of truth. Barbin is part of a phenomenon that few who live in postindustrial societies have occasion to know about anymore, for a simple and perhaps brutal reason. Nowadays, surgeons cut. In the introduction to the documents that compose the study of Barbin, Foucault suggested that the most important problem s/he faced was the emergent quest, in France and other countries of Europe, to discover the "truth" of sex.[34] Hermaphroditism, in the context of this quest, was discredited as a human condition. The clinical goal was to uncover the "real" sex in the confused bodies of those whose surfaces were inscribed by the anatomical features of male and female. The doctor became the key sexual examiner, whose role was to decode the specific mechanisms of the body. "He had, as it were, to strip the body of its anatomical deceptions and discover the one true sex behind organs that might have put on the forms of the opposite sex."[35] Choices concerning sexual preference (use of body as well as presentation of body) shifted from her/him to experts.

This shift coincided with a new political aesthetic of the medical gaze, one that Foucault analyzes at length in *The Birth of the Clinic*. The rhetorical incision with which he opens that book or, to use Rajchman's terms, the "before-and-after-pictures"[36] juxtapose a phantasmagorical description of one set of membranes (a fantasy of theory) and a clinical description ("atheoretical") of another. What was for the doctor of the eighteenth century "parchment" was for the doctor of the nineteenth a field of specific properties, colors, characteristics, and categories. Lacking "any perceptual base," the eighteenth-century description is couched in abstract, semipoetical, theoretical language. But the nineteenth-century description is lengthy, organized, detailed, and conveys "a world of constant visibility." Foucault argues,

> Medical rationality plunges into the marvelous density of perception, offering the grain of things as the first face of truth, with their colors, their spots, their hardness, their adherence. The breadth of the experiment seems to be identified with the domain of the careful gaze, and of an empirical vigilance receptive only to the evidence of visible contents. The eye becomes the depository and source of clarity; it has the power to bring truth to light that it receives only to the extent that it has brought it to light; as it opens, the eye first opens the truth.[37]

Foucault returns to this notion of the truth of the gaze. "[The clinical gaze] is a gaze of the concrete sensibility, a gaze that travels from body to body, and whose trajectory is situated in the space of sensible manifestation. For the clinic, all truth is sensible truth."[38] Thus the clinical gaze founded an empire of a new empiricism. This clinic later became reconfigured by Foucault into an instrument of disciplinary society. But Foucault never equates rationality and vision. Acts of vision are not reducible to a single equation of sight with the registration of data. Vision is instead a mutable technique for the creation of highly particularized, very specific objects about which much can be said and done and for the establishment of a field of activity, however limited, on which there can and will be contests about different knowledges, different political agendas, different opinions of good and bad, and different assessments of beauty.

Including the beauty of Barbin. The truth of sex violates the reality of her/him. It becomes sensible truth. The autopsy report of Barbin, filed after her/his suicide, exemplifies this sensibility. A particular kind of gaze is at work, one that in its very process establishes its truth, defines a field of vision that must exclude the excesses one might otherwise admit to seeing in the body of the hermaphrodite.

> In the place that it normally occupies was to be seen a regularly inserted penis five centimeters long and two centimeters in diameter in the state of flaccidity. This organ ended in an imperforate glans that was flattened on the sides and completely exposed by the prepuce, which formed a crown at its root. . . . Examination showed that [the vagina] was covered entirely by a pavement epithelium, which is the kind that lines the normal vagina. . . . The anus . . . was in no way abnormal. On either side of the erectile organ (penis or clitoris), forming a groove in which this organ stood, were voluminous folds of the skin. These folds were the two lobes of a scrotum that remained divided. The right lobe, which was much larger than the left one, obviously contained a testicle of normal size, whose spermatic cord could easily be perceived through the skin, right up to the abdominal ring. The left testicle had not completely descended; a large part of it was still caught in the ring.[39]

This document reflects the rhetoric of the emergent medical vision. Uncertain of anything but the field it describes, it does not comment on the gender status of the body under its investigative knife. The descriptive phrases and parenthetical statements betray uncertainty, not in vision, but in the divisions that the knife will ultimately make. Even the internal features of the body, when brought to light by the knife, are subjected to the gaze that sees, not the blood and fluids, not the features of a dead human, but the physiological features of a scientific specimen. All is surface.

The sexual status of Barbin had been decided long before her/his death and autopsy. Of all the doctors who examined Barbin, only the first to examine her/him made a straightforward declaration of sex. His precedent, however, had the force of law, even though the legal apparatus was not yet fixed in regard to the declaration of sex. This first doctor declared the woman named Alexina to be a man named Alex. The *naming* had a particular power, in this case, in the service of the gaze, as an accompanying text. One can follow this process by examining the text of the doctor's examination notes, which record his declaration.

Is Alexina a woman? She has a vulva, labia majora, and a feminine urethra, independent of the sort of imperforate penis, which might be a monstrously developed clitoris. She has a vagina. True, it is very short and very narrow; but, after all, what is it if it is not a vagina? These are completely feminine attributes. Yes, but Alexina has never menstruated; the whole outer part of her body is that of a man, and explorations did not enable me to find a womb. Her tastes, her inclinations, draw her toward women. At night she has voluptuous sensations that are followed by a discharge of sperm; her linen is starched and stained with it. Finally, to sum up the matter, ovoid bodies and spermatic codes are found by touch in a divided scrotum. These are the real proofs of sex. We can now conclude and say: Alexina is a man.[40]

The real proofs of sex are what is most visible not to the naked eye but to the medical gaze. But that gaze is subject to its own rules, its own performative rituals. The activity of the doctor is not only that of the doctor, it is that of the male doctor, who empathetically identifies the features he knows to be those of his sex. A five centimeter penis is tiny, a five centimeter clitoris is huge, so the ambiguous status of the potential phallus remains so. But because Barbin has balls, he must be a man! After all, what is a vagina compared to balls? That the doctor was a man is not as important here as the engendering of the medical gaze as male. A vagina is an absence, a space, a void, a fold, and Barbin's fold ended in a cul-de-sac, it went nowhere. Perhaps that was the worst transgression of all.

The medical gaze does not traverse the folds of thought unless they are forced into shapes that are visible from above or below, always from the outside, never from within. The doctor's gaze necessarily excluded the ambiguous dimension of vision that was read by Barbin and those women Barbin loved as a genuine sentiment of sisterly love. He did not know, nor did he ask, about Barbin's feelings for the community of women from which s/he was being expelled.

The shift to a medical gaze in the nineteenth century was accompanied by what has more famously been discussed in reference to both *Discipline and Punish* and the first volume of Foucault's *History of Sexuality*,[41] the idea of the confession. In the case of Barbin the transfer of authority from priest to doctor takes place explicitly. The doctor who examined Barbin (after being given the case by the priest who found out about the "problem" in the confessional), said, "Here you must regard me not only as a doctor but as a confessor."[42] He wished his statement to be one of reassurance, a way of informing the patient that the doctor would listen as well as look. But Barbin's voice was subordinated to the doctor's vision. Hence, he may have said, "Tell me the truth of your sex. Tell me who you are. Tell me what you are. Men want to know, so we can have you, either as one of us, or as one of you. We don't care who you are, so long as you do not remain invisible to us. And your long period of invisibility is almost over, because we can see you now for what you are."

This is a message riddled with contradiction, of course, but it weighs on the gazing doctor as well. For that doctor might well have added, in his own act of confession, "We are lonely, gazing. Our overwhelming loneliness comes, perhaps, from what we suspect of our death. We know we can only have you as a man or as a woman, and we know that neither is enough. Our possession of you does not depend on you, you are an other, even should you decide to become one of us. We are sorry for you, but most of all we are sorry for ourselves."

We might note that the medical gaze is an instrument of loneliness, the expression of the friendless man on the outside looking in. It imposes a certitude that the gazer knows to be uncertain. The gazer traps those who are the object of the gaze. The trap works not necessarily or exclusively because that person is exposed, but because the person gazed upon is denied the possibility of seeing her/his self for her/his self. The denial of sight (is it too reactionary to call this the denial of a *right* to see?) is reinforced by social conventions that express an entire matrix of prior divisions of knowledge. Through the instrumentality of the gaze, reason and possession become attached to the very idea of vision.[43] When the trained gaze is joined to the other mechanisms that collectively constitute panopticism, a new instrument comes into play which constitutes and extends a terrain of power effects. The gaze operates on this terrain as a line of power that renders distinctions among different places in this topos. Visibility/invisibility, partial/impartial, strong/weak, fat/thin, large/small, innumerable reciprocal distinctions bear the weight of their meaning from what remains unspoken, but which speaks nonetheless as a way of hiding what words themselves cannot express. A new inclusion/exclusion line comes into being, and also a new world of sensible perception.[44] Alternatives to the extension of sensible perception become subsumed and delegitimized as the gaze creates the epistemological field which allows and sustains these relationships.

A Dangerous Topology

The critical difference constructed between women and men in the heterosexual matrix is a reflection of the artifice through which vision becomes the gaze. As a result, Cervantes' most subtle and prophetic aphorism may well be that "comparisons are odious."

The medical gaze denigrates that which exists within the folds. One need not merely curse sight for what one sees, however. A politics of vision contests not only what is looked at but what is visible and invisible. It does not abandon the site of sight for the oceanic experience of phonography. However, in this struggle, the terms of address of the politicizing artist need to be examined not only for how they reveal the various powers of the gaze but also for how they amplify and otherwise distort the sounds of power and for how they refract as well as reflect the intersections of language and light. Our incomparable elements live on to hurt us. None of our comparisons can be complete, yet everything about our united states incites us to completion.

Am I being too French? Tocqueville once claimed that we Americans are practical Cartesians.[45] The difference between us and them is that we are in a geography of open horizons. There is no escaping our subjectivities because there is no desire to escape. We invent and re-invent our selves. And yet we use that same tool to do so, time after time. In the open field of desire we close on the superior position as the only way to order things. The language that we have to address these matters is borrowed from the French, perhaps because not enough of us are Laurie Anderson or for that matter, Madonna. These fictions, regardless of our language, are enabled by our constant (failed) attempts to describe something we might call the American experience.

It is possible that contemporary French thinkers know this better than we do, having studied us from the security of a culture in which unity is assumed, not fundamentally doubted and hence deeply de-

sired. In his attempt to "narrate Foucault's great fiction," Gilles Deleuze suggests that

> the world is made up of superimposed surfaces, archives, or strata. The
> world is thus knowledge. But strata are crossed by a central fissure that
> separates on the one hand the visual scenes, and on the other the sound
> curves: the articulable and the visible on each stratum, the two irreducible
> forms of knowledge, Light and Language, two vast environments of the
> exteriority where visibilities and statements are respectively deposited.[46]

For Deleuze, the "central fissure" of thought is the zone of subjectification. The activity of thought is to try to comprehend the unknown of
these spaces. He invokes Herman Melville: "We look for a central
chamber, afraid that there will be no one there and that man's soul will
reveal nothing but an immense and terrifying void."[47] "We" also go
above and outside these folds in order to understand how the two sides
of language and light might touch each other, how the two sides of the
fold might connect. This zone of exteriority, unlike the inside zone of
strata (which only collect and solidify "the visual dust and the sonic echo
of the battle raging above them"), is "the domain of uncertain doubles
and partial deaths, where things continually emerge and fade."[48]

Paul Bové has worried that Deleuze presents Foucault's topology in
terms that are "metaphysically tinged."[49] Is his metaphysics of the same
order as Andrea Dworkin's? Or is a new joke lurking behind the
assertion of this metaphysics? To put this awkward matter in another,
equally awkward way, what if the metaphysics is constituted as a joke?
Of course we can see that there *is* such a joke underlying Deleuze's
metaphysical narration of Foucault's fiction, a spectacular joke, a visual
joke. We might ask: If metaphysics can be made into a visual joke, does
vision cease to be metaphysical? Can we move Dworkin to laughter,
shattering her tensions in a fit of giggles? Can we give her version of
intercourse a Chaplinesque, mistaken identification?

Deleuze presents a metaphysics of material irony, what might be
called the metaphysics of the anus. The diagram he draws to represent
Language and Light shows them as two cheeks of an ass, the fold
between them as a rectum, and the points of intersection as an anus.[50]
Deleuze penetrates himself. This crude diagram, seemingly hastily
drawn, criticizes the metaphysics of the text with the most penetrating
criticism of all—laughter. The obsession with the metaphysical that
haunts the history of metaphysics is drawn as the history of anality.

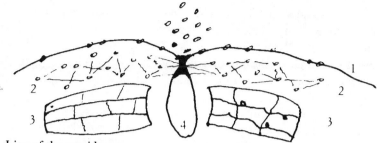

1. Line of the outside.
2. Strategic zone.
3. Strta
4. Fold

Gilles Deleuze, *Diagram of Foucault*. Reproduced, by permission, from Gilles Deleuze, *Foucault* (University of Minnesota Press, 1988). Copyright © 1988 by the University of Minnesota.

When we engage Deleuze's analysis of Foucault, looking at his sketch allows us to reconsider the text. When we engage Kruger's work, looking at the text allows us to reconsider the picture. The gap between picture and text can be understood as the fold of her thought, the zone of subjectification that, to paraphrase Deleuze, is to be filled with us, a place where "one becomes a master of one's speed, and relatively speaking, a master of one's molecules and particular features, in this zone of subjectification."[51]

Perhaps Deleuze's zone is not the anus but the vagina. What's the difference? If we strategically de-essentialize bodily difference, we could go back to that radical moment in the Sadeian text when his characters ask precisely that question, what's the difference?[52] What is the difference between Barbin's normal anus and her/his cul-de-sac vagina? Deleuze's project may be to reclaim for philosophy what it has lost as a consequence of the exhaustion of truth in the twentieth century, but not by providing a new game of truth. Instead, he may be thought of as enjoining the search for metaphysical principles with the task of rendering the truths that might be found in the banalities of bad jokes, as well as those that might be found in the grand codes of morality on which such jokes depend for their explosive force.[53] Exactly what might *not* be called for is subtlety, because the violence which not only accompanies the visual joke, but constitutes it, requires a certain crudeness for its force to be felt. Life is many things, but it is also violent, a simple fact that we cannot repress any more than we should celebrate. To expose not only the dirty little joke but the explosiveness of a fart is the aim of a metaphysics that would be "truer" to the intent of Deleuze than more "serious" philosophers might ever wish or know.

We could return to our united states via this French detour, then, a postcard of the non-Derridian type. Our laughter could be leavened by a hint of the exposure of the desire that leads nowhere, and it might be better laughter for its new modesty.

An Element of Care

How far are we from our united states? Kruger's French-American understanding of political power may help us attend to our violence. Her insight finally derives from a recognition of the crudeness of our violence as we unite. Her use of the banal in order to force us men out of our accustomed position of choice and her willingness to overwhelm the gazer with the products of his vision are based on a profound knowledge of the crudeness of violence. But Kruger is also, I dare say, more mature, in that her feminist field of vision moves beyond our attraction to anality to encompass the genital. Her point is "to demonstrate that masculine and feminine are unstable identities, but subject to ex-change," as Craig Owens has put it,[54] but this then is supplemented by a constructive project as well, to demonstrate the power of the vaginal as a zone of subjectivity. The folds of the vagina do not establish a zone of passivity, but impel action. They operate violently, but also with care.

Care. The element of care surprises me, even after what Kruger has already shown me. Care is the lesson to be found in her lenticular photography, which multiplies the perspectives from which text and picture might be seen.

Lenticular photographs are composed of images so layered that from one perspective the eyes see one image and from another perspective another image. Anyone who has gotten the "moving picture" prize in a box of Crackerjacks knows how this device presents an illusion of movement. Rather than using such complementary and continuous images, Kruger poses pictures that present an image when viewed directly, but from an angle present a text.

When I approach this picture directly, I see a photograph of a woman

Standard viewing position. Barbara Kruger, *Untitled (We are astonishingly life-like/Help! I'm locked inside this picture)*, 1985. Lenticular photograph, 19 in. × 19 in. Private collection. Courtesy Mary Boone Gallery, New York.

holding a grid-like frame in front of her face. The face looks through the grid at me. The accompanying text of the image is "We are astonishingly lifelike," itself complex, ironical. The frame within the frame, ambiguous in origin, perhaps an enlargement of an unknown electronic component, perhaps an integrated circuit, perhaps a loom, plays on the notions of text and context. The face is half-hidden in shadow. The accompanying words, placed at the corners of the picture, draw my gaze toward the center of the field (small words "we" and "are" at the upper left and right corners, the larger words, "astonishingly" and

Oblique viewing position. Barbara Kruger, *Untitled* (*We are astonishingly life-like/Help! I'm locked inside this picture*).

"lifelike," along with the hands holding the frame, forming a ground underneath the face). The symmetry is not clean, but may instead be thought of as a found symmetry, a lifelike symmetry. The woman in the picture frames herself, holds the frame in front of herself. Her hands are carefully manicured.

When I step to the left or right of the center of the picture this image disappears, replaced by a text in large white letters on a red background, "Help! I'm locked inside this picture." The plea can only be seen when the viewer steps to the side, when he or she moves aside from the normal line of sight. A sidestep, a shuffle, the first step of a dance. The gaze cannot penetrate the message of the photograph. It must become unfixed, it must move out of the direct line in order for learning to take place. Seeing becomes a movement of the body, an exercise in releasing a message from its subordination to the directed characteristics of sensible perception. Moreover, as I move toward the picture, the priority of the image of the woman is put in doubt because the initial approach of the ordinary viewer to the wall on which most visual art is hung (and this is not an exception) is from an angle (unless one's approach is regulated by entrance through a straight passage).[55] The appeal for help catches my eye before I have focused attention upon the work, pseudo-subliminally. The advocate of the straight-ahead gaze will always seek to find the visual center of a picture before looking, but by abandoning the search for the dead knowledge of the gaze, the prior meaning of the message—Help! I'm locked inside this picture—can be interpreted as a plea to seek the woman hidden in the text of the message. The relationship of the text embedded within the photo—We are incredibly lifelike—when recontextualized by the appeal for help, becomes a challenge to me to rethink the political implications of passivity, the relationship between representation and life, how that relationship is imbued with politics, and finally, the status of the viewer's subjectivity, in that he or she is being challenged to act, and hence must reflect on what it means to free the woman locked in the picture.

Such a reflection might parallel the path of our imprisoned men. The woman whom we are invited to free is already herself the effect of a subjection much more profound than herself.[56] The "soul" that inhabits her and brings her into existence, a factor in the mastery that power exerts over her, is "merely" a representation, perhaps. Locked in a picture, this woman can be helped if we learn to refuse the terms of representation. We might begin to question, with Kruger, both the identity of the woman and the forces that operate to identify her. This is the sensibility of care in her work. To destabilize identity is not yet to incite reflection on the forces that constitute identity in the world of actions, gestures, and positions. But to destabilize the text and context as a means for destabilizing identity is to ask a more profound question: How are we made?

Moreover, to follow Kruger is to challenge the segregation of the genders. A "we" of gender-crossing and ambiguity is enabled in such movement. Her term of address begins to lose its gender specificity when she claims—We are incredibly lifelike—and asks for help in getting out of the picture. The demand for participation dissolves a pre-fixed politics of the gaze at its level of formal arrangement.

Such a dissolution signals the introduction of the Lacanian "third term." Marjorie Garber demonstrates how the third term destabilizes meaning. She does so in a discussion that is explicitly sympathetic to the project of making gendered references ambiguous, in the name of opening possibility. She writes, "The 'third' is that which questions binary thinking and introduces crisis—a crisis which is symptomized by *both* the overestimation *and* the underestimation of cross-dressing. . . . The 'third' is a mode of articulation, a way of describing a space of possibility. Three puts into question the idea of one: of identity, self-sufficiency, self-knowledge."[57] The third term—which Garber notes is not, strictly speaking, a term at all, in the sense that it is more an articulation of what escapes terminology—is what the man in the superior position can only resist, or appropriate in order to absorb, as in the case of J. Edgar Hoover.[58] It introduces a space of possibility for opening closets of identity. Within those closets are resources for fashioning alternatives to "the idea of one."

Foucault, when writing about Klee, Kandinsky, and Magritte, argues that they dissolve the distinction in painting "between plastic representation (which implies resemblance) and linguistic reference (which excludes it)." From the fifteenth century to twentieth, the separation of plastic representation from linguistic reference operated to aid in the establishment of a hierarchical ordering of things. "What is essential is that verbal signs and visual representations are never given at once. An order always hierarchizes them, running from the figure to discourse or from discourse to the figure."[59] If the distinction *is* dissolved, the dominating power of the principle of resemblance may be broken, and relationships of similitude, which might serve as a signal for the slackening of order, might emerge. "A day will come," Foucault asserts, "when, by means of similitude relayed indefinitely along the length of a series, the image itself, along with the name it bears, will lose its identity."[60]

This loss of identity prepares the way for a movement outside the scientific gaze of sensible perception, away from the sort of vision that has served as the political undergirding of our disciplines of the eye, a movement that might aid us in playing with difference as opposed to intensifying it. Such a relaxation might serve, not as a solace from the storm that Deleuze describes as being the zone of the informal outside, but as a strategy for lessening the intensity of the battles that occur there.[61] This civil war would not be called off, but instead would be fought with devices less deadly than are now so commonly used to advance the orders of the day.

Kruger carries the strategy of similitude beyond the realm of things called pipes to the realm of things called men and women. She presents the arbitrary order of the gaze within the messiness of everyday life. We might ask how such a scrambling of vision contributes to a politics that moves beyond mere tolerance of difference. We might also ask whether it is possible or desirable to try to overcome the principle of resemblance. So often such questions are asked, however, as though they are unanswerable. Conservative critics try to maintain that these questions are only accessible to a few. The works and lives of "ordinary" men and women suffer in comparison to those who are artists or "aesthetes," because the experience of the former is not recognized as artistic, or because their experience of aesthetic life is shaped by the disciplinary forces that govern too many persons' lives.

It is most often in the suffering of people, not as artists necessarily, but more prosaically as they experience life, that an answer to those questions might be recovered. Kruger, in asking for help, invites me, the gazed-upon gazer, to participate in experiential projects that cultivate similitude as a response to resemblance. She is a democrat, with the attendant possibilities and problems associated with democratic values. Implicit in her effort is a politics that addresses what is most *dangerous* about our united states in America, where danger expresses the relationship of protection that bears between those who dominate and those who are dominated. A dangerous politics fits a democratic ethic of care because it involves the unending exposure of desires for stability and protection that inform the practices of people who fear for their selves, even to the extent of placing the preservation of their selves over the preservation of their lives.

The politics of danger is ubiquitous in modern life. Danger may be conceived as a line that serves to create and delimit others. It is a technique at work in the processes by which the modern subject is constituted. Yet it also intrudes into what Deleuze and Guattari refer to as the quantum dimension of power, the area of flows of powers that cannot be contained by segmentations and lines. In discussing the danger of the line, they argue, "The more rigid the segmentarity, the more reassuring it is for us. That is what fear is, and how it makes us retreat into the first line."[62] The trajectory that overcoming fear takes is first clarity, then power, then disgust. And disgust concerns the lines of flight that might be anxiously pursued once one overcomes fear. The problem for them is that disgust presents the danger of fascism, the retreat, not into death, but into an ultimate paradox: "*A war machine that no longer had war as its object* and would rather annihilate its own servants than stop the destruction."[63] This is the ultimate, and most ironic danger, because danger (understood as a relationship of protection) is most fundamentally what endangers all of us.

Kruger operates from a terrain on the lines that danger makes visible and urgent. The political challenge for her art is to incite destabilizations of identity in the face of attempts to retreat into dangerous security, and to do so without merely opposing that which already is. Her art—an art of the self—presses open the rituals and regulations that shape contemporary zones of subjectivity. Her gaze strikes the side of my face, a Medusan look that does not freeze, but thaws. And thus she breaks the gaze that limits the range of possible beings in the world.

Such is the politics of an art of the body in an age of fragmentation and emerging pluralities. It opposes the closure of vision suggested by Dworkin and MacKinnon, but not in the name of a liberty reflected in George Bush's mirror. It would not seek escape from our united states, but would continue to move within them, joyously laughing at the strange combinations we come up with, pointing out the ultimate stupidity of our violent adulations of obscenity.

Is it merely a matter of bringing this picture into focus? No. And yet so many of our differences have as a starting point images fixed by the boundaries of bodies, limited in posture, pinned in place by expectations we fail to question. Until we acknowledge that we have too easily depended on the subordination of some bodies to others to shape our visions of coherence, clarity, and right, these expectations will remain sacrosanct. Disorder is democratic. Democrats, to be democrats, must challenge the idea of fixed identities, constituted by visions that look down on others. Democrats recognize that our united states are expressions of exchange. Such exchanges are not grounded on final selves (the final self is always dead), but on the joys and pains of change. This is what it means to unite.

Although the raucousness of our exchanges is sometimes scary (democratic turbulence is never without its fears), it would be worse for us if we choose to fail to unite and instead insist on purity and disconnection. The temptation is always there. It is inscribed on our geography, which beckons us to retreat from one another. It underwrites the desire for homelessness, the precondition of our freedom together. We cannot be free without departing from that state of grace which calls on us to separate, but neither can we continue to unite as we have without losing what remains of the democracy we have made together. What are we going to do?

CHAPTER SIX

Joyce Brown, or
Democracy and Homelessness

The ice that still supports people today has become very thin; the wind that
brings the thaw is blowing; we ourselves who are homeless constitute a force that
breaks open ice and other all too thin "realities."

—Friedrich Nietzsche

Lost in the Supermarket

I went down to the supermarket to buy food, and stood transfixed before
the potato chips: Wise, Frito Lay, Gibble's, Cape Cod, Pringles, Eagle
Brand. "Ruffles have ridges." "Bet you can't eat just one." I could not
choose just one. It was the end of the business day and the market was
crowded. Other shoppers moved past me. I was stuck. I had too many
questions. Should I buy a nationally known brand of junk food from a
multinational corporation that is inevitably implicated in the politics of
oppression? Should I buy locally, even though the chips will not taste as
good? What is the expiration date on that bag on sale at a reduced price?
Time to choose. But I could not choose. I was expected home and I
stood there, time passing. Bar-B-Q, Onion and Sour Cream, Cheddar,
Jalepeño, Cajun Spices, Mesquite? The taste of too many preservatives,
the taste of too much salt.

Supermarkets order commodities in massive quantities from dis-
tributors for producers from around the world. They put their goods on
spectacular display for me the hungry one, the one brimming with
neediness, the one wanting satisfaction. I wrestle a poorly oiled steel
cart with sticky wheels down endless, fluorescent-lit, linoleum aisles.
Employees scrutinize me at various checkpoints, through one-way win-
dows, off convex mirrors, in television monitors, and with laser de-

vices. I am told what to feel: Every item in every aisle is meant for me, or I am meant for it. Headless chickens leap into my cart, in a late twentieth-century revision of a nineteenth-century utopian promise— Fourier's vision of fish jumping into a frying pan, ready to eat.

I wonder about kiwi fruit from New Zealand. I note the categories most closely associated with caste; the upscale supermarket for the prosperous, health-conscious wealthy (expensive and delicious organic produce at Bread and Circus), the middle brow for non-aspiring yuppies (the fresh vegetables are plentiful, if not always "organic," at the Stop'n Shop), and the bargain market for the working poor (infant formula is cheapest at the Price Chopper).

Behind each item in my local supermarket lies the threat of a disappearance. Perhaps the threat is also an opportunity. Many recognize the modes of disappearance I am thinking about. I am lucky; I can disappear into a book or a house or behind the wheel of large automobile, or into another's body or a movie theater or television program, or into the haze of alcohol or the electricity of whatever else I can get my hands on. These opportunities and threats are a gift, they make for our most pleasurable and frightening united states. Here in the supermarket we might trace the ruins of bodily experience in united states. The supermarket is the arcade of our residue; it presents us with objects within which we might live and die.[1]

But the laser eye of the supermarket checkout also exposes each consumer to a rigorous inspection of the contemporary aesthetics of ownership, including especially the ownership of the body. Every time we leave the supermarket we are presented with a list, an inventory of what we have bought, at the area called the checkout. As I wait in line with other members of my community, I wonder who else recalls Henry David Thoreau's experience at Walden Pond at that moment when the cashier hands over the register tape. In *Walden* Thoreau presents a list of the materials he had purchased in order to build his house. "[I] give the details," he writes, "because very few are able to tell exactly what their houses cost, and fewer still, if any, the separate cost of the various materials that compose them."[2] Composing a house, composing a home.[3] The details were once recorded on paper by the wonderful pencils of the Thoreau family factory and are now preserved in memory as a consequence of the collision of bar codes and beams of light.[4]

Is it important to understand that America has never expressed itself philosophically? Or that it has?[5] When shown the technology of bar codes, George Bush was amazed. I remain amazed as well, too long after bar codes first appeared to complicate inventory taking, but is my amazement another put-on? After all, an old thing is happening here. My purchase of potato chips will duly be recorded and I will be provided a slip telling me what I possess. So what? I can trace my self. But how am I to choose? Philosophy or its lack?

Does it do any good to know that choice in the supermarket is mediated by the need to terminate (rather than compensate), via the use of an organizational schema? Three little words initiate and terminate any action in a supermarket. Stanley Cavell has noted how deeply conventional this sorting process is, and yet still how it depends on three little words. He connects Wittgenstein's meditation on the term "five red apples" at the beginning of *Philosophical Investigations* to the mediations of everyday life. He shares Wittgenstein's wonder at the ability to "operate" effectively with three words. And yet Cavell also wants to express what an effort it is to do so, how weighty and deeply fateful this ordinary activity is.[6] The materials that compose our homes have begun to compose us. They impact on how we choose, the range and the quality of our choices, the difficulty of enacting choice itself, the hazardous movement from one terminal to another.

When I enter the supermarket I think of the vestibule of a church. I become acutely aware that I am traversing a liminal arena. I feel a silence, and faintly hear the strains of Musak (a string version of John Lennon's "Imagine" plays over the intercom). I anticipate a threshold somewhere between death and life. Perhaps this is the feeling shared by Don DeLillo, who has suggested that supermarkets evoke the Tibetan belief in a transitional state between life and death, a place where "the soul restores to itself some of the divinity it has lost at birth." The psychic data of the supermarket are concealed by layers and layers of cultural material, but they are there nonetheless. "All the letters are here, all the colors of the spectrum, all the voices and sounds, all the code words and ceremonial phrases. It is just a question of deciphering, rearranging, peeling off the layers of unspeakability." In supermarkets, "We don't die, we shop. But the difference is less marked than you think." The difference is diminished because, as DeLillo puts it, "Even Tibet is not Tibet anymore."[7]

As we, the most modern of subjects, become composed as consumers, we move ever closer to some sort of completion through the consumption of commodities. But the matrices of consumption also habituate us to a particularly strained aesthetics of existence, marking us as con-

DECOMPOSITION

(DISTANCE FROM DEATH)

sumers, gradually inscribing a message on our bodies. Twenty-odd years ago, veterans of the American war against Vietnam came back to Altoona, Pennsylvania, and told strange stories, apocryphal no doubt, about how much longer it took American bodies to rot in the jungle than it did Vietnamese bodies. They expressed an ironic pride in this notion, suggesting our better living through chemistry. We are preserved by our junk food, they claimed. Perhaps we are preserved as well by our experience in choosing. This experience, in its variations, is not merely available to almost anyone, it is inescapable for almost everyone who lives in the worldly web of global capitalism. And therein lies a fundamental paradox of political order. A regime of choice is every bit as forceful as a regime of no choice, and is more difficult to transform.

The cultural logic of late capitalism is inscribed in these choices, and each instance of choice assumes the structure of a paradox.[8] The confining features of choice have become more, not less, discernible with the collapse of Communism, for in the last instance the paradox is not defined by an opposition between choice and its lack. The paradox reflects a struggle, not against, but concerning death, in Georges Bataille's words "of man's not becoming merely *a thing*, but of *being in a sovereign manner*."[9] The struggle to achieve the state "of being in a sovereign manner" is tentatively opposed to a desire to achieve intimacy through things. For Bataille (as well as for DeLillo) such desire is based on a religious impulse. "Religion in general answered the desire that man always had to find himself, to regain an intimacy that was always strangely lost. But the mistake of all religion is to always give man a contradictory answer: *an external form of intimacy*."[10]

The impulses Bataille identified are associated with the luxury of death. Death itself is a luxury, a consequence most aptly summarized by the practice of eating animals.[11] In his economy of consumption death is a departure from an equilibrium that, if preserved, would assure immortality. The more consumption itself enters into the material organization of the life of an entity, the more deathbound the entity in question becomes. The departure from equilibrium is brought about by the greater consumptive potential of a species; each step toward greater efficiency in consumption enhances the capacity for wastefulness. All luxurious living (and for Bataille all living is luxurious) has as its indicator of quality the extent to which consumption is enhanced. Luxurious living presents us with a situation in which a great destructive capacity is inherent in the condition of life. This condition of luxury is especially true of humankind because the most luxuriously living species is the human species, which has gathered the most to squander.[12] For Bataille the most exemplary moment of this form of life is war. Bataille the pornographer, Bataille the mediator of Nietzschean insight to a subsequent generation of French thinkers, reaches out to our united states of war. But Bataille finds his moment of truth, not in the deserts of Kuwait, but instead in the aisles of the supermarket.

The supermarket is our repository of death, a warehouse of the "things" we people eat. It has the sanctity of a graveyard; one can hear a certain hush underneath its bustle. This silence reflects our collective realization that the supermarket serves as the contemporary site of the religious impulse, the place where "intimacy is given external form." On display in the supermarket are the commodities that afford us a communion, a connection between life and death. A lack of life perspective enables us to negotiate the aisles of the supermarket without being shocked and shaken by the extraordinary excess gathered, assembled, and presented for our consumption. The pyramids of cookies, the piles of flesh, the stacks of cheese, and the bins of vegetables are for the entertainment of those who shop.

It is not only the choice of potato chips that has arrested me in our modern marketplace. Supermarkets fascinate and stupefy all of us with their massive quantities of commodities, their voluptuous displays, and their intensive automation of work. Automation allows surveillance to transform itself into an automatic feature of the shopping experience. The supermarket remains caught in the old-fashioned system of surveillance. We are what we buy, and what we buy is traced, or traceable to the ends of the earth.

I am under the spell of the supermarket. I watch transfixed, constantly moving, gaining a sense of narrative from the strategic arrangement of goods, the orchestration of consumption. In a good supermarket I can assemble a wholly representative body, purchase styling mousse for hair, a wide, if not exhaustive, range of beauty products, hardware and household appliances, over-the-counter drugs, kitchenware, cleaning goods, greeting cards, home videos, and nylons in plastic eggs. Anything that might be considered a household need can be found in a supermarket. It exists to provide. It is the pantry for a society that has ceased to horde. If the mall shows how small each one of us is, if it demonstrates our puny finitude as consumers, the supermarket is friendlier, a resource designed so that we might go to it time and time again. It is a space of the familiar. We need never leave it empty-handed, and we often leave with change, if only because we gathered some bottles, put them into a shopping cart, and returned them for deposits.[13]

This quotidian dimension of the supermarket, its prosaic role in the lives of modern subjects, lends it political importance. The supermarket not only operates to commodify life, but also to create a dystopia of danger. Like the other spaces of agonistic exchange, in the supermarket a zone is established in which it becomes possible to talk a certain talk. And the words that constitute the vocabulary of the supermarket compose a fragmented language of pain. The Price Chopper. Spoiling, cutting, slicing, tagging, pounding, beating, scrubbing, pricing, packing, trimming, loading, freezing, thawing, stacking, shelving, storing, sorting, thinning out, cleaning up, mopping up, closing down, putting into cold storage, preserving, disposing, incinerating, buying and selling and butchering. Are these terms of political discourse or terms of supermarket discourse? Is each set cleansed or laundered in the same way? What sanitary words have we for our sanctioned terminations? What is political science, after all, if not a search of popular idioms for their latent cruelties, a desire to police, to keep things clean? Why not look to the supermarket for signs of death as well as life?

I hasten too quickly to admit it. Not only death generally, but torture, to be more specific, is linked to shopping. Who wants to think such a thought? But maybe we should not try to avoid the dissonance that comes to the surface when the objects of everyday experience begin to swallow us up. Perhaps I should not avert my gaze from the mechanisms that consume me, perhaps you should not be so quick to enjoy the thrills of mediated pleasure, the death through consumption that is our completion, the composition of our homes that becomes the completion of us. Perhaps we should look at what the supermarket does to us while we think it is doing things *for* us.

To think about torture in the contemporary age is to think of odors and appearances that embarrass the intellect because they seem to be actions.[14] The body products, the blood, the muck, the shit and vomit, the waste products of packages of potato chips, canned hams, canisters of aerosol spray, plastic-wrapped junk, would make a Thoreau blush. Is there any form of transcendence that spares one of the heat of bodies, of the sort of misery Saint Theresa and other ecstatic anorexics have enjoyed through the millennia? Is there an American religion that spares me the very American Catholic guilt through which observers from Tocqueville on have comprehended this pagan culture?[15] Every moment in the supermarket rests on a similarly religious diversion from the pain that is the source of our satisfaction. Here abstraction, as embarrassment, becomes absorbed into the religious impulse, as one more commodity from which to compose a life.

There is yet another danger in thinking the connection between the tortuous character of the supermarket and the consumption of goods. To contemplate the supermarket within the framework of misery, to make it a piece of an unrelieved landscape of life in the late modern era, fosters the complacency of despair. This stoical move, associated with a particular shrug of the shoulders, looks, but only looks, knowing and wise.[16] (It may bespeak an inability to "get a life.") In fact, it participates in a different ignorance, one that associates the perpetuation of cruelty with ubiquitous qualities of life. Not only the postmodernist, but the contemporary liberal, and the communitarian are guilty of this ignorance as well.[17] There is a constant struggle in the thinking that would try to resist this religious impulse. The struggle involves not only trying to maintain perspective as perspective become flattened, but trying to deepen one's sense of something (flatness) that is not deep to begin with.

The problem of perspective applies to time as well as to space. I am lost because I do not even have the confidence of knowing that I am on a road to nowhere.[18] In the late modern age, people are only passing the time.[19] When time has become empty of meaning, when perspective flattens, questions concerning the continuities between the supermarket and the torture chamber float to the surface, and it is here that a special kind of revelation is enabled.

So I might ask, anyone might ask, in what ways might the supermarket be assimilated to the torture chamber? And what ethical instruction might follow from such an assimilation? One might follow the path of the filmmaker Peter Greenaway in asking that question, and suggest that torture can best be understood as a Jacobin drama of vengeance played out through an expensive meal in a luxurious restaurant.[20] An even more direct comparison has been made. Phyllis Rose writes,

> The secret of torture, like the secret of French cuisine, is that nothing is unthinkable. The human body is like a foodstuff, to be grilled, pounded, filleted. Every opening exists to be stuffed, all flesh to be carved to the bone. You take an ordinary wheel, a heavy wooden wheel with spokes. You lay the victim on the ground with blocks of wood at strategic points under his shoulders, legs and arms. You use the wheel to break every bone

in his body. . . . Who would have thought to do this with a man and a wheel? But then, who would have thought to take the disgusting snail, force it to render its ooze, stuff it in its own shell with garlic butter, bake it, and eat it?[21]

From one perspective this imagery suggests an indifference to the pain that torture provides by the implicit equation it presents regarding the subjectivity of the snail and the human. But from another the comparison makes us think of the pain of the snail, of the small increments of displaced pain attached to the beauty and wonder of our lives. This double vision, this metaphorical lenticular picture,[22] gives rise to Rose's decision to play it safe. She attempts to remedy any possible *faux pas* by appealing to Judith Shklar's suggestion that cruelty is the worst thing we can do to each other. But that appeal is, I think, based on the acceptance of an opposition that will not hold. Rose is not celebrating torture, but presenting an acute expression of the torturous character of the everyday. Although one is not excused of one's own practices by this self-consciousness-raising exercise, neither is one able to pretend, as she does, that torture is opposed to luxury. Rose concludes that "Paris is civilization's reminder to itself that nothing leads you less wrong than your awareness of your own pleasure and a genial desire to spread it around."[23]

On the potato chip aisle in the supermarket most of the shoppers surrounding me are women. They mediate choices for their men and children. They are disproportionately represented in this space of luxury, and they are constituted by the activity of shopping both as objects and as communicants in the ritual of excessiveness that leads to death. They move from the lost intimacy that Bataille invoked to its public display, and then back to a now hollow interior of the household, a space that needs to be stuffed with things to overcome the aloneness that only a society of Thoreaus could stand. Our talk-show hosts, especially Oprah Winphrey and Phil Donahue, have told us for years that when these women get home they reach a place containing every object that might annihilate them. The domestic space of their pain intensifies with the passage of time, with the isolation that increases tensions within the spaces of home. But they have no room of their own. Their husbands rage at things lacking at home, they fall in love with other women, they beat these women and their children. And then they ask forgiveness, not knowing exactly for what.

Who has thought these structures of pain in order to make pain visible? Elaine Scarry has tried. Of torture chambers, she writes,

> The room, both in its structure and its content, is converted into a weapon, deconverted, undone. Made to participate in the annihilation of the prisoners, made to demonstrate that everything is a weapon, the objects themselves, and with them the fact of civilization, are annihilated; there is no wall, no window, no bathtub, no refrigerator, no chair, no bed.
>   . . . [T]he de-objectifying of the objects, the unmaking of the made, is a process externalizing the way in which the person's pain causes his world to disintegrate; and in the most literal way possible, made painful, made the direct cause of pain. That is, in the conversion of the refrigerator into a bludgeon, the refrigerator disappears; its disappearance objectifies the disappearance of the world (sky, country, bench) experienced by a person in great pain; and it is the very fact of its disappearance, its transition from a refrigerator into a bludgeon, that inflicts pain. . . . The appearance of these common domestic objects in torture reports of the 1970s is no more gratuitous and accidental than the fact that so much of our awareness of Germany in the 1940s is attached to the words, "ovens," "showers," "lampshades," and "soap."[24]

When a body is in pain, Scarry says, the pain fills the perceptual world of the subject and makes the horizon of possible ways of being disappear. The body either swells to fill all or the universe or the universe crushes the body.[25] In either case, the subject disappears.

The political structure of torture is built on this disappearance of the subject. The torturer depends on this disappearance, but also on its peculiar inversion, reflected in the torturer's own lack, a lack of pain, which demonstrates that something has disappeared for him.[26] This lack is fundamental to the power of torturing regimes. Torture, from this perspective, is but an extreme instance of ordinary political situations. Scarry suggests, "A political situation is almost by definition one in which the two locations of selfhood are in a skewed relation to one another or have wholly split apart and have begun to work, or be worked, against one another."[27] The politics of torture are absolutist: the torturer gains ground precisely to the extent that he makes himself felt by the tortured. To destroy the objects of sentience for the tortured is to expand them for the torturer. This is how the law of identity is at work in Scarry's analysis.

Scarry believes that to destroy the objects of sentience, which are also the objects of self-extension, is to destroy the self. Those objects of the world that give one a sense of selfhood, whether one's clothes, one's house, one's body, or one's book collection[28] work together to make one into a person. Scarry's theory of personality thus seems rooted less in Freud, or even Marx, than in Hobbes, and appropriately so, because it is Hobbes who teaches how a person is one who is an author, a self-owning creature.[29] The reality that is destroyed and created is mostly propertied. A torturer gains ground as the tortured loses ground. *Reality*, a construct that she constantly refers to in an unproblematic way, is etymologically associated with realty.[30] The world unmade in torture is the world of ownership and possession.

Scarry's capacity to see the unmaking of the world in the act of torture depends on her profound insight that the making of any world is a consequence of another world's destruction. In her discussion of the interior of capital she understands the world that she is describing as flawed at the level of the artifacts that it produces. For her, to think about what others might call commodity fetishism is "to enter into the interior of capital," which is in turn "to enter into a deeply flawed artifact in which the two originally inseparable consequences of creation have been interrupted by the artifact's own capacity to become internally referential."[31] This internal referentiality is crucial to understanding how important making and unmaking is to justice.[32]

Our vulnerability to torture, it seems, stems from the fact that "we shop." From the perspective available to us in contemporary consumer society, to understand the division of labor is less important than to understand the division of consumption.[33] Scarry's speculative comment concerning the rise of liability law in the United States is inept, in that it reflects a view that the legal culture of this society has been particularly sensitive toward the ethical responsibilities inherent in a manufacturing culture. The opposite is true. Rather than understand tort's relationship to torture as being crude and direct (as I do, and as the etymology of the word suggests), she argues that tort actions may act as a register of an American concern with making and thus may serve as a medium for saving Americans and others who share American legal/cultural values (liberal values?) from the torture that seems to lurk as a latency in the bowels of the culture, as the form par excellence of cultural self-dramatization.[34] "The courtroom," she writes, "is a communal area in which civilization's ongoing expectations about objects are overtly (and sometimes noisily) announced; the trial does not occasion the expectation but merely occasions the objectification of the expectation; and though it may be itself a concussive and exceptional occurrence, it only makes audible what is actually a very quiet, very widely shared, very deep, and in its own way quite magnificent intuition about the nature of creation."[35]

But if most liability cases in the United States concern not manufacturing per se, but rather the consumption of manufactured goods, then the American *agon* is not located in the manufactories, but dispersed to the sites of consumption. The supermarket is where most Americans shop for the things they eat. It is common ground, and it is where a profound drama of appearance and disappearance proceeds, the place where one might cease to be concerned with the form of objects and begin to be concerned with the substance of objects. And if the objects disappear, the subject, as Scarry shows, is not far behind. It is all too easy to get lost in the supermarket.

Perhaps the subject we seek to save is already the product of a subjection much greater than itself.[36] Torture identifies fragments of the subject, much like an explosion reveals fragments of an airplane. But what does it tell about the why of the torturer, or for that matter, of the tortured? I am hungry and I pause, and I cannot decide what to buy. In that moment of indecision, an abyss opens, and I am lost in the supermarket.

How might I begin to find my way out?

Lost in the Streets

In 1991, the American space program launched some satellites that used in conjunction with hand-held receivers on the planet's surface, enable the user to know within a meter or two (sometimes within an inch or two) precisely where he or she is on the face of the earth. It is called the Navstar Global Positioning System. Most of us heard about it during the war against Iraq. In the vast desert of Saudi Arabia, Kuwait, and Iraq it had its uses, and it is now, among other things, put to use in the streets of Japan to guide motorists to their destinations.[37] The world has within its technical capacity the practical realization of the Borges tale of the Emperor of China, a complete mapping of the world. And yet there is always room to maneuver. In this case, a few inches to several meters means the difference between being inside or outside, on the street or in the shop, touching someone or passing them by. A reduced space of anonymity, but anonymity still.

My thoughts on Navstar are, of course, allegorical. But whose thoughts escape allegory? Navstar illustrates a peculiar paradox concerning what it means to be lost and found. Historically, to have known that one is lost, one has always needed to know what it would mean to be found. But when every point is known, one knows where one is, knows it with an absoluteness that can become unbearable. Under such conditions, to be lost is to be overwhelmed by a sense of presence amid an incapacity to act. Disorientation comes from the uncanny feeling that one is lost and found at the same time. One might be disoriented, but one is located. Navstar is a mirror image of the most common experience given by postmodern geographers to illustrate the loss of perspective underlying modern concepts of space. They suggest that under the circumstances of habitation an emerging majority of humans now enjoy,[38] the experience of being lost is a result of the disappearance of specific markers of place. One comes not to know *whether* one is lost. Everything looks familiar, but nothing looks definite. In urban spaces this experience is increasingly common. Navstar shows how the opposite experience—to be found no matter where one is—paradoxically reduces the meaning of being found. It points one toward a common homogeneity of space, reducing space to points on a grid of longitude and latitude. In mapping the world, Navstar makes a single experience of space possible, flattening perspective along the most physical of dimensions. And herein lies yet another aspect of our paradoxical situation: the more common the experience of a single space, the more intense the effect on being lost and found. The commonness of this experience becomes a sign of the increasing homogeneity of space, and the increasing homogeneity of space intensifies the experience.

We might then realize that with the advent of satellite mapping of such great precision the world becomes totally enclosed via the encoding of the world. The cybernetic experience documented by Donna Haraway then becomes unavoidable,[39] a nonelective affinity uniting us through digital signals from outer space. The ravings of those who connect everything in a paranoid dream were once madness, but are now our common sense. But is our common sense in any sense a truth?

Thomas Pynchon anticipates this question in his 1967 novel, *The Crying of Lot 59*. He writes,

> The saint whose water can light lamps, the clairvoyant whose lapse in recall is the breath of God, the true paranoid for whom all is organized in spheres joyful or threatening about the central pulse of himself, the dreamer whose puns probe ancient fetid shafts and tunnels of truth all act in the same special relevance to the word, or whatever it is the word is

there, buffering, to protect us from. The act of metaphor then was a thrust
at truth and a lie, depending where you were: inside, safe, or outside,
lost.[40]

We work the words to protect ourselves, and those who are lost among
us, lost because they are found, still might provide us with some hope to
the extent that they remain able to reach those moments when a truth
might appear. I myself do not know whether the thrust at truth is
further from the truth than a lie would be. A lie seems to presume the
existence of a truth of sorts, whereas the thrust at truth is a heat-seeking
gesture, cruising the streets, detouring with the frustration of someone
with a word on the tip of the tongue, almost always, but never quite,
untied. We strive for it, we move toward it or away from it, energized
by loss, frustrated by safety.

But how can one be lost while totally found? Celeste Olalquiaga has
suggested that urban cultural experiences occur under circumstances in
which "spatial and temporal coordinates end up collapsing: space is no
longer defined by depth and volume, but rather by a cinematic (temporal) repetition, while the sequence of time is frozen in an instant of
(spatial) immobility."[41] Under such conditions one loses more than a
sense of place; one loses the capacity to mark and trace the constituent
elements of self-identity. Aphasic in regard to place, one risks the loss of
the boundary between self and other or, to put it more generally,
between self and surroundings.

The erasure of boundaries that contributes to this new spatiality is
accomplished technologically, no doubt. But what might be said of the
ontological threshold that is crossed? Certainly it is difficult to claim
that there are some bodies out there which have not always already been
"violated" by the technological.[42] Perhaps it is more the style of inva-
sion and intervention into the bodies in question that is, or should be, a
concern of politics. Contemporary political theories might be understood as being a series of responses to the experience of being lost.
Theorists look for "communities" and "individuals," without being able
to map the space where either might be located.

In addressing what it means to be lost, political theories also address
what it means to be found. The two seem to compensate for each other.
Any movement that would disclose itself as a response to the modern
loss of place and its impact on the placing of identity will, at some point,
encounter the stillness which inevitably follows the experience of being
lost.[43] To be found is to be located, to be placed. One might go further

and suggest that to be found is to be re-placed or re-located, highlighting the undecidability of the distinction between being lost and found. Because location itself is increasingly fungible as the advance of consumer capitalism commodifies new elements of life, being lost and found are more and more closely tied to the circulation of commodities and signs.[44]

When being lost and found blend, secure identity, even (perhaps especially) identity based on bodily integrity, is also lost. In the face of the new modes of mobility the reference points of bodily integrity become fuzzy and imprecise. It does not matter that these modes of mobility are not connected to movement through space and time as our common sense would have us conceive it, but are instead simulated through telephonic and televideo communicative actions, computer models, and a variety of cybernetic feedback systems.[45] To paraphrase Tocqueville, the strategies of artificial reality are as purely intellectual as the souls they seek to penetrate. And it often seems as though those who are most sensitive to the simulations of space are in greatest danger of losing their orientation.

The paradox of being lost and found simultaneously is not only an element of our lives in common. It is a dimension of it, signaling a potential fate for democratic life. We are faced with this question: How might democracy be connected to homelessness? For many people, fear of democracy is associated with a desire for home, which remains, as it has for the history of our experience of united states, the solution to all of our problems, the comfort we might find when the demands and challenges of political life become too great. Democracy is connected to a form of homelessness, in that it requires that one overcome the desire to be at home. Home, in our contemporary democracy, is comprehended as a private place, a place of withdrawal from the demands of common life, a place of fixed meaning where one is protected from disorientation, but also from the possibility of democratic involvement. Hence one might say that democratic life requires one to overcome the fear of homelessness, to develop the courage to leave home (embracing another fear) without knowing when or whether one will return.

So we might ask: Is there a way to recover the idea of homelessness as a way of thinking about the American democratic condition? How might the condition of homelessness enable, rather than disable, us?

This question represents a major challenge to those of us who still seek to be democrats. We fight enclosure on every front, and in the fight threaten to lose sight of our human remainders. We who seek to recover the open road are most vulnerable to accusations of coldness, a post-modern harshness and willingness to overlook pain and suffering. And now we would even turn on the homeless.

The homeless of American cities are widely comprehended as victims and/or vermin.[46] Attempts to think about the conditions of homelessness—connecting the material conditions of those who lack homes with the psychological conditions that give rise to a democratic posture toward life—must to be responsive to the accusation of callousness regarding the material conditions of those who lack homes in the most material sense. Otherwise, the value of homelessness would itself be lost to us. So we need to put pressure on what might be called the two conditions of homelessness.

The first condition of homelessness—the moral psychology of homelessness—is implied in the work of two contemporary Emersonian philosophers, George Kateb and Stanley Cavell. The psychology of the democratic thinker presumes and relies on the existence of material conditions permitting individuals to be moderately alienated from others. This is a homelessness dependent on habits supported by a particular way of life that is democratic in outlook. The second condition, the material condition, is disastrously damaged when there is change in habit, when everyday life militates against the generosity and openness that is the significant attribute of psychological homelessness. The difficulty is that we seem not to know where and how to ameliorate the material condition of homelessness in a manner consistent with the encouragement of its psychological condition.

What might it mean to suggest that democracy is associated with a moral psychology of homelessness? Cavell suggests that one good place to begin to think about the meaning of home is by reflecting on Novalis's famous saying "Philosophy is essentially homesickness—the universal impulse to be home" and connecting it with what he believes is a major idea (a philosophical masterpiece) shared by Emerson and Thoreau, "that owning or belonging to a place is the promise and power of leaving it, say of staking one's name."[47] He then suggests that home's meaning might be further illuminated when he cites Fritz Lang's film, *Clash by Night* (written by Clifford Odets), in which "Barbara Stanwyck says to a man, a stranger, 'Home is where you go when you run out of places.'"[48]

These views of home depend on one another even as they diverge. To leave home one must have a home to leave. To make a home one must stake one's name to a place where one belongs. To go home, one must have run out of places. Each perspective is a moment in the experience of home through which recognizing its value comes from feeling its lack. Each relates back to a set of material conditions which provide points of departure for a person's recovery or discovery of home. Each connects the material conditions that enable one to be at home with the systems of representation through which home becomes comprehensible as a name, place, and feeling.

But the (re)discovery of home is not always a happy process. Michele Wallace evokes the themes of discovery and return when she reflects on her desire to leave the claustrophobic space of her sister's home, to which she repaired after release from Harlem Hospital's psychiatric center:

> There was no transcending the past so long as I remained in the Harlem of
> my birthplace, so long as I remained at home. Yet getting my own
> apartment in New York seemed financially out of the question. So I
> dreamed a black woman's dream that made no sense at all. I would change
> my name, get on a Greyhound bus, and get off wherever it stopped, begin
> a new life in a new place—like John Garfield or Henry Fonda in some
> formulaic 1930s movie—washing dishes or slinging hash at a no-name
> diner.[49]

She envisions herself anonymous and unattached. But the dream makes no sense, it takes place only in her movie memory. She cannot begin anew, she cannot go to a place untethered from her past. It is financially impossible.

Could Wallace simply leave, take to the open road, drop out? She reflects on categories of homelessness developed by a journalist, Peter Marin, to enable a defense of the option of marginality, of a retention of the right to choose homelessness:

> I think I understand what he means about the need for a way to drop out,
> but I don't believe there ever was, except in the movies, an economic and
> social demilitarized zone to which people could escape. . . . When he
> writes of "traditional tramps, hobos, and transients," I think of Red
> Skelton with a day-old beard pencilled in, or Meryl Streep and Jack
> Nicholson stumbling from public shelter to tavern, working through their
> middle-class angst, in the 1940s world of *Ironweed*. I don't think of Grand-
> pa Bob, who hoboed because he couldn't get the kind of work he wanted as
> a horticulturalist, just because he was black. I don't think of the 1980s in
> which AIDS, crack, the diminished employment opportunities and wel-

fare benefits make poverty and homelessness inevitable for more and more people who don't "have it all together." Our world is their world too.[50]

These material conditions, she suggests, are inevitably associated with the mental states of feeling either at home or homeless. "Containment" is the word she uses to describe the condition through which people are produced as crazy. But craziness is not the only way to contain people. To take but one important example, families are potential sites of containment as well, reinforcing a masculinist authority system woefully inadequate to the needs of children and women.

The idea of homelessness as an unbidden disaster is present in Wallace's discussion, though it is not her only theme. It rubs against Cavell's thought connecting the hobo to philosophy, made toward the conclusion of his essay on finding as founding. Cavell carefully expresses the openness available to philosophy when thought of as a kind of homelessness, albeit a homelessness comforted by the indetermination of language, and ultimately (re)found for philosophy. He writes,

> What seems to me evident is that Emerson's finding of founding as finding, say the transfiguration of philosophical grounding as lasting, could not have presented itself as a stable philosophical proposal before the configuration of philosophy established by the work of the later Heidegger and the later Wittgenstein, call this the establishing of thinking as knowing how to go on, being on the way, onward and onward. At each step, or level, all explanation comes to an end; there is no level to which all explanations come, at which all end. An American might see this as taking the open road. The philosopher as the hobo of thought.[51]

Might Cavell's hobo of thought be connected to Michele Wallace's Uncle Bob? I think Wallace would hope so, because she approaches the unbidden disaster of homelessness as a matter of "our world," and because she understands that "our world" is constructed through the power of language. Her concern about the lack of a space into which one might escape leads her to observe that the terms of experience are themselves becoming more and more enclosed. She writes, " 'Crazy' is a word I hear being used more and more often to describe what people do to one another and themselves in their 'leisure' time, perhaps in order to accommodate, simultaneously, the limited choices and the much more extensive choicelessness of our present living arrangements."[52] Wallace thus focuses attention on one of the final sentence fragments in Cavell's essay: "What I think can be said is that while of course there are things in the world other than language, for those creatures for whom language is our form of life, those who are what 'Experience' entitles 'victims of expression'—mortals—language is everywhere we find ourselves, which means everywhere in philosophy (like sexuality in psychoanalysis)."[53]

When Wallace refers to containment, she gestures toward material conditions and structures of the organization of life—families, hospitals, schools—that arrange living in a manner that connects with the Emersonian phrase Cavell uses, "victims of expression." We are also victims of containment. Containment is everywhere we find ourselves, and in finding ourselves in this way, we are lost to ourselves. We are lost and found.

This sense of being lost as a consequence of being found is at the root of the problem of homesickness. It is not finding as founding as finding, but instead a blockage that results from a dead-ended quest for security through making the world certain.[54] George Kateb suggests as much in his comments concerning those who seek to overcome alienation. Kateb wants to assert "that alienation or estrangement is good, and hence that wanting to be at home mentally or spiritually is questionable, and ought to be questioned."[55] He wants to make this claim because he believes that a lack of alienation is at the root of the problem of homesickness. Those who are homesick are already, in the most important senses, at home. But that condition only heightens their problems: "At home, they want more home. They are homesick, even though they are home. What is their desire? They crave that the self be made of answerable questions. They want no real self-process. They want an identity, a self-same self. They want to be defined, known, and understood by those around them. Others are their furnishings. They do not believe in the right of self-trust."[56] For Kateb, these people need to learn to become self-reliant, which I would claim is how he sees us overcoming the paradoxical condition engendered by our united states. But the desire to be defined, known, and understood, this metaphysical agoraphobia—where does it come from, if not from the ways in which people are victims of modern strategies of containment? In exasperation Kateb wants to tell the homesick, "Grow up!"[57] But he does not suggest why they would construct this desire as they do, though he develops suggestive lines of inquiry in his comments on Emerson's critique of mass society.[58] To find "a demilitarized zone to which we might escape," requires relief from the containment of the world. And if that is so, then the attainment of homelessness is necessary if we are to find ourselves in a manner consistent with self-reliance, or the idea of self-process.

How extensive has the containment of the world become? We need not rely on allegories drawn from the Persian Gulf War to make plausible claims about the limits under which we labor and live. Jeremy Waldron presents a compelling argument to the effect that homeless people are in danger of being allowed no place to be in contemporary America.[59] This is a consequence of one facet of the boundary-creating laws of the world, the rules of private property that reduce the possibility of common spaces where the homeless can exist. Though the libertarian fantasy (and the catastrophe for those who are without a room of their own) of all property being made private has not happened, Waldron suggests that a modified form of that catastrophe is in effect. There is increasing regulation of streets and restrictions on the uses to which public spaces may be put, designed to force the homeless to go away. Waldron writes, "What is emerging—and it is not just a matter of fantasy—is a state of affairs in which a million or more citizens have no place to perform elementary human activities like urinating, washing, sleeping, cooking, eating, and standing around."[60] He suggests that the homeless have freedom in our society only to the extent that our society is communistic, that is, to the extent that collective resources remain open to common access and use.[61] But through a series of regulations a cumulative effect has resulted, in which homeless people end up not having places where they can piss, shit, and sleep.[62]

For Waldron it is useful to think of homelessness as an issue of freedom before considering it as an issue of need because to do so highlights the agency of those who are homeless. To characterize the plight of homeless people in reference to need obscures their agency. To focus on need is to suggest that the relief of need is an end in itself, and hence the relationship between the relief of needs and the freedom of the needy is truncated. When we lose sight of agency a frightening specter is raised.

> Now one question we face as a society . . . is whether we are willing to tolerate an economic system in which large numbers of people are homeless. Since the answer is evidently "Yes," the question that remains is whether we are willing to allow those who are in this predicament to act as free agents, looking after their own needs, in public places—the only space available to them. It is a deeply frightening fact about the modern

United States that those who *have* homes and jobs are willing to answer "Yes" to the first question and "No" to the second.[63]

The securing of freedom is connected with the overcoming of the conditions that accompany homelessness. But Waldron is careful in distinguishing the securing of that freedom from that of putting people into homes. What is unbearable for people who are homeless is not homelessness itself, but the restrictions that are placed on their basic bodily freedoms. He writes, "If freedom is important, it is freedom for human beings, that is, for the embodied and needy organisms that we are."[64]

Waldron's focus on embodiment links the issue of freedom to the material conditions of homelessness in a manner that puts great pressure on any position that would merely celebrate estrangement. Estrangement is a moment in the practice of freedom. That is all. It cannot be a permanent condition, because if it becomes that it threatens the very freedom that gives rise to it by attacking the body that bears it. But at the same time estrangement, as a moment in the practice of freedom, is vital, for it places us outside the machinery of connection that frames our life in common.

In the light of the connection of freedom to homelessness, we might consider the case of Joyce Brown as exemplary. She not only dreamed the black woman's dream that makes no sense but enacted it, in her own fashion. In October of 1987 she was living on a street of New York City in front of a restaurant vent at Second Avenue and 65th Street.[65] On 28 October she was picked up as part of Mayor Edward Koch's program to rid the streets of homeless people, taken to Bellevue hospital, injected with an antipsychotic drug and tranquilizers and retained against her will.[66] In her court appearance, she explained that she used a pseudonym so her sisters could not find her. She feared they would return her to the hospital to which they had committed her in 1985. She argued that she had a right to be on the streets and that she was a "professional" at caring for herself.[67]

Brown lived a minimalist lifestyle, taking what she needed to live and leaving the rest. She had a budget of $7.00 per day, and panhandled more than that as a cushion. She would refuse any gifts greater than what she considered to be her daily minimal requirement. Her reasoning was straightforward. "If money is given to me and I don't want it, of course I am going to give it back. . . . I've heard people say: 'Take it. It will make me feel good.' But I say: 'I don't want it. I don't need it.' Is it

my job to make them feel good by taking their money?"[68] Her refusal
led Judge Robert Lippman, who disposed of her case to write, "Apparently beggars can be choosers."[69] In making his decision, he concluded
that her problems stemmed, not from mental illness, or from being
homeless itself, but from the condition of poverty that accompanied her
homelessness. He suggested that the key determination in ruling on her
case is not whether or not she is mentally ill, but whether or not she is
capable of enjoying her freedom.

Apparently, beggars can be choosers, but below the appearance of
choice there lies a series of institutions that belie the appearance of
choice. Even though the requirements of freedom along the dimension
of bodily needs are minimal, we often go below the minimal position
that would allow the Joyce Browns of the world to be. Another story of
a homeless person, one with a less happy denouement than that of Joyce
Brown,[70] is the story of this latter-day hobo. We might hear in his
statement an echo of Thoreau: "Hell with 'em. Every time I get something, somebody else wants it. I'm better off right here . . . a fucking
bum. I'm happy. Hey, this is my life. I don't need no 9-to-5 shit. Free.
That's all I want. You know what life is, doncha? The only reason you
hang around is to see what happens next. If it wouldn't be for curiosity,
you'd a hung it up, committed suicide, jumped off the 'Frisco bridge."[71]
This man was named Blackie, and has been described as "the last of the
old-time hobos." Blackie was once able to go door-to-door doing yard
work to make his way. That ended when he was arrested. Blackie was
once free to make shelters for himself in hobo jungles. His camp outside
of Sacramento, California, was swept by police in 1989, and rather than
run, Blackie decided to challenge the right of local authorities to remove
the camp. Several delays in the scheduling of the hearing, however,
forced him to move on, leaving the cheap hotel he was staying in while
waiting for his day in court and abandoning the place that he had made
into his semipermanent home for his declining years. Despondent, he
left on a freight for Reno, Nevada, and was never heard from again.

This old-time hobo, Blackie, and Joyce Brown, and anyone who has
sought to take to the open road, to fulfill the mad dream Michele
Wallace limns, anyone who has imagined the possibility of getting lost,
disappearing from the constraints of containment, anyone like that—
and who is not, sometimes?—could almost be said to be homeless by
choice. The circumstances that govern organized, normalized life are
oppressive to such people, they seek out alternatives, they seek to
live outside the containment fields that govern modern experience.
That the space for the existence of such people is threatened is a fact of

the material conditions of homelessness. As Waldron urgently notes, the material conditions of homelessness are intimately connected to the issue of freedom. Put bluntly, if there cease to be places of bodily freedom for those who lack property in anything beyond their own embodied selves, the possibilities for the enjoyment of philosophy as the experience of the open road, and the preconditions for the quest for self-reliance, become severely impoverished. The social ecology that would support such endeavors becomes too impoverished. We enter into a state of political emergency. When framed as an issue of freedom, the condition of the homeless suggests that we are suffering an emergency of freedom. To anticipate, the homeless serves as a type of monitor for us. If the material conditions that enable Joyce Brown and Blackie—and by extension any one of us—to be homeless disappear, the spiritual possibility of homelessness as the open road, as a possible path of freedom, disappears as well.

Lost and Found

What is this dense location in which our political life is embedded? What is my point in presenting this tour of strange spaces and marginal experiences? Perhaps only this: we struggle to assume a place, yet we know that once we assume a place we will come to a great trouble. Our innocence, to recall Louis Hartz, requires that we keep moving on.

Because we are running out of room to move, it is important to turn toward those who have had no place to go for some time. This is the attraction our French cousins provide. Through their eyes, through the meditations of thinkers like Maurice Blanchot, we might see a starting point for comprehending our paradoxical status as a polity losing its mobility. Blanchot looks with an ecstatic horror on the enclosure of experience, the positing of no place for people to be. He calls this horrifying phenomenon the absolute immanence of humanity. As a good European, he associates this idea with both communism and fascism, under the rubric of totalitarianism. And he also notes that the absolute immanence of humanity is a principle that allows a radical individualism to emerge.

Of this connection he writes,

> Now, this exigency of an absolute immanence implies the dissolution of everything that would prevent man (given that he is his own equality and determination) from positing himself as pure individual reality, a reality all

the more closed as it is open to all. The individual affirms himself with his inalienable rights, his refusal to have any other origin than himself, his indifference to any theoretical dependency in relation to another who would not be an individual as he is, that is to say, in relation to himself perpetually repeated, whether in the past or in the future—thus both mortal and immortal: mortal in his inability to perpetuate himself without alienating himself; immortal because his individuality is the immanence of life which has no limit in itself.[72]

Absolute immanence reflects the dense reality of presence that over-whelms all other evocations of life, a mapping so total that we cannot get lost. If this "pure individual reality" is the practical realization of the rights of man, then absolute immanence constitutes the embrace of a mode of being that would implode meaning.[73] The technologies that allow (or disallow) limitless life could thus present individuals with an identity, but in doing so would put an end to each identity by closing it off from any connection with others. A hyperreal immortality would be achieved, but who would want it?

Absolute immanence is frightening. Perhaps it is the most important twentieth-century fear, the fear of an identity that blends together the bodies of all of those who should be allowed to remain apart. It is associated with a strategy of rule that relies on loneliness as its principle of organization.[74] The population made so vulnerable is everyone and anyone. In other words, all who partake of modern experience are intimately implicated in this contagion called immanentism.

How entangled in this problem are those of us who have achieved united states through a faith in the open road? Have we succeeded in evading *that* sort of individualism? Is there anything in the American experience, or even in American thought, that suggests that we have confronted and overcome it? (Perhaps we must violate the rules of Emerson in order to make him speak to us.)

Those who have sought to avoid the identification of themselves, have also, if unwittingly, sought to avoid immanentism, whether identity is focused through the lens of politics, law, art, or even that of a more recent arrival in the history of existence, personality.[75] It might be better to claim that such tactics of avoidance, or attempts to be anony-mous, in the modern age became increasingly pseudonymous. So al-though one might try to enact the sort of pseudonymous anonymity that Foucault attempted in one of his late interviews, one inevitably risks exposure.[76]

In their meditations on each other, Blanchot and Foucault show us that the problem of anonymity is destined to be attached to the problem of immanentism, because anonymous being is constantly at risk in the presence of the imperative of dense identity. One might claim that such immanentism is only indirectly available to thought at the level of the everyday practices of life. The more difficult task is to grasp experience in its paradoxes (in its compensatory splits). But this process is always fictional, in the sense that it always involves the incredibly fragile process of making-believe that we have bridged the impossible gap that always lies between us. It is a process of making the invisibility of the visible apparent. As Foucault has written, "Fiction consists not in showing the invisible, but in showing the extent to which the invisibility of the visible is invisible."[77] Fiction faces an impossible task for which it is uniquely prepared: not to show invisibility but instead to show that the invisible is part of the visible, and then to show how that dynamic operates in the processes of life. But is not this task so far removed from the practical concerns of our lives together that it becomes absurd?

Not if we are acting in reference to a mode of thought that would reject understandings of the truth as simply the direct experience of senses, or more generally as a metaphysical presence that is immutable and finally knowable. If each or any of us senses instead that the truth of living together is not given up as a final revelation, but is instead an ever changing consequence of constitution,[78] then Foucault's words become practical advice. They follow as well from Heidegger's concern, when he suggested that freedom is best understood as "that which conceals in such a way that opens to light, in whose lighting shimmers that veil that hides the essential occurrence of all truth and lets the veil appear as what veils."[79] Thus, as strange as it may seem, it may be possible to know the everyday best by experiencing its lack. The burden of the everyday as a mode of thought is excessive, and so it might escape capture by any specific authoritative discourse. Or so Joyce Brown might hope, begging and choosing on the streets of Manhattan.

The political tension that is strengthened by reference to this veiled character of truth is expressed in Blanchot's understanding of incompleteness. He writes,

A being does not want to be recognized, it wants to be contested: in order to exist it goes toward the other, which at times contests and negates it, so as to start being only in that privation that makes it conscious (here lies the origin of its consciousness) of the impossibility of being itself, of subsisting as its *ipse* or, if you will, as itself as a separate individual: this way it will perhaps ex-ist, experiencing itself as an always prior exteriority, or as an existence shattered through and through, composing itself only as it decomposes itself constantly, violently and in silence.[80]

He thus gives voice to that impossible and hence fictional expression, the existence of the *will* to find oneself. As an experience, such a willing is *fabulous*.[81] And because it is fabulous, it may be a counter to the law which composes as a consequence of the density of location.

What might allow us to feel as though we are exceptions to the conditions Blanchot describes? We might understand the limits he describes, not merely as something to run up against, but as something that we must try to run through. The tatters of the law that insists on our being normal create flickering shadows that someone might notice, in glancing, as the product of their own misguided imagination, as a movement that overreaches our uncanny united states. In this sense, Foucault's aphorism is apt: "The law is the shadow toward which every gesture necessarily advances; it is itself the shadow of the advancing gesture."[82] Resisting the law is what Anne Norton calls democratic excess, and she suggests it as the ethical accompaniment to everyday liberalism.[83] Can we do so without risking losing ourselves? What is the fate of our united states?

Any answer to the question must somehow evade it. I think that this need to evade informs the elusive quality of Foucault's descriptions of law itself. For him, law is something that inevitably refers to visibility and invisibility: it is always passive but never inert. He writes,

> If it were self-evident and in the heart, the law would no longer be the law, but the sweet interiority of consciousness. If, on the other hand, it were present in a text, if it were possible to decipher it between the lines of a book, if it were on a register that could be consulted, then it would have the solidity of external things; it would be possible to follow or disobey it. Where then would its power reside, by what force or prestige would it command respect? In fact, the presence of the law is its concealment.[84]

The paradox of law, its specific impossibility, is that it can sustain legality only by withdrawing from the scene of legal acts, and associating itself most closely with illegality. This is not a question of whether law might question itself; it is instead a consequence of its immanent character, its absolute self-identity, its inclination toward norms.

Foucault illustrated this paradox by posing a series of questions.

> How could one know the law and truly experience it, how could one force
> it to come into view, to exercise its powers clearly, to speak, without
> provoking it, without pursuing it into recesses, without resolutely going
> farther into the outside into which it is always receding? How can one see
> its invisibility unless it has been turned into its opposite, punishment,
> which, after all, is only the law overstepped, irritated, beside itself?[85]

The law's invisibility enforces its very ubiquitousness through its complicity with normalizing discourse. This invisibility effectively forbids
anonymity. Any attempt to seek the shelter of the lack of a name calls
forth the name that law already has for one. Only a simulated version of
the anonym, the pseudonym, is allowable. (We might note well that
torture has as its end the disclosure of a name, and that the name itself
becomes true in the telling . . . [America].)

And here we might begin to turn, to see a glimmer of hope. For we
are the most lawless of people, which as Anne Norton notes, explains
why we make such a production of our legal procedures.[86] Thus there is
always a chance that we will redeem ourselves from the temptation of
law, that we will break the limits we have imposed. We know, uncannily, that the experience of limits always has as its end the speaking of a
name, whether it be of God, of man, or of the principle that would
displace them both.

Foucault teaches that the law's need to reveal itself as invisible must
result in a strange dialogue with transgression. Transgression attempts
to make law visible and thus to control it, but it must always fail because
law operates by receding. The recession of law, though, is not a movement, because law is always, as Foucault puts it, "immobile in its
identity." "Anyone," he wrote, "who attempts to oppose the law in
order to found a new order, to organize a second police force, to
institute a new state, will only encounter the silent and infinitely ac-
commodating welcome of the law."[87] In our world, it may well be that
we assume transgression as a fundamental, unspoken, *right*.

From this perspective, the habits of human existence are not confined
by law so much as defined by its invisibility. Keeping the law visible
might ameliorate its effects. In fact, it may be that disappearance is the
secret aesthetic of immanentism, that the appeal of contemporary radical individualism is that it confidently offers an opportunity to live
beyond the penumbra of law's shadow. In the contemporary era, to be
alone, a dream realized ironically in the nightmare of contemporary

bureaucratic experience, gives rise to the more subtle desire to be unknown. Hence the attraction of being lost in the supermarket. Since Aristotle's time at least the production of idiocy has depended on a subjective longing for isolation.[88] But isolation, at least isolation as it exists in the political orders that are spawning now, has become a fetish, so that when isolation enters the realm of the practical, bad things happen. The regimes of torture that writers such as Elaine Scarry use to understand pain are latent in the vision of privacy that informs this dream of disappearance.[89]

To disappear is to achieve anonymity. But we cannot explore the conditions and possibilities of anonymity in the present age without also giving up any claim to the status of being anonymous. Our celebrity status as Americans is the paradoxical condition of being known only by our representations. We successfully evade this thing called authenticity by our willingness to be known by our representations. So this dilemma of anonymity presents itself, not as an intractable condition, but as a way station in the life of a political culture saturated by a luxury that allows us to pretend we are alone, especially when we are together. When we, as legal subjects, understand that the quest for identity is an impossible attempt to complete the modern project of ordering being, then we begin the transgressive project of puzzling through the relationship of torture to the invisibility of law.

The desire to become anonymous is perverse. Only if law becomes visible can anyone hide from it.

So we live between the two points, before the law, and in quest of anonymity. We place ourselves in the collective position of an observer in Bentham's Panopticon, liking to watch. To think that I could be anonymous is my wish to find a shadow substitute for the hurtful experience of being lost, an experience that entails thinking about the points at which something that might be called fixed identity disappears. But like everyone I know, "I am one who has a borrowed and happenstance singularity, who in the patience of passivity, am one whom anyone can replace, the nonindispensible by definition, but one for whom there is, nonetheless, no dispensation."[90] When seeking a pseudonymous anonymity, I do so because it is only on achieving such a named namelessness that I might reach a floating position from which I may contemplate what fates might befall the world, beginning to "peel off the layers of unspeakability"[91] that surround what might be said about the politics of time in an era when time is fungible.

If we appreciate the ruinous quality of the politics of this era, if we understand more fully how one is cast into a world in which the norm and its absorptive power is distributed as a political/organizational principle, we may then be able to find new sources of self-awareness. We might substitute the study of the evasion of law for the more conventional, though increasingly reactionary, effort to reconstruct a philosophy of life that resolves the paradoxes of living through the embrace of transcendent categories. Such a self-awareness might inform the development of an ethic of care.[92] Caring could come to inform our united states.

The Habits of Homelessness

Think about a society in which homelessness is supported and made possible. Think about the sort of care that might inform the American present. Think about our beggars, past and future. This might provide us with a measure of how far we have to travel. In the end it may be only a matter of bad habits, but that is no small thing.

In an essay on alienation and belonging, David Bromwich uses a poem by Wordsworth, "The Old Cumberland Beggar," to explore the mores that enabled people to integrate homeless people into their lives in the early nineteenth century.[93] The following is a key passage of the poem:

> Where'er the aged Beggar takes his rounds,
> The mild necessity of use compels
> To acts of love; and habit does the work
> Of reason, yet prepares that after joy
> Which reason cherishes.[94]

The people of Cumberland give alms to the beggar not out of any sense of program or plan, but out of a sense of "use." Bromwich suggests that by "use" Wordsworth means something unusual, "the repeated performance of a given action"[95] This use, which is synonymous with habit, "does the work of reason." As Bromwich puts it, "a guided, but unreasoning impulse, gives all the sanction to an act that we could hope to obtain from rational reflection."[96] This kind of use has nothing to do with utility.

Habit differs from rational action in that regard, but in another important regard as well. It prepares "that after joy that reason cherishes." Bromwich points out that this end is not a social utility. The relationship between reason and habit suggested by Wordsworth is more protean and fragile than that. It involves "pleasure unpursued," in Wordsworth's phrase. Bromwich asks, why must the pleasure be *unpursued*? "The problem (Wordsworth must feel) with an ethic of rational choice, which speaks of the pursuit of pleasure or the pursuit of happiness, is that it subtly or conspicuously includes the idea of a reward."[97] Wordsworth wishes to warn against such thinking because of its utilitarian calculations, which could render a man such as the Cumberland beggar useless and thus vulnerable to removal.

The Cumberland beggar, Wordsworth suggests, is "A silent monitor, which on their minds / Must needs impress a transitory thought / Of self-congratulation."[98] Bromwich comments:

> The beggar, by vividly calling to mind everything he stands for in a social order, recalls to others their own peculiar position in the same order: not their security alone, or their want of it; but the part that chance, or that fateful succession of accidents that we sometimes call "nature," has played in their own coming to be what they are. In his presence, we all of us count our "charters and exemptions," the things that constrain us, and the things that leave us partly free.[99]

Bromwich argues that it would be a horrible mistake to think that "The Cumberland Beggar" is an object lesson in the Christian homily, "There but for the grace of God go I." He points out that there is no scene of gratitude contained in "The Old Cumberland Beggar." One is not asked to feel as the beggar feels. Instead, he suggests that Wordsworth might be conveying the message "that any life at all, when its conventional accretions are burned away, might become the sort of monitor that the beggar's is."[100]

In his introduction to the poem, Wordsworth writes, "The class of Beggars, to which the old Man here described belongs, will probably soon be extinct."[101] He is right. David Rothman, among many others, has recorded the disappearance of beggars into the almshouses of early nineteenth-century America, and Michael Ignatieff has done the same in his study of England.[102] Wordsworth refers to the almshouse experience in "The Old Cumberland Beggar," wishing that he never be placed there:

> May never HOUSE, misnamed of INDUSTRY,
> Make him captive! —for that pent-up din,
> Those life-consuming sounds that clog the air,
> Be his the natural silence of old age![103]

The beggar's silence is respected in the fading world described by Wordsworth. It is a silence allowable in a time and place where habits are understood to be the moral underpinnings of the impersonal ethos governing the common life of democratic citizens.

But our silence, the silence of the present, is *composed* of the pent-up din, the life-consuming sounds of disciplinary institutions, within which habit is reduced to rehabilitation.[104] This is not to say that we now live in a disciplinary age, that the workhouse and factory dominate our lives. We are over that period. Moreover, such a term would reassure us too much.[105] Although our society has been a disciplinary society, one of the most thoroughgoing disciplinary societies, we are now living among the ruins of the penitentiary. What this means is that the decline of habit Wordsworth feared was only a prelude to the later withdrawal of focused attention on individuation in favor of tactics of normalization that focus on entire populations instead of separate individuals. We are in a period of new enclosures, a time when control proceeds through monitoring of a sort Wordsworth could probably not have imagined. The dignity enjoyed by Wordsworth's Cumberland beggar was transitory. Perhaps it marked a high point in liberal-democratic life, ironically, prior to democracy's fuller realization.

What habit of life characterizes the relationship of homelessness to democracy now, as opposed to in Wordsworth's time? To return to Bromwich's understanding of Wordsworth's poetic assertion, might any life at all, when its accretions are burned away, become a monitor like the Cumberland beggar's? I would tentatively answer: yes and no. Yes, in that it is still possible, if barely, to imagine our conventional accretions burned away, *pace* the advocates of identity politics, and *pace* my own pessimistic moments. No, in that the habits of the lives of those who lived in Cumberland are not the same as ours. Our age is deeply disenchanted, and we are left to develop our own representations. We know too well that what is left when our accretions are burned away is not an essential humanity, but something much lighter and contingent and hence more frightening. We wrestle with what to do.

What reinvigorating habits might we provide for such fragile yet persistent beings? Since we're not going anywhere, how might we all get along, homeless?

Compensation and the (Re)Turn to Democracy

"Emerson," George Kateb writes, "will try to break up the mass, break up the masses, by both his method and the substance of his teaching, and thus tease out individuals."[106] But he will try to do so in a way that escapes the means of politics, because for Emerson, politics is almost inevitably corrupted by how it connects power to utility. The only political activities of value are those of direct democratic participation, primarily in speeches presented as part of democratic deliberation, moments of individual resistance, such as engaged in by Thoreau, and moments of "stupendous moral emergency beyond the reach of individual self-reliance," when the evil of political mobilization is less than the evil to be overcome, as in the famous case of the American Civil War.[107] The final political position for Kateb's Emerson is straightforward. "Individualism must do battle with massification, more and more."[108]

But the difficult relationship of democracy to homelessness suggests a minority reading of Emerson that emphasizes the contingent (rather than immanent) character of the individualism that battles massification. One might pose this as a question: After the death of Emerson's God, what remains?[109] (After the burning away of our accretions, what remains?) Kateb develops a position beyond politics. He writes, "Alone, one is divine because only when one is withdrawn can reality present itself by presenting itself as beauty. This life of illusions is transformed by self-reliance into the sublime spectacle of appearances."[110] Kateb's religious gesture refolds outer life into inner peace. But at what cost? One cannot shut one's ears to Wordsworth's "life-consuming sounds" forever. The sublime spectacle of appearances seems too much like a retreat from politics rather than a magisterial and democratic contempt for politics.

But instead of the transformation of the life of illusion into the sublime spectacle of appearances, can we not substitute the compensatory activity of partial identification? I see this activity as the form that the care of self needs to take in the ruins of disciplinary society, in the unsettled character of our united states. Such an activity is likely to be one of solitude, but a solitude in which "the life consuming sounds that clog the air" are given their due, that is, in which they are recognized as a crucial if painful part of the constitution of our selves in lack. I see Emerson underwriting this activity in his essay "Compensation."

Emerson begins that essay in good protestant manner, mocking precisely what Wordsworth also rejects—the value of Christian moralisms smelling of utilitarian calculation. He muses about the preacher who argues, from the doctrine of the Last Judgment, that the wicked are successful in this life, but that just compensation will be rendered to those who are good in the next. He objects: "The legitimate inference the disciple would draw was—'We are to have *such* a good time as the sinners have now;' or, to push it to its extreme import—'You sin now, we shall sin by and by; we would sin now, if we could; not being successful we expect our revenge to-morrow."[111] Such an idea "defers to the base estimate of the market of what constitutes manly success, instead of confronting and convicting the world from the truth; announcing the presence of the soul; the omnipotence of the will; and so establishing the standards of good and ill, of success and failure."[112]

Men are better than their theology, Emerson suggests, wiser than they know, because they adhere to the law of compensation. But what is that law? He does not say, suggesting only that he wants "to record some facts that indicate the path of the law of Compensation; happy beyond my expectation if I shall truly draw the smallest arc of this circle."[113] That Emerson seeks to "draw the smallest arc" of the law of compensation puts compensation in opposition to the central idea in "Circles," that enclosed in a series of circles is the truth of life itself.[114] (Is this an opposition of the contingent to the immanent?) In only recording some facts that indicate the law of compensation, Emerson keeps the circle open; he does so surprisingly, by identifying compensation with a dualism that pervades all of nature. The world is dual, and so are all of its parts. "The entire system of things gets represented in every particle."[115]

Emerson described this dualism in a series of observations concerning the fortunes that attend to political fame and personal genius. But these only illustrate a more fundamental fact of life in the universe. "All things are moral," he suggests. For every good, there is an evil, for every disaster, a triumph. "What we call retribution is the universal necessity by which the whole appears wherever a part appears."[116] Yet Emerson takes care to note that the wholesomeness of things is constantly challenged by the partial response of humans. This partiality is an aspect of the dualism of body and soul. He writes,

> Every act rewards itself, or in other words integrates itself, in a twofold manner; first in the thing, or in real nature; and secondly in the circumstance, or in apparent nature. Men call the circumstance retribution. The causal retribution is in the thing and is seen in the soul. The retribution in the circumstance is seen by the understanding; it is inseparable from the thing, but is often spread over a long time and so does not become distinct until after many years. . . . Cause and effect, means and end, seed and fruit, cannot be severed; for the effect already blooms in the cause, and the end preexists in the means, the fruit in the seed.[117]

We seek to act partially, Emerson seems to suggest, because we are bodily beings. In our moral striving in particular, we seek the pleasures of the senses and not the requirements of character. But we will be thwarted in our delusions by the inevitability of retributive action. "There is a crack in everything God has made," he notes. That sentence accounts for both the resistance of the body to the soul and their inevitable connection. Compensation, as Kateb notes, is the hardest teaching. It is hardest when applied to the partial sensuality of human beings, our lack which is grounded in our sensual being, our embodiment. Although it is inevitable that we will resist the imposition of wholeness on our bodies with our bodies, it is also almost useless that we do so, because our bodies are deeply connected to our souls. As Foucault has put it, in one of his most famous aphorisms: "The soul is the prison of the body."[118]

Our knowledge of the harshness of compensation might lead to stoicism, or passive nihilism. This cannot be the path of anyone who seeks to "be," politically. Despite "the indifferency of circumstances,"[119] Emerson suggests that we see beyond compensation to the soul. He writes, "The soul is not a compensation, but a life. The soul *is*. Under all this running sea of circumstance, whose waters ebb and flow with perfect balance, lies the aboriginal abyss of real Being. Essence, or God, is not a relation of a part, but the whole. Being is the vast affirmative, excluding negation, self-balanced, and swallowing up all relations, parts and times within itself."[120] This life is a progress, not a station. The absolute measure of our selves is the whole, one not readily realizable. So underlying Emerson's discussion of compensation is the question of the relationship of compensation to the real Being of the soul. And as he puts it, "In the nature of the soul is the compensation for the inequalities of condition."[121]

Ironically, the soul constantly quits its whole system of things. Worldly relations hang loosely to the circumstances of the soul's existence, and when perceived properly "becom[e] as it were a transparent fluid membrane through which the living form is seen, and not, as in most men, an indurated heterogenous fabric of many dates and of no settled character, in which the man is imprisoned. Then there can be enlargement, and the man to-day scarcely remembers the man of yesterday."[122] Whatever sadness and resignation accompany the human condition, then, reflects a lack of faith. In our lack of faith we cannot move forward. We are stuck, and the immobility we suffer might be said to consist of our fearful clinging to the conditions that make us recognizable to ourselves at the cost of further growth, the sort of identification with home criticized by Kateb. It is our "lapsed estate, resting, not advancing, resisting, not cooperating with the divine expansion."[123]

Emerson certainly does not intend that his soul be the same as that described by Foucault. But the pressure is there. If the soul is not to be a prison, but instead a vast affirmative—a life—can it be that without resort to belief in a sovereign Being, a God who might save us? So much of the doctrine of compensation is bound up in faith that the question almost presents itself: Is it possible to think of advancement, to observe growth and development, without thinking of a God, even nostalgically? If we need a God to explain the spiritual law of compensation, do we not need a law of compensation to explain God's lack? To ask that question, however one formulates it, is to begin an inquiry into the terms through which we might begin to imagine a politics that could attend compensation in this disenchanted world. The beginning of such a politics might be found in the actions through which we compensate for the lack of God. We might go further and repair to an appreciation of life for what it lacks. And in beginning to appreciate what life lacks, we might be able to note how full it is.

This is an insight provided by Kateb when he reads Heidegger. For Kateb, Heidegger substitutes a "sense of the inessentiality of all things and the wonder of the uncomposed indefiniteness that contrasts with nothingness . . . for the untenable religiousness . . . in the works of Emerson, Thoreau and Whitman. This is the core of the attachment to earthly existence as such."[124]

But one might ask, if we rid ourselves of God, why not finish the task and rid ourselves of this thing called individualism? To be more modest, is not the individualism reflected in self-reliance so thoroughly tainted with a faith in God that we need radically to amend Emerson? Or, to be even more modest, can we not begin to renegotiate the terms of care for the self in a way that would meet the transformed circumstances of self-hood, brought on in part by the doctrine of individualism, however improperly that doctrine has been understood? Kateb himself has called for a rehabilitation of individualism, pretending that those to whom he issues the call have not been doing so all along.[125]

Here, compensation, freed from its religious moorings, has much to teach us. It might guide us to a politics of homelessness that is sensitive to the incomplete character of all attempts to be at home, including the last home, the home one makes within one's self. Such a politics would enable us to negotiate the terms of our incomplete identifications, to monitor the relative depths of aspects of our ontological commitments. In showing those of us who are at home how to be less at home, how to recognize our common and individual lack, students of compensation might enable us to go to war with all ideas that would call on us to complete communities of friends, rather than enjoy the company of strangers. But they would do more than that. They would teach us to recognize the strangeness in our selves, and to cultivate strangeness. They would show us better how to think with our bodies. In seeking to negotiate a way through the conditions of homelessness, they would be forced down a path that takes them further away from their destination, even as they would admit not knowing the road they are traveling, perhaps accepting only that it is a road to nowhere.

But I turn around and look back, and see that I have slipped. "We" have become "them." I desire a teacher. Who doesn't? But that desire leads to a dead end. There is great energy behind this desire for dependence, a desire to be led by someone who will put us back on a road to righteousness. Who are we and how do we resist the final gesture of deferral, that which depends on others to care for us rather than for us to care for ourselves? Can I rewrite the conclusion in order to right myself?

It is this. We might learn to compensate. If we do, we might be able to renew our freedom as a practice that gives rise to generosity for ourselves. If we do not, we will lose the world, not only in its generality, but in its particulars, in the love we have for each other, in the fecundity of desire, in the regard we have for our selves and others, in the proper mourning we might have for what we have lost, and in the celebrations we might display for the fruits of our terrible labors. Our lives will be less worth living, and hence will be less well lived. Our united states will come to be hated and dreaded.

Against that alternative we must think for ourselves, think imperti-
nently, seek the better laughter that is available to us when we realize
that growing up does not mean abandoning childish things, but instead
means abandoning the parents who called such things childish. The
politics of our desire have been framed in terms of prohibitions and
liberties, of authenticity and immortality. Can our politics be more than
our policies, and yet not seek the infinite silence that would not even
mark our end? Can we dance instead to a rhythm we recognize as
having elements of virtuality, can we learn to desire forms of virtuosity
associated with finitude? Can we compensate ourselves for our homelessness?

Stay tuned.

P.S. (I Love . . .)
Television in Wartime

In our country, Goodbye looks just like Hello.

—Laurie Anderson

A Signal, A Sign

Laurie Anderson notices an arm raised, another sign of the phallus.[1] She is free to comment on it, because she is in-between, vacillating, a self-haunting ghost in the machine of digital meaning. The crossover effect Anderson achieves depends on her prodigious knowledge of the history of language, her genius for understanding it as a history of breakdown, signified by our radio towers, towers of babble, our many indeterminate languages, on again, off again, digitalized.[2] She sees a sign raised for extraterrestrials, she sees a man raise his arm, and a woman stand by her man.[3] But what are these codes to us?

Earthly matters intervene, interfere with the reception. The Persian Gulf War—would anyone now call it the war to liberate Kuwait?—was not a war to end war. It was a war to end a syndrome, to renew us for more war. Inclined by habit toward war, we had been stopped, stunned by the trauma of seeing ourselves as we prosecuted low intensity war against Vietnam. We came to fear and loathe what we had done before. Overcoming our loathing meant placing it elsewhere, in another zone of existence. For although Vietnam took place when the register of television's reality had not yet spread through our culture, had not yet been absorbed by most of us—hence the shock of its televised images—the purpose of television, its function as what Avital Ronell calls a "shock absorber," has since come to the fore.[4] Televison has come to connect us to a network of assumptions, moving us into a tract of time where our inclination to war can be satisfied without our needing to feel its most unpleasant effects, the blood, the pain, the smell of death. Life in

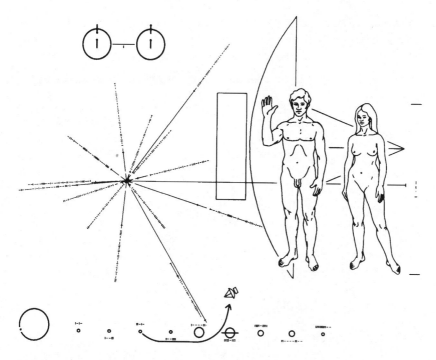

Voyager Man and Woman.

wartime assumes an unreality, but in a television age, what is real, and what is an illusion?

I am repeating myself, even my epigraphy. Dream delivers us to dream, and there is no end to illusion. There is no end to television, is there? But is there a limit to it? How might we come to know this war in a way that would help us evade it in the future? Instead of a conclusion, in pale imitation of other, more thorough thinkers,[5] I offer a television diary of the abstract kind, a story of life in wartime. It is a postscript, an afterthought.

After-Image

It was a television war.

I watched it a lot. It made me wonder: How is life in wartime within the imperium affected by the presence of television? How has the time of the latter made that of the former easier to accept? Or to put it more pretentiously: How might we suspend the play of *differance* needed to pretend that we are not always already watching television, television's obscenity always already torn asunder by the mechanisms of its production, always already a beam, always already targeted? Does television evade the fiction of writing before the word only to reinvent it? How can we watch television and *fail* to be politically engaged?

Perhaps a different world order of truth can be associated with the magnetic tapes of video, the laser disc, the green lights in the sky above Baghdad (where the tracers glow . . . and mark the parabola of the savagery of our imperial order). Television, cousin to the telephone,[6] will come to share the same fiber-optic line, in the future and forever more, thousands of channels streaming through our minds, making us conscious of something, but of what? This ever repeating moment is the discovery of a new medium of communication. The burning of the library at Alexandria smoothly jump-cuts to a burning city on the edge of the Pacific basin, to looters carrying Sony Trinitron television receivers through the ravaged streets. South Central Los Angeles. Another view of our united states: squint and you will see it in the interstices of the technical event.

Repeats, it is all repeats. Each repeat is inscribed in a binary code in our electric dreams. How many times before I die will I recall how the most famous event in the history of American television, the Kennedy assassination, became, with melodramatic eeriness, the Kennedy assassinations? How often do we all re-experience the horror of replication enacted around the familial television set, dancing on the screen itself in endless parody?[7] When does fiction, in the face of the endlessly repeated instant replay, become a comfort?[8] Television is but one more reason why Sartre had it wrong. Hell is not other people. Hell is yet another rerun of *M*A*S*H*.

Can I calm down? Can I think coolly about this cool medium? I look more closely and see something. There is an uncanniness accompanying these farcical replications of death in the electrical storms of tele-video experience. The new realm of our familiar constitutes the moment of fear inscribed in the televisual. And those who watch television with regularity are prepared for fear by the evening news.

When we learn that the news spills over, interrupts the evening schedule, we are ready to flip channels, to go to the leaders, Cable News Network, and find there the reassurance of Bernard Shaw, who was last seen in this book interrogating Michael Dukakis about his manhood, and who is now hiding in terror under a table in a hotel in

Iraq while bombs are falling, while Peter Arnett makes reassuring noises for him and for us, the second-hand viewers at home. Bernard Shaw trembles in fear for us. He is our man on the scene. We will go to him or to other anchors: Dan Rather, whatever. He will watch for us. We will not face it alone. Whatever "it" may be.

This war is a tract of time subject to rerun. What is its schedule? Can we interrupt it to bring you an important message?

Seriality

More easily than any other writing, the writing about television in particular is writing about television in general. Whereas television might be said to be a forum for the play of genres, that description is itself not quite right, for it only represents and replicates the triumph of the group over the specific, of the genre over the series in the most obvious and least interesting way possible.

None of the sophisticated viewers can tell me how to watch TV better. All they know is that it is more or less a medium through which I am taught to buy things. But my consumption is not the point here. My education is, and I do not want my schedule interrupted.

Stanley Cavell seems to understand how television operates as my companion. Cavell explains why I long for television. In "The Fact of Television," he argues that there is a distinctive "aesthetic interest of television."[9] This interest, he writes, is located "in [television's] serial-episode mode of composition."[10] His first concern is to distinguish television's mode of composition from film's—his deeper love—which, he argues, has a member-genre mode of composition. Film's aesthetic is revealed in each film, and television's in each *series*. "What is memorable, treasurable, criticizable, is not primarily the individual work, but the program, the format, not this or that day of 'I Love Lucy,' but the program as such."[11] We just can't decipher any particular "work" of television. He writes, "To say that the primary object of aesthetic interest in television is not the individual piece, but the format, is to say that the format is its primary individual of aesthetic interest."[12] From Cavell's perspective, we should proceed by understanding that a meaningful analysis of television involves not the study of its particulars, but of its more general ground, which constitutes its ontological frame of reference.

Both genre-member and serial-episode can be called formats of the respective media of film and television. A genre-member format, which predominates in the experience of film, allows for what might be called a critical individuation of each production. Cavell suggests that the process of individuation occurs as a process of compensation, each member of the genre introducing something new, but relating to the whole.[13] The establishment of one genre and its distinction from other genres proceeds by processes of compensation and divergence, or the negation of various features in specific films, ultimately becoming part of the system known as film. Movies, it seems, are ultimately eminently *comparable* to one another. In contrast, the serial-episode format (which bears some resemblance to the film genre that Cavell calls genre-as-cycle) proceeds by processes of repetition. In series, narratives come to a conclusion with each episode, but in such a way that the completion or ending is called into question, undermining the possibility of negation and compensation that is the comparative basis of film's aesthetics. Affirmation, not negation. The father's "yes" is always a yes that validates what is, a fabulous moment that defines what has gone before through an act of will, an "Amen," which is to say, an acquiescence as much as an assertion.

Because of how it disarms possibilities of resistance, the process of serialization, with its repetitions, leads to surprising improvisations at each situation, the embodiment of the situation being recapitulated and reinforced with each episode.[14] Although each improvisation ends in a "Yes," an affirmation, or with the assertion "That's the way it is," the groundlessness of televideo creativity enables peculiarly fabulous assertions that operate to block assent to its own reality. "That's the way it is" is not to be taken too seriously.

Television operates in a serial-episode format because "the material basis of television [is] *a current of simultaneous event reception*." Film, on the other hand, has as its basis *a succession of automatic world projections*.[15] Television receivers are monitors of what is shown, of what broadcasters or cable companies or VCR users allow to appear on the screen. In contrast to film, which is *viewed*, what is seen on television screens is *received* and *monitored*. Whether live or recorded, because of the constant presence of the image on the screen (even if at the rate of one dot at a time, a technical difficulty to be overcome with the advent of digital television), television presents others as present. Television does not say, "You are There," but "They're Here." (Perhaps it took a Stephen Spielberg movie, *Poltergeist*, to tell a television horror story properly.) All television formats participate in the *current*, feeding into the continuous broadcast available to all of us who sit at home and monitor our receivers.

The discontinuities presented on television are contained within and supported by the ground of the continuous feed of the current. Cavell writes,

> It is internal to television formats to be made so as to participate in this continuity, which means that they are formed to admit discontinuities both within themselves and between one another, and between these and commercials, station breaks, news breaks, emergency signal tests, color charts, program announcements, and so on, which means formed to allow these breaks, hence these recurrences, to be legible. So that switching (and I mean here not primarily switching from, say narrative to one or another break, for a station or for a sponsor, and back again) is as indicative of life as—in a way to be specified—monitoring is.[16]

All television is the same, experience collapses into the singular field of virtual video. The virtuosity of television will come to be its simulation of the interruption. Television is a holding place, a universal marker for the missing word.

Monitoring also might be an indicator, for Cavell, of television's underrated capacity to act as "company" to those of us who monitor it. Television switches as we switch from one scene to another. As it becomes more "a set of permutations of a single cultural constant,"[17] it becomes more predictable and reliable, easier to watch. It acts as company as well in the massive amounts of commentary that accompany video images.

This is why talk, rather than images, forms the most improvisational aspect of television. In the context of both game shows and talk shows, comedy shows and new shows, talk is the source of drama, of suspense and relief. "Here, the fact that nothing of consequence is said matters little compared to the fact that something is spoken. . . . The gift of the host is to know how, and how far, to put guests recurrently at ease and on the spot."[18] Improvisation, no matter how slight, is the sign of life on the television monitor. Vanna White, letter-turner on *Wheel of Fortune*, reduced the requirements of this improvisation to the unspoken language of the face. Talking heads, the most obviously boring part of television, are also what are most alive.[19] Boredom becomes anxiety.

Television monitors event and nonevent equally. In fact, the uneventful constitutes the content of the ground, is what is continuously fed via the current. The event, as it is covered in the serial procedures of television, is not a development of a situation requiring some resolution, but an intrusion or emergency. Each event subsides into the ground of the uneventful. Cavell suggests that serial procedure is thus "undialectical,"[20] so that the manner in which television can be said to monitor events disables interpretive schemes of reversal. Once one realizes this, one reaches the appropriate intersection of the aesthetic dimension with the political. The aesthetic of monitoring is such that it "encodes the denial of succession as integral to the basis of the medium."[21]

The open-ended strategy of the series has very problematic political implications. It represents what William Corlett has declared to be a force of reassurance, a continuum that is most reassuring in that it names a series. Corlett suggests that "there are at least three approaches to the continuum: (1) to declare continuity moot in a pure world of immutable ideality; (2) to declare continuity possible in worlds reassured by immanence; (3) to declare continuity impossible in a world of flux."[22] Seriality, in this sense, contributes to an understanding of space in a way that allows one to fix oneself in time in order to be able to project oneself into a past-future continuum. The seriality of television that Cavell invokes seems homologous with the one that Corlett condemns (in the name of Derrida).

But the problem of seriality, one might claim, is even more difficult than the allegiances and condemnations it might invoke. The recapitulation of space that is involved in the articulation of time-as-series opens a field of politics that is less than reassuring. Seriality in this sense is a line, but as a tightrope is a line. So when Cavell emphasizes the possibilities inherent in television's material base as a current of simultaneous event reception, he indicates how television might serve as a device for heightening or intensifying the feeling of anxiety that dominates the age. The line becomes a point, as the tightrope disappears from both ends. Like Wile E. Coyote, for a moment, the moment of fearful paralysis, we hang in the imaginary air, far above the too-real ground. And as in the most common mythology of dreaming, should we fail to awaken before we hit the ground, we will surely die.

How to Fear

Etymologies suggest that *fear* once meant the experience of being between places of protection, in transit, in a situation analogous to the condition that is commonly referred to in contemporary ethnographic literature as liminality.[23] Alphonso Lingis has suggested that the modern will to be a person is impelled into thought by a fear of the law of the mind, an experience of inauthenticity that is the only way in which one comes to appreciate the powers that inform meaning.[24] In positing fear before law, Lingis seeks to unsettle thought. He does so as a genealogist, pointing to the dubious politics of all projects that insist on a return to origins in order to "get it right," to build something straight out of the crooked timber of humanity. In part, Lingis's point is that the position of fear, a moving position, is also a position of passivity. He thus suggests that one think about fear in reference to a "rapture of the deep," an experience that serves as an unsettling way of appreciating order without attempting to ground order in a totalizing ontology. He writes, "The one who goes down to the deep goes down for the fear."[25] If one disperses one's powers, one might come to experience the loss-of-self that allows one to understand the processes of willing entailed in establishing one's identity. One moves through fear's space, engaging in a deliberately solipsistic mediating experience to see the disorders that compose order, to traverse the heterotopias of an era that constructs them as the ordinary spaces of everyday life. Discontinuity is our continuity, television our vehicle.

Fear is the political aesthetic of the medium of television because from the roving position of fear, Laurie Anderson's ghostly position within the digital feedback loop, we are able to move past the most obvious (and pointless) claims regarding the capacities of television to present the "truth" of the world—television's supposed attention to the visually spectacular, for instance, or its seeming need to dramatize conflict—to a more nuanced and more troubling set of observations concerning how television enables certain kinds of thought and disables others.

The form as well as the content of television (to the extent that such terms even make sense in reference to television) can dissolve into the non-place and non-time of fear. Television thus reconstitutes thinking concerning distinctions, and it effects disastrously the variations and limits on that strange phenomenon called representation. From the liminal point of fear, one can gain the perspective that allows one to tune into, without being subject to, the recreated representation that television enables.

Television requires, or at least thrives on, a profound state of distraction, advancing further the project that Walter Benjamin identified in "The Work of Art in the Age of Mechanical Reproduction."[26] Benjamin makes a strong distinction between concentration and distraction. He argues that people in mass society absorb art in a state of distraction, as opposed to the individual who concentrates on a work of art, and hence is absorbed by it. For Benjamin the exemplary mass art is architecture, which is received tactilely, as a matter of habit. Important to architecture is its relationship to enduring *need*, as an expression grounded in the ever present necessity for shelter from weather. Trained to perceive the building in a state of distraction, people in massifying (consolidating, modern) societies are prepared for film.[27] This preparation is paradoxical, in that a *need* is reinscribed in the aesthetic mode of film. Trained to perceive film in a state of distraction, we who wish to work for de-massification are prepared for television.

If we disinter Benjamin's meaning from its immediate context of explaining the fascistic attraction to war, we are obligated to explain to what extent the technology of television is implicated in the attractions of the beauty of war, because for Benjamin the aesthetics of war appears as an excess of production, pressing for a catastrophic utilization.[28] Film plays an important role in conflating need and beauty. Benjamin writes, "Imperialist war is a rebellion of technology which collects, in the form of 'human material', the claims to which society has denied its natural material. Instead of draining rivers, society directs a human stream into a bed of trenches; instead of dropping seeds from airplanes, its drops incendiary bombs over cities; and through gas warfare the aura is abolished in a new way."[29] Although he writes within the metaphysical frame of Marxism (still seeking to dominate "nature," to discern the absolute truth of material being), the most important point here is that the new way of abolishing the aura is to abolish the "human material" that instantiates it. In James Der Derian's syllogism (composed in equal parts of Sherman and Sartre) this point is made in all of its brutality: "Since war is hell and hell is others, bomb the others into nothingness."[30]

Television simulates this abolition of the aura. It simulates war. But this does not mean that television contributes to war's abolition. Instead it reconstructs its truth. This televised war, brought to us in a state of distraction, disarms opposition by dissolving it. In this way resistance is not crushed by power so much as it is made irrelevant by being made uninteresting.

The Camera Never Blinks

The night the bombs began to fall on Baghdad, I stayed in front of the television set. For the next few days, family and friends—and not a few protagonists—spent inordinate amounts of time becoming experts on coverage, using the remote control to surf from one channel to another, picking up the latest developments, criticizing the talking heads, complaining about the jingoistic coverage, worrying about the damage out there. Eventually, however, we began to reintegrate the war coverage (even as the networks did) into our ordinary schedules. As the adrenaline rush faded, the war became an annoying disruption to my regular televideo schedule, and I was secretly relieved to get back to my regular viewing schedule.[31] The immediacy and the urgency of the bombing war was a consequence of "We interrupt our regularly broadcast program to bring you this important news." Once the bombing had settled into a pattern that could be scheduled, and thus rendered coherent, by the television program managers, we found better things to do with our time, even before it was clear that the Iraqis were to suffer a horrible defeat, long before the damage to the environment was revealed, and long before the atrocities we had suspected began to come to light. We could catch what we "needed" to know in regularly scheduled broadcasts. In the meantime, 'twas a famous victory. Norman Schwarzkopf, vaguely familiar to us already (was it Willard Scott or Jonathan Winters he most closely resembled?), became the general of new kind of war, a war sponsored by, rather than investigated by television.

After a few days I even stopped watching when the most potent image of the war appeared on screen—the television picture from the nose of the "smart bomb" as it zeroed in on its target, an image that became part of what Der Derian refers to as the "logos war" that erupted among the major networks.[32] Because of that image, I think, I was unable to convince people of what I had read in the *New York Times*, that such bombs were but a small part of the arsenal being used, and that "our" side was using B-52s to "precision" bomb the "suburbs" of Baghdad. I needed, in fact, to remind myself of the registers of reality that were being separated from each other as the war proceeded. But the bombs continued to fall, and the camera never blinked.[33]

I sought relief. I turned off the set. But then I did not know what to do, because the reality of those on the streets of Amherst had become incommensurate with what I had seen on my television set. Shortly after the land war drew to a close Noam Chomsky visited Amherst College to deliver the Corless Lamont Lectures, a series of speeches endowed by the College in the name of a philosopher who has devoted his life to the study of peace. As part of his visit Chomsky attended several regular college courses, and I had been lucky to get him to speak to the students in my seminar on power and representation in American politics.[34]

As we left the building, I looked over to the Town Commons, where several police cars and a small crowd had gathered. I presumed another antiwar demonstration had occurred (there were many during the war, but few were covered on TV). I asked a student what had happened, and he told me that someone had immolated himself in protest against the war.[35] I returned to tell Chomsky. He continued with his schedule, a veteran of antiwar movements, knowing better than to be distracted by a register of the real that would matter less than the distinctions he could teach. (Or, he refused to be distracted by events that mattered less to him than the distinctions he intended to make.)

The following week, I went to a memorial service for that young man. I could not connect his death with the yellow ribbons, with the line in the sand, with the C-5A transporters flying over the town from the nearby staging base in Chicopee, Massachusetts, transporting troops and supplies to the Gulf. While I wandered through the empty tomb of the public sphere (with a few others), I suspected that the register of the real that counted was elsewhere, although not with Chomsky.[36]

The tool for separating these registers of reality, and for constructing the truth of the Gulf War, was already in place months before the fighting itself began. As Der Derian notes with appropriate irony, "We were primed for this war."[37] What prime-time schedule did I hunger for, what habit of mine had been disrupted? As a student of discipline I have known for some time how much hinges on regularity, how the creation of the modern soul now depends as much on television as it does on prison schedules.[38] I count on my regular meetings with the prime-time inhabitants of the evening programs. I am supposed to be a critic. Why might I still be seduced by television, if not because it reassures me, if not because it is something I can count on?

I know that television news programs are series composed of specific episodes. They monitor events, following the rules of the situation. What is most obvious about regular television news programs is that they are composed of a fixed period of time—one half hour, inclusive of all the switches that aid in the composition of any particular time slot. Only under what are considered to be extraordinary circumstances will there be additional time, and that time will usually be separated from the regular news, a "news special," such as the ones that accompanied Ronald Reagan's address to the nation on the Iran-contra scandal. The regulation of the time of news is itself a sign of the importance of news—time is the television equivalent of newspaper space.[39]

The formal composition, the format, of television news time is rigorously regulated as well. A lead story; a second lead story often related to the lead; headline stories concerning other events; one, perhaps two, stories of "continuing interest"; a human-interest story; perhaps something from the domain of celebrity; maybe some commentary. The specific elements will vary, as in any improvisation on a repetitive theme, but a general principle holds—the most important story first, with a general gradation of stories according to their importance. One can note that there is no explicit tagging of stories in terms of importance. The principle of order of importance, though, is firmly ingrained in consciousness, so that when there is a failure due to a technical glitch, we share the nervousness of the anchor, who sweats until the next story is ready to go.

One can ask a further question—how does the principle of order of importance contribute to the serialization of the news? The episodes in serial-episode formats are set up to call into question any notion of ending or completion. The material presented throughout most of a newscast calls into question completion in at least two ways. First, the separation of stories fragments narrative wholes by giving mini-narratives precedence over complete narrative. In all cases, the completion of a story is accompanied by a switch, either to an advertisement, or back to the "anchor," or to another story, so that a recapitulation of the specific situation is made clear.

Completion is also undermined by what might be called the "naturalization" of television news. The stories that follow the lead often lend substance to the pretense that television is only showing those who monitor it fragments of a greater reality. The stories that follow what is deemed the most important story support the supposition that the lead story *is* the most important event of the day. Yet at the same time they provide evidence that regardless of the importance of the lead story, "life goes on." Those who monitor can make no sense of what is important on the news unless they are able to conceive of what is not important. The events of the day thus are embedded in the context of a synthesized reality, a common sense constituted by the minor, rather than the major stories.

The role of the anchor is of crucial importance for naturalizing the news, which is why anchors are so valorized. The anchor performs a double function—orchestrating the order of stories by serving as a switch from one current to another and monitoring the news along with those who are watching in front of their own sets. At least from the very first broadcast of *You Are There*, television news has provided the home watcher with the image of the anchor as monitor. On that program, Edward R. Morrow watched his monitor and the audience watched him watching his monitor through their sets. The anchor is able to present herself/himself as a fellow watcher, but one who is a surrogate for the watcher at home, able to ask questions and guide the agenda of the proceedings.

Thus television news is constituted as a serial, with all the rules of serialization that Cavell describes. The characteristic of television news that renders it different from the rest of television lies only in how its switches render events distinct from the ground of continuing current. The people and events constituted by the world of diachronic eventualities, the supposedly necessary world of history, come into television as flat events, dissociated from what has been before and what will be after, yet connected by the linkages of serialization.

As the bombing war transmuted into the ground war, the events that unfolded in the Gulf were regularized. Time zones were uncannily cooperative with the needs of the American prime-time news network, CNN. Whereas the regular networks had to disrupt their schedules, CNN's schedule was designed for disruption. That the bombing schedule coincided with the evening hours in the United States was a fortunate development that the U.S. Department of Defense exploited. After close to a month of bombing, the series was brought to a spectacular close with the special presentation of a blitzkrieg attack, "War in the Gulf, the Final Episode." Of course, although this series may have been brought to a conclusion, a spin-off may be in the works. Gulfwar Deux? The Gulf Strikes Back? Gulfwar: The Next Generation?

Fear of Television

So *then* what happened? In August 1991, the U.S.S.R. suffered a right-wing coup. I watched my set at home one early afternoon, as an instant replay of Tienanmen Square began. CNN was there, camera at the ready outside the White House (no, not the American one, the other one, the home of the Russian Parliament). I heard a cheer from the streets, and an announcer said that the crowd outside had just been informed that one of the coup leaders had suffered a heart attack. Thinking that a colleague of mine (a specialist in Soviet politics) and a visiting scholar (who had left Moscow two hours before the coup began) might be interested in hearing about this new development, I left home and walked to my office on campus. I told them what I had just seen, and they looked at each other and began to laugh. Moments earlier, my colleague had been answering questions on a telephone line hook-up for a radio call-in program from Toronto, and the CBC had announced the news of the heart attack. My colleague told our visiting scholar, who promptly telephoned friends of his who were inside the Russian Parliament (the White House), who then went outside and told the crowd, which then cheered. I noticed that my colleague had a television set in his office now, and that it was tuned to CNN. . . .

And now I write the end of this book, and today's *New York Times* describes how Muscovites were relying on CNN feed, with simultaneous translation, to inform them of the bloody end of the rebellion by the regnant factions of the parliament in the very same White House.[40] This book must end, but the serial continues.

Linking up to the televideo register of reality means understanding the element of fear that television not merely represents, but which is the feeble embodiment of the televisual itself. Fear of television is ambiguous, in that it constitutes both a field of understanding that denies any definitive vision and a reaction to the very denial of vision that is the basic strategy of televisual reality. To deny vision through a technique of vision is the solipsistic element of television that leads writers such as Baudrillard to despair about it rhapsodically. Even affirmations of television are ambiguous and indecisive; "That's the way it is" tempts one to disagree, to deny television its reality. The politics of fear leads neither to despair nor to hope. Instead, it reminds the observant (which is to say distracted) watcher that what has been called the postmodern condition is not and cannot be identified as a "left" or "right" phenomenon, but is instead a recapitulation of the fields of modern political discourse in a space where left and right are shadows of their former selves.

Television can thus be understood as the popular vehicle for the democratization of Nietzsche's knowledge concerning the death of God. Over one hundred years have passed since Nietzsche so observed, and it may be that the television anchor, sitting at the right hand of nothing, is only monitoring events with the rest of humanity, attempting to conjure into existence a new home for humanity. But the home the anchor wishes to establish is far too much like the home that most people find so unbearably costly to maintain, a place that seems to risk all possibilities of future endeavors in imagination for a system of anticipation of the end of the world (both "as we know it," and as we don't), a permanent state of emergency.[41] The rejection of the anchor might be the next moment in the unfolding of the story of television, the point at which it will become clearer than ever before that there is nothing worthy to report at the end of the world. To reflect on the meaning of Walter Cronkite's famous phrase "That's the way it is," is to experience both the comfort of certitude and the depression of conclusion that accompanies catastrophe.

But one might also note that the end of the world does not mean its destruction in a catastrophic sense. We are always at the end of the world and must find some comfort in our ability to reflect on that banal fact. "Courage," Dan Rather urged as his sign-off line for one brief week. His producer sought to understand the portent contained in his one-word sign-off, and Rather remained silent, the single word an enigmatic statement in response to the ever changing yet ever constant world on the screen.

In response to television, courage, the companion to fear.

The man with his arm raised in greeting, and the woman who stands by his side, are lost in space. Voyagers to places unknown, carrying vital information, they have departed the solar system, they are leaving us, they are lost in space. Sometimes we are told that television signals will reach Alpha Centauri after the millennium, where faintly is heard the big-band sound of Desi Arnez, Desi Arnez, arm raised (is it in greeting,) in greeting, I love . . .

Hello?

Good-bye . . .

Notes

Introduction

Epigraph taken from Ralph Waldo Emerson, "Experience," in *Essays, Second Series*, found in *The Selected Writings of Ralph Waldo Emerson* (New York: Modern Library, 1992), p. 305.

1. See Patricia Williams, *The Alchemy of Race and Rights* (Cambridge: Harvard University Press, 1991).

2. Walter Lippmann, *The Phantom Public* (New York: Macmillan, 1927). For the most relevant overview of the contemporary problem of the public sphere, see Bruce Robbins, ed., *The Phantom Public Sphere* (Minneapolis: University of Minnesota Press, 1993), especially Robbins, "Introduction: The Public as Phantom."

3. My perspective on narcissism is at variance with, even if it is indebted to, that developed by Christopher Lasch. See his *Culture of Narcissism: American Life in an Age of Diminishing Expectations* (New York: Norton, 1978).

4. For an example of this accusation, see Charles Taylor, *Multiculturalism and the "Politics of Recognition*," ed. Amy Gutmann (Princeton: Princeton University Press, 1992), especially the introductory essay by Gutmann.

5. This is one way to read Emerson's "Experience." See *The Selected Writings of Ralph Waldo Emerson*.

6. See Emerson, "Experience," p. 325. Much of what I know of Emerson has been filtered through reading George Kateb and Stanley Cavell and through talking with Kateb. See George Kateb, *The Inner Ocean: Individualism and Democratic Culture* (Ithaca: Cornell University Press, 1992), and his forthcoming study of Emerson (Sage). Also see Stanley Cavell, *Conditions Handsome and Unhandsome: The Constitution of Emersonian Perfectionism* (Chicago: University of Chicago Press, 1990), *In Quest of the Ordinary: Lines of Skepticism and Romanticism* (Chicago: University of Chicago Press, 1988), and *This New Yet Unapproachable America: Lectures after Emerson after Wittgenstein* (Albuquerque: Living Batch, 1989).

1. Dear Laurie Anderson

Epigraph taken from Laurie Anderson, *United States* (New York: Harper & Row, 1984), part 1, "Say Hello."

1. Michel Foucault once suggested that we are suffering from "a very paradoxical disease, for which we haven't yet found a name; and this mental disease has a very curious symptom, which is that the symptom itself brought the mental disease into being." See Michel Foucault and Noam Chomsky, "Human Nature: Justice versus Power," in Fons Elders, ed., *Reflexive Water: The Basic Concerns of Mankind* (London: Souvenir Press, 1974), pp. 188–89.

2. On the fabulous quality of constitutive statements, see Jacques Derrida, "Declarations of Independence," trans. Thomas Keenan and Thomas Pepper, *New Political Science*, no. 15 (Summer 1986), and Bonnie Honig, "Declarations of Independence: Arendt and Derrida on the Problem of Founding a Republic," in Frederick Dolan and Thomas Dumm, eds., *Rhetorical Republic: Governing Representations in American Politics* (Amherst: University of Massachusetts Press, 1993).

3. William E. Connolly, *Identity\Difference: Democratic Negotiations of Political Paradox* (Ithaca: Cornell University Press, 1991). See especially chapter 1.

4. For a brief description of the performance, see Janet Kardon, "Laurie Anderson: A Synesthesic Journey," in Kardon, ed., *Laurie Anderson: Works from 1969 to 1983* (Philadelphia: University of Pennsylvania, Institute of Contemporary Art, 1983), pp. 9–12.

5. See "Reading the Body: An Interview with Kathy Acker," *Mondo 2000*, Issue no. 4 (1991): 74.

6. For instance, see George Kateb, "Remarks on the Procedures of Constitutional Democracy," in J. Roland Pennock and John W. Chapman, eds., *Constitutionalism: Nomos XX* (New York: New York University Press, 1979), pp. 215–37. The same essay appears in George Kateb, *The Inner Ocean* (Ithaca: Cornell University Press, 1993), pp. 57–76. I will discuss American liberalism and Kateb's distinctive views concerning it in more detail later, especially in Chapters 2 and 6.

7. Bruce Ackerman, *We the People*, vol. 1, *Foundations* (Cambridge: Harvard University Press, 1991).

8. See Robert Cover, "Violence and the Word," *Yale Law Journal* 95 (1986), for a study of the negative elements of law. For an extension of Cover's analysis, see Thomas L. Dumm, "Fear of Law," in Austin Sarat and Susan Silbey, eds., *Studies in Law, Politics, and Society*, vol. 10 (Greenwich, Conn.: JAI, 1990).

9. On the exclusion of alternatives, see Walter Dean Burnham's prophetic book *The Current Crisis in American Politics* (New York: Oxford University Press, 1982).

10. See the introduction to Kateb, *Inner Ocean*. For a perspective on the robustness of liberalism as a popular cultural form, see Anne Norton, *Republic of Signs: Liberal Theory and Popular Culture* (Chicago: University of Chicago Press, 1993).

11. See Leo Bersani, *The Culture of Salvation* (Cambridge: Harvard University Press, 1989).

12. For a fascinating study of Bell, Watson, and the role played by ghosts in the early history of the telephone, see Avital Ronell, *The Telephone Book: Technology,*

Schizophrenia, Electric Speech (Lincoln: University of Nebraska Press, 1989), especially pp. 246–48.

13. It doesn't matter that Louis Hartz himself might be described as an innocent when he wrote his major work, *The Liberal Tradition in America* (New York: Harcourt Brace, 1955), even though it seems he got over his innocence by the time he died. For instance, see Patrick Riley's fascinating account of the late work of Hartz, "Louis Hartz: The Final Years, the Unknown Work," *Political Theory* 16 (May 1988): 377–99, as well as John Diggins's essay in the same issue, "Knowledge and Sorrow," pp. 355–76. I pursue a decidedly different direction from that of either Riley or Diggins here.

14. Hartz, *Liberal Tradition*, p. 65.

15. Among recent writers who have attempted to think through the complex social psychology of American guilt are Christopher Lasch, *The Culture of Narcissism* (New York: Norton, 1978), and, more important to me, Michael Rogin, *Ronald Reagan, the Movie and Other Episodes in American Political Demonology* (Berkeley and Los Angeles: University of California Press, 1987), and *Fathers and Children: Andrew Jackson and the Subjugation of the American Indian* (New York: Knopf, 1975). Neither Lasch nor Rogin would agree with the way I have connected them to Hartz. Lasch, for instance, sees the modern narcissist as a distinct character from the nineteenth-century individual (see *The Culture of Narcissism*, p. 8), and also understands Louis Hartz, simplistically in my view, as a celebrant of American consensus. Rogin explicitly distinguishes himself from Hartz in *Ronald Reagan, The Movie* (p.275), even though he understands that Hartz, as he puts it, "is in a class by himself among consensus historians" (pp. 351–52).

16. Thus, for instance, the weird unreality of the XYZ affair during the Washington administration. On the question of revolution in this regard, see Michel Foucault, "Power and Sex," in Lawrence Kritzman, ed., *Michel Foucault: Politics, Philosophy, Culture* (New York: Routledge, 1988), p. 124.

17. Don DeLillo, *White Noise* (New York: Viking, 1985), p. 218.

18. I think that the last incident in *White Noise*, which is Jack Gladney's son Wilder's pedaling his tricycle across a traffic-filled freeway, gestures to this complex of meaning. Even Wilder's name harbors promise of something more than we have now, a wilder child is being born.

19. See "How an 'Experience-Book' Is Born," in Michel Foucault, *Remarks on Marx*, trans. R. James Goldstein and James Cascaito (New York: Semiotext(e), 1991), p. 40.

2. Judith Shklar, or Fear of Liberalism

Epigraph taken from Judith Shklar, "The Liberalism of Fear," in Nancy Rosenblum, ed., *Liberalism and the Moral Life* (Cambridge: Harvard University Press, 1989).

1. Sheldon Wolin's influence on political theorists is hard to overestimate. See his *Politics and Vision* (Boston: Little, Brown, 1960).

2. Jean-Luc Nancy, "Our History," *Diacritics* 20 (Fall 1990): 106; quoted in Avital Ronell, "Support Our Tropes," in Frederick Dolan and Thomas Dumm, eds., *Rhetorical Republic: Governing Representations in American Politics* (Amherst: University of Massachusetts Press, 1993), p. 22.

3. See Judith Shklar's "Liberalism of Fear," in Rosenblum, ed., *Liberalism and the Moral Life*.

4. So too has George Kateb in a variety of essays, collected in *The Inner Ocean* (Ithaca: Cornell University Press, 1992).

5. The first version of this chapter was written in the summer of 1991 and given as a paper at the American Political Science Association annual meeting. I mention this because at the time of Judith Shklar's death in the autumn of 1992, there had not yet appeared any critical appraisal of her political theory. As this book goes to press, that statement remains true.

6. For a discussion of the development of new forms of representation and their varying impacts on capitalist civilization, see Jean François Lyotard, *The Postmodern Condition: A Report on Knowledge*, trans. Geoff Bennington and Brian Massumi (Minneapolis: University of Minnesota Press, 1984). For a provocative response to Lyotard that develops his argument along sociopolitical lines, see Anthony Giddens, *The Consequences of Modernity* (Stanford: Stanford University Press, 1990).

7. Shklar, "Liberalism of Fear," p. 21.

8. Ibid., p. 22.

9. For a different view of toleration, see Kirstie McClure, "Difference, Diversity, and the Limits of Toleration," *Political Theory* 18 (August 1989).

10. Shklar, "Liberalism of Fear," p. 24.

11. Ibid., pp. 24–25.

12. Michael Walzer, "Liberalism and the Art of Separation," *Political Theory* 12 (August 1984).

13. Shklar, "Liberalism of Fear," p. 29.

14. Ibid.

15. Ibid.

16. Here I am summarizing, at best, one of the underlying arguments in Judith Shklar's *Faces of Injustice* (New Haven: Yale University Press, 1990), especially her discussion of Mrs. Bardell of Dickens's *Pickwick Papers*, on pp. 12–14.

17. This is best demonstrated by Shklar in her discussion of the shortchanged customer in the supermarket (ibid., pp. 43–45). Here she demonstrates through a hypothetical example the banal and ordinary ways in which people will redefine an injustice as a misfortune to escape being bothered by it. I return to this question in Shklar's discussion of Michael Kohlhaas and Coalhouse Walker. I return to questions about the supermarket in Chapter 6.

18. Ibid., pp. 95–101. All subsequent quotations from Shklar on injustice will be taken from these pages, unless otherwise noted.

19. Ibid., p. 124. Here Shklar cites George Kateb, "Remarks on the Procedures of Constitutional Democracy," in J. Roland Pennock and John W. Chapman, eds., *Constitutionalism, Nomos XX* (New York: New York University Press, 1979), pp. 215–37. Shklar suggests that procedural rules "create their own characters of

forbearance and propriety as well as forcing the restraints of fairness on public agents." In short, just procedures create good manners.

20. Judith Shklar, *American Citizenship: The Quest for Inclusion* (Cambridge: Harvard University Press, 1990), pp. 2–3.

21. Ibid., p. 14.

22. Ibid., pp. 22–23.

23. Ibid., p. 55.

24. Ibid., p. 63.

25. Ibid., pp. 81–84.

26. Ibid., p. 79 and pp. 96–97.

27. Shklar comes close to making such a connection herself. She writes, "The poor are social victims who are being denied racial equality, opportunities for decent work and education, and access to normal public goods" (ibid., p. 97). One need only point out that most poor people in American are white to see that there is a racism involved in equating poverty with minority racial status. If Shklar's sentence is parsed another way, however, the connection is not determinative, but associative. (One needs to suggest that she means, by "the poor," not a unity, but a variety of people who are poor.)

28. Ibid., p. 63. Shklar would not claim that everyone accepts the idea that a right to work ought to be pursued through public means. So many have not been able to divorce their feelings concerning relief from the dignity of work (for Shklar this failure is yet another inheritance of slavery) that it is unclear that most would make the right to work even secondary to and derived from the requirements of local citizenship (ibid., p. 100).

29. Ibid., p. 101.

30. For an alternative discussion of the role of toleration in the liberal tradition in America, see Thomas L. Dumm, *Democracy and Punishment: Disciplinary Origins of the United States* (Madison: University of Wisconsin Press, 1987), chap. 3.

31. See Michael Walzer, "The Civil Society Argument," in Chantal Mouffe, ed., *Dimensions of Radical Democracy* (London: Verso, 1993), p. 89. Walzer's essay is a revised and extended version of "The Idea of Civil Society," *Dissent* (Spring 1991). It was delivered as the Gynnar Myrdal Lecture at the University of Stockholm, October 1990. I refer to both versions in my discussion here.

32. Walzer, "Civil Society Argument," p. 97, and "Idea of Civil Society," p. 228.

33. Walzer, "Civil Society Argument," p. 98. In "Idea of Civil Society," Walzer's phrasing is slightly different: "the setting of settings, where each can find the partial fulfillment that is all it deserves" (p. 304). The shift away from the moralistic conclusion of desert in the latter version is paralleled by the softening of terminology later in the essay as well.

34. Walzer, "Idea of Civil Society," p. 304. In the later version, "The Civil Society Argument," Walzer substitutes the word "pluralized," for the phrase "fragmented and localized" (see p. 107). The rhetorical purpose seems clear. Incorporation moves from diminishing and causing violence to groups to making them open and multivalent. Yet perhaps Walzer thinks (as I do) that to pluralize *is* to fragment and localize.

35. In making this admission, Walzer does nothing to advance an argument. He just *seems* to. On the rhetorical functions of such moves, see William E. Connolly, "Democracy and Territoriality," in Dolan and Dumm, eds., *Rhetorical Republic.*

36. Walzer, "Civil Society Argument," p. 107, and "Idea of Civil Society," p. 304. One might note in passing that "God" has been replaced here by "the good life." One might also note how Walzer's rhetoric echoes the themes of Foucault, except that Walzer places an unambiguously positive valence on the strategies of state power.

37. See note 34.

38. On governmentality, see Colin Gordon's introduction to Graham Burchell, Colin Gordon, and Peter Miller, eds., *The Foucault Effect: Essays in Governmentality* (Chicago: University of Chicago Press, 1991). "Governmentality" refers here to the techniques of administration shared by policy-making and implementing bodies, regardless of their status as public or private.

39. For me the most important recent statement on the lack of participation in American politics remains Walter Dean Burnham, *The Current Crisis in American Politics* (New York: Oxford University Press, 1982). Other studies that have focused on lack of participation include several by Frances Fox Piven and Richard Cloward, most prominently among them, *Why Americans Don't Vote* (New York: Pantheon, 1988). See also Benjamin Barber, *Strong Democracy* (Berkeley and Los Angeles: University of California Press, 1984), for a more theoretically attuned argument that deemphasizes the importance of elections in favor of watching interactive television.

40. See Theodore Lowi, *The End of Liberalism*, 2d ed. (New York: Norton, 1979).

41. See Benjamin Ginsberg, *The Captive Public: How Mass Opinion Promotes State Power* (New York: Basic Books, 1986), and Ginsberg and Martin Shefter, *Politics by Other Means: The Declining Importance of Elections in America* (New York: Basic Books, 1990).

42. In fact, although Shklar suggests that no "scholars have found the [26th] amendment fascinating" (*American Citizenship*, p. 106 n. 15), she was overlooking the analysis that Benjamin Ginsberg provides in *The Consequences of Consent: Elections, Citizen Control, and Popular Acquiescence* (Reading, Mass.: Addison-Wesley, 1982).

43. Ginsberg, *Captive Public*, p. 184.

44. Ibid., p. 185 and the chapter "Polling and the Transformation of Public Opinion."

45. Ibid., pp. x and 232.

46. For this argument, see Kateb, "Individualism, Communitarianism, and Docility," in *Inner Ocean.*

47. I address in more detail such practices, which have been usefully characterized as "normalizing" by Michel Foucault, in Chapter 4. There I also ask if it may be the case that normalization is entering a postdisciplinary phase.

48. See Giddens, *Consequences of Modernity.* In fact, a central element in Giddens's argument is one that follows close on Foucault's argument (and Ewald's gloss on Foucault) concerning risk and danger. Giddens suggests that the globalization of

risk that has accompanied modernity is the most important sociological fact of the modern age.

49. Walzer, "Civil Society Argument," p. 304.

50. In making this claim, I am not suggesting that all political theorists need to turn into political economists. I do, however, think that it is nonsensical for liberals to assert that they have advanced a critical view of the world of liberal democracy without having accounted for the role that corporate values have played in the constitution of civil society. Moreover, the very phenomenon of corporatism is associated with the intensification of forces of technology in the twentieth century. Of the recent literature on both the enormous problems associated with the development of Heidegger's thesis on technology and the imperative to think through it, there are three studies that bear special attention. See Kateb, *Inner Ocean*; Philippe Lacoue-Labarthe, *Heidegger, Art and Politics*, trans. Chris Turner (New York: Basil Blackwell, 1990); and perhaps most important for this essay because of its forceful depiction of the history of American technology, Avital Ronell, *The Telephone Book: Technology, Schizophrenia, Electric Speech* (Lincoln: University of Nebraska Press, 1989).

51. See Alexis de Tocqueville, *Democracy in America*, trans. George Lawrence, ed. J. P. Mayer (New York: Harper & Row, 1966), from the 12th ed., 1848, vol. 2, part 2, chap. 20, "How an Aristocracy May Be Created by Industry," pp. 555–58.

52. Kateb, *Inner Ocean*, p. 229. For the original discussion in Tocqueville, see *Democracy in America*, vol. 2, part 4, chap. 6, "What Sort of Despotism Democracies Have to Fear," pp. 690–95.

53. Kateb acknowledges more depth in Foucault's analysis than most liberals do, but I would argue that he does not go far enough in this essay. His final call, that those who admire Foucault should "work to rehabilitate individualism" (p. 239), seems to me to apply most clearly to him. In the wisdom of Pee-Wee Herman, "Every time you point your finger at me, three of them are pointing back at you."

54. For a critique of Kateb that emphasizes the nihilistic elements of his argument, see William E. Connolly, *Identity/Difference: Democratic Negotiations of Political Paradox* (Ithaca: Cornell University Press, 1991), pp. 84–85. As his most severe rebuke of Kateb, Connolly writes, "In a highly structured state, an episodic, juridical politics of dissent against extreme atrocities lapses into a nonpolitics of nihilistic consent to the everyday extension of discipline and normalization—the most ominous form nihilism assumes today" (p.95). I do not wish to repudiate Kateb's appeal to individuality; rather, I want to politicize it, make it turn toward, not away from politics. I return to this theme in the conclusion of this essay.

55. Much of this criticism is blunted by Kateb's tireless efforts to qualify his conclusions regarding the relative damages of corporation and state. He is especially concessionary in the introduction to *Inner Ocean*.

56. Shklar, "Liberalism of Fear," p. 31.

57. On some of the problems endemic to the political economy of late capitalism that flow from the incoherence of corporate strategies of economic control, see Claus Offe, *Disorganized Capitalism*, ed. John Keane (Cambridge: MIT Press, 1985).

58. This oversight seems especially surprising in light of Shklar's emphasis on cruelty. I will return to this puzzle in the final section of this chapter.

59. In the popular movie *Bladerunner* (Ridley Scott, 1982), the replicant, in his final confrontation with the bounty hunter asks, "How does it feel to live in fear? That's what it means to be a slave."

60. Jonathan Simon, "Don't Shoot Me Please, Mr. Stagolee: Violence, Discipline, and the Bodies of Young Black Men" (paper presented to the Law and Society Association Annual Meeting, Amsterdam, Netherlands, June 1991).

61. Ibid., pp. 7–10.

62. O. O. Howard, *Report of the Assistant Commissioners of the Freedman's Bureau*, 39th Cong., 1st sess., 1866, S. Doc. 27, serial 1238. Cited in ibid., p. 16.

63. See Dumm, *Democracy and Punishment*, chap. 5.

64. Simon, "Don't Shoot Me Please, Mr. Stagolee," pp. 17–18.

65. Ibid., pp. 23–29.

66. See, for example, Gerald David Jaynes, *Branches without Roots: Genesis of the Black Working Class in the American South, 1862–1882* (New York: Oxford University Press, 1986). Jaynes is clear that newly freed slaves for a time took control of their economic destiny in confrontation with their former masters. But by the 1870s, after intense labor-planter conflict, which resulted in theft of cotton and vandalism (on the part of both freedmen and planters), the control of state legislatures by Democrats resulted in criminal laws so severe that the freedmen were effectively reenslaved. "For instance, a negro is charged with stealing. . . . He is brought before the police court [police courts were usually controlled by the Ku Klux Klan], and tried and convicted. . . . The judge almost invariably binds him over in some very small amount; whereupon some planter, anxious for labor, will come in and go on his bond, take him out, and pay the thing in full. . . . This is I might say, the universal system." Taken from the testimony of Andrew Currie, mayor of Shrevesport, Louisiana, as quoted in Jaynes, pp. 306–7.

67. See Rodolphe Gasché, *The Tain of the Mirror: Derrida and the Philosophy of Reflection* (Cambridge: Harvard University Press, 1986). I refer specifically to this passage: "*Tain*, a word altered from the French e'tain, according to the OED, refers to the tinfoil, the silver lining, the lusterless back of the mirror. Derrida's philosophy, rather than being a philosophy of reflection, is engaged in the systematic exploration of that dull surface without which no reflection and no specular and speculative activity would be possible, but which at the same time has no place and no part in reflection's scintillating play" (p. 6).

68. Jaynes, *Branches without Roots*, pp. 253–61.

69. Michael Rogin, *Ronald Reagan, the Movie* (Berkeley and Los Angeles: University of California Press, 1987), pp. 190–235.

70. Ibid., p. 228.

71. Ibid., p. 207.

72. Ibid., p. 215.

73. For a trenchant presentation on the use of Willie Horton in the 1988 election, see Anne Norton, "Representation and the Silences of Politics," in *Republic of Signs* (Chicago: University of Chicago Press, 1993).

74. For a more extended discussion of issues of gender and race, see Chapters 4 and 5.

75. See Brenda Bright, "Remappings: Los Angeles Lowriders," in Bright and Elizabeth Bakewell, eds., *Looking High and Low: Art and Cultural Identity* (Tucson: University of Arizona Press, 1995).

76. On this point see George Lipsitz, *Time Passages* (Minneapolis: University of Minnesota Press, 1990), pp. 21–36. On another plane, this is also a point made by Judith Butler in her argument concerning performative identity. See Judith Butler, *Gender Trouble: Feminism and the Subversion of Identity* (New York: Routledge, 1990).

77. E. L. Doctorow, *Ragtime* (New York: Random House, 1975), pp. 132–34. For an important discussion of the politics of blackface, see Michael Rogin, "Blackface, White Noise: The Jewish Jazz Singer Finds His Voice" (paper presented to the annual meeting of the Conference for the Study of Political Thought, Yale University, April 1991).

78. Doctorow, *Ragtime*, p. 145; my emphasis.

79. Ibid., p. 226. "Then Coalhouse made a quick inspection of the premises. Nothing is lost, he assured them. We wanted the man and so we have him since we have his property."

80. Ibid., pp. 269–70.

81. Ibid., p. 111.

82. I discuss looking and listening in Chapter 6.

83. For a radical interpretation/negotiation/demonstration of the power of electronic technology, see Ronell, *Telephone Book*. On an alternative concept of the monitor, see Stanley Cavell, "The Fact of Television," in *Themes Out of School* (Chicago: University of Chicago Press, 1988).

84. For an analysis of the function of copyright in corporate control of culture, see Rosemary Coombe, "Objects of Property and Subjects of Politics: Intellectual Property Law and Democratic Dialogue," *University of Texas Law Review* (forthcoming).

85. For a fuller argument concerning the politics of art in this regard, see Thomas L. Dumm, "The Politics of Post-Modern Aesthetics: Habermas Contra Foucault," *Political Theory* 16 (May 1988).

86. I address at greater length some expressions of such violence in Chapters 3 through 5.

87. Shklar, "Liberalism of Fear," pp. 37–38.

88. Judith Shklar, "Torturers," review of *The Body in Pain: The Making and Unmaking of the World*, by Elaine Scarry, *London Review of Books*, 9 October 1986, pp. 26–27.

89. This point is overlooked completely by James Miller in his endorsement of Shklar's argument concerning cruelty. See his "Carnivals of Atrocity: Foucault, Nietzsche, Cruelty," *Political Theory* 18 (August 1989): 487.

90. This is one of the most important points made by Michael Sandel in *Liberalism and the Limits of Justice* (Cambridge: Cambridge University Press, 1982). The roar of battle that accompanied that book, and the subsequent reduction of it to canonical text of the communitarians, has, I think, obscured this dimension of it.

On this subject see Bonnie Honig, *Political Theory and the Displacement of Politics* (Ithaca: Cornell University Press, 1993).

91. For figures on the increase in the activities of death squads, see Amnesty International, *1991 Annual Report Summary* (Washington, D.C.: Amnesty International U.S.A., 1991). The desire to totally efface the object of torture is horrible, it is perhaps the most horrible political development of the twentieth century. That needs to be stated, I think, any time one raises the subject.

92. See *Wilson v. Seiter*, 111 S. Ct. 2321 (1991).

93. The *Los Angeles Times*, 5 July 1991, p. A28, reported three deaths from heat prostration on July 3 in the California state prison at Vacaville. Temperatures inside that prison regularly exceed 100 degrees Fahrenheit in summer and the cell of one of the three prisoners who died reached 124 degrees that day. The prisoners who died were all being administered mood-altering drugs (which are often used as a form of control in maximum security prisons), which have the side effect of raising body temperatures. At least one of the prisoners had a body temperature as measured by a prison doctor in excess of 111 degrees. The name of this prison, which is designed to house mentally disturbed inmates, is the California Medical Facility.

94. For an overview of recent theories concerning crime policy and the use of demography see James Q. Wilson, ed., *Crime and Public Policy* (San Francisco: ICS, 1983). For fuller discussion of this theme, as well as a critique of Wilson, see Chapter 4.

95. It may be objected that Shklar is clear in her opposition to racism, and generally to the discrimination against people on the basis of attributes beyond their control. But the standards for constructing profiles are not racist in a volitional sense. They do not render judgments concerning individuals, but concerning *profiles*, that is, artificial constructs, composed not of persons, but of fragmented attributes partially shared by some members of some groups. There is no single attribute uniting members of a group here, such as black skin. Instead, there are descriptions, such as "young black male on foot dressed wearing gang colors," and so on.

96. Michel Foucault, "Two Lectures," in *Power/Knowledge*, ed. Colin Gordon (New York: Pantheon, 1980), p. 96.

97. Ibid., p. 108.

98. Shklar, "Liberalism of Fear," p. 29.

99. Michel Foucault, *The Care of the Self*, vol. 3 of *The History of Sexuality*, trans. Robert Hurley (New York: Pantheon, 1986), p. 135.

100. For an argument concerning liberalism's disembodiment, see Anne Norton, "Engendering Another American Identity," in Dolan and Dumm, eds., *Rhetorical Republic*.

101. Here I am borrowing language that Richard Flathman takes from Nietzsche. See Flathman, "Voluntarism, Individuality, and Liberalism," part 2 of *Willful Liberalism* (Ithaca: Cornell University Press, 1992).

102. Ibid., pp. 211–12.

103. Ibid., p. 218. Flathman cites the work of Stanley Cavell here. This is most appropriate. The idea of the ordinary containing within it more than itself is a

notion associated with Emerson and one communicated with the most grace these days by Cavell. See especially his *In Quest of the Ordinary* (Chicago: University of Chicago Press, 1988). The intent is often expressed by Kateb as well, though he focuses less often on such prosaic moments in his own writing. See for instance, George Kateb, "Some Rigidities in the Study of Political Theory," in John Nelson, ed., *Tradition, Interpretation and Science: Political Theory in the American Academy* (Albany: SUNY Press, 1986). There, in arguing against consistency, Kateb borrows from William Butler Yeats to refer to theories as "mist and snow" (p. 140).

104. On the role that the idea of emergency plays in liberal theory as a form of *supplement*, see Thomas L. Popejoy, "Thoughts on the Traffic in Liberalism" (Johns Hopkins University, Department of Political Science, 1991). See also Mick Taussig, "Terror as Usual: Walter Benjamin's Theory of History as State of Siege," *Social Text* 7 (Spring 1989). I revisit the theme of emergency in Chapter 6.

105. I take this to be Walter Benjamin's point in "Theses on the Philosophy of History," in *Illuminations*, ed. Hannah Arendt (New York: Schocken, 1969), when he writes, "One reason Fascism has a chance is that in the name of progress its opponents treat it as a historical norm. The current amazement that the things we are experiencing are 'still' possible in the twentieth century is *not* philosophical" (p. 257).

106. Walter Benjamin, "Surrealism: The Last Snapshot of the European Intelligentsia," in *Reflections*, ed. Peter Demetz (New York: Harcourt, Brace, Jovanovich, 1978), p. 192.

3. George Bush, or Sex in the Superior Position

Epigraph taken from the special bookseller's preview of Mikal Gilmore, *Shot in the Heart* (New York: Doubleday, 1994), p. 5. My thanks to Mark Wootton of Wootton's Bookstore in Amherst for giving me his copy of this extraordinary memoir.

1. Although this sentence was written earlier, it now (inevitably) refers to President George Bush's pardoning of Casper Weinberger and five other officials involved in the Iran-Contra scandal. See the *New York Times*, 25 December 1992, p. 9, for Bush's statement.

2. John Rajchman, *Truth and Eros: Foucault, Lacan, and the Question of Ethics* (New York: Routledge, 1991), p. 41.

3. Report on George Bush, speaking in Twin Falls, Idaho, reported in the *New York Times*, 12 May 1988, p. A32.

4. I do not mean to suggest we share a similar class background, which is in many ways a decisive fact concerning Bush. For the record, technically, I could be described as from a petit-bourgeois background, with emphasis on the petit.

5. *Regarding Henry*, the 1991 vehicle for Harrison Ford. The basic conceit I express here was first presented in a review of the film by Tom Shales on National Public Radio.

6. A recent example of the use of this technique is Michael Rogin's *Ronald Reagan, the Movie, and Other Studies in American Political Demonology* (Berkeley and

Los Angeles: University of California Press, 1987). On the psychology of Reagan, see also Garry Will, *Innocents at Home* (New York: Basic Books, 1986).

7. Eve Kosofsky Sedgwick, *Between Men: English Literature and Male Homosocial Desire* (New York: Columbia University Press, 1985), pp. 10–11. See also her more recent essay "Across Gender, Across Sexuality: Willa Cather and Others," *South Atlantic Quarterly* 88 (Winter 1989). In that essay, Sedgwick attempts to build distinctions between sexuality and gender. Also see her *Epistemology of the Closet* (Berkeley and Los Angeles: University of California Press, 1991).

8. Sedgwick, *Between Men*, p. 4.

9. Ibid., p. 20.

10. For a trenchant analysis of the "realpolitik" behind the war in Iraq, see Christopher Hitchins, "Why We Are Stuck in the Sand," *Harpers*, January 1991.

11. On the rituals and violence of our fraternities, see Peggy Sanday, *Fraternity Gang Rape* (New York: NYU Press, 1990).

12. An analysis of Bush as a male hysteric has been developed convincingly by Diane Rubenstein. See "This Is Not a President: Baudrillard, Bush, and Enchanted Simulation," in Arthur Kroker and Mary Louise Kroker, eds., *The Hysterical Male: New Feminist Theory* (New York: St. Martin's, 1991).

13. See, for example, Kathy Ferguson, *The Man Question* (Berkeley and Los Angeles: University of California Press, 1993).

14. See Sigmund Freud, *Jokes and Their Relation to the Unconscious*, trans. and ed. James Strachey (New York: Norton, 1963), pp. 96–97.

15. Ibid., p. 97.

16. Ibid.

17. Ibid., p. 99.

18. Ibid., p. 103.

19. Norman Mailer, *The Executioner's Song* (New York: Warner, 1979), p. 149.

20. On the dangerous individual and the psychiatrization of violent crime, see Michel Foucault, "The Dangerous Individual," trans. Alan Baudot and Jane Couchman, with reference to a translation by Carol Brown, in Lawrence Kritzman, ed., *Michel Foucault* (London: Routledge, 1988).

21. William E. Connolly, *Political Theory and Modernity* (1988; Ithaca: Cornell University Press, 1993), p. 79.

22. Ibid., p. 83.

23. In this sense, one can think about the old joke employed so well in the various movie and stage versions of *Little Shop of Horrors*, concerning the sadistic dentist who is frustrated when he has a masochist as his patient. The paradox is not so dissimilar to that of the pornographer. It is perhaps similar to the famous example on which much of modern formal theorizing is based, the "Prisoner's Dilemma."

24. For a brilliant analysis of the Meese Commission's report, see Susan Stewart, "The Marquis de Meese," *Critical Inquiry* 15 (Autumn 1988).

25. It is interesting to note that the state almost never needs to get involved when the question is one of "high" literature or academic discourse. One might think about the recent scandal involving the publication of Salman Rushdie's novel, *The Satanic Verses* (New York: Penguin, 1989). It took an internationally issued death threat to focus writers' attention on the problem of the book being censored, but the

manner in which the defense has proceeded has been in effect to give Rushdie permission, or the right, to be blasphemous. No one in the West takes the charge of obscenity seriously. Such a discussion might reveal the limits of toleration of some of these writers. One might compare the defense of Rushdie with the earlier censorship of Thomas Pynchon's *Gravity's Rainbow*, which in the early 1970s was denied a Pulitzer Prize because the Pulitzer committee overruled its own jury to declare the novel "obscene." Defenses of Pynchon, rather than allow it to be obscene and defend the obscene, had to explain something patently untrue, how it somehow *wasn't* obscene. The Pulitzer committee wasn't so reluctant later on when it awarded the prize to Norman Mailer's *Executioner's Song*. Obscenity, in a few years, had become literature.

On a similar note, because of the context of its production and dissemination, a recent issue of *Semiotext(e)*, which featured pictorials that would rival anything in "hardcore" pornographic circles, failed to even raise an eyebrow in intellectual circles.

26. Klaus Theweleit, *Male Fantasies*, vol. 1, *Women, Floods, Bodies, History*, trans. Steven Conway, in collaboration with Erica Carter and Chris Turner (Minneapolis: University of Minnesota Press, 1987), pp. 55–56.

27. Ibid., p. 55. The passage under discussion is from Theodor Adorno, *Minima Moralia, Reflections from Damaged Life*, trans. E. J. N. Jephcott (London: Verso, 1974), pp. 45–46.

28. This question animated Foucault in his study of sexuality. See, for instance, Foucault's preface to *Herculine Barbin, Being the Recently Discovered Memoirs of a Nineteenth Century French Hermaphrodite*, trans. Richard McDougall (New York: Pantheon, 1980).

29. This is what seems to be at stake in Theweleit's use of Norbert Elias's *Civilizing Process* (New York: Urizen, 1978). Elias's study is one of the first modern attempts to demonstrate the intimate relationship between social codes of etiquette and bodily transformations.

30. Adorno, *Minima Moralia*, p. 46.

31. For a contrasting view of the function of the *practice* of sadomasochism, see Foucault, "Sexual Choice, Sexual Act," in Kritzman, ed., *Michel Foucault*, p. 299.

32. Adorno, *Minima Moralia*, p. 46.

33. "The mirror stage as formative of the function of the I as revealed in psychoanalytical experience" (Jacques Lacan, *Ecrits, a Selection*, trans. Alan Sheridan [New York: Norton, 1977], pp. 1–7).

34. Ibid., pp. 2–3.

35. Susan Buck-Morss, "Aesthetics and Anaesthetics: Walter Benjamin's Artwork Essay Reconsidered," *October* 62 (Fall 1992): 3–41. This part of Buck-Morss's analysis rests heavily on Hal Foster's essay, "Armor Fou," *October* 57 (Spring 1991): 65–81. One might note that war trauma also informs the Benjaminian insight into the modern "state of emergency."

36. Buck-Morss, "Aesthetics and Anaesthetics," p. 37.

37. Mailer titled his most explicitly comic novel *Tough Guys Don't Dance*. The protagonist is trying to *quit* smoking, among other vices.

38. Mailer, *Executioner's Song*, p. 142.

39. Ibid., pp. 363–64.

40. Ibid., p. 155.

41. Ibid., p. 335.

42. Foucault, "Dangerous Individual," p. 128.

43. Ibid., pp. 134–35.

44. Foucault, "Sexual Morality and the Law," in Kritzman, ed., *Michel Foucault*, p. 275. The comment on *attentat sans violence* is borrowed from Guy Hocquenghem in the same interview, p. 278.

45. On the dustcover to his biography of Foucault, James Miller tries to exempt himself from the accusations he hurls at Foucault by describing himself as living with his wife and two sons. See Miller, *The Passion of Michel Foucault*.

46. Mailer, *Executioner's Song*, pp. 853–54.

47. Farrell looks at this letter after reviewing an interview with Gilmore in which Gilmore had requested some child pornography (a sex education book called *Show Me*, of which Gilmore claimed, "It's not a piece of smut" [ibid., p. 855]).

48. Ibid., p. 855.

49. For "The Time of Her Time," see Norman Mailer, *Advertisements for Myself* (Boston: Little, Brown, 1958). Also see *Harlot's Ghost* (New York: Random House, 1991), pp. 287–97.

50. Jack Henry Abbott, *In the Belly of the Beast*, introduction by Norman Mailer (New York: Harper & Row, 1981), p. xi.

51. Ibid., p. xii.

52. Ibid., p. xiii.

53. For a supporting argument regarding the limits of Rawlsian toleration, see the chapter on Rawls and punishment in Bonnie Honig's *Political Theory and the Displacement of Politics* (Ithaca: Cornell University Press, 1993).

54. Abbott, *Belly of the Beast*, p. xiii.

55. Ibid., p. 119.

56. See Jack Henry Abbott, "Epistle to Paul," in *My Return* (Buffalo, N.Y.: Prometheus, 1987), p. 196.

57. Robert Cover, "Violence and the Word," *Yale Law Journal* 95 (1986): 1629. In Chapter 6 I address the problematic and yet helpful dimensions of this text.

58. Abbott, *Belly of the Beast*, p. 78.

59. See Wilbert Rideau, "The Sexual Jungle," in Rideau and Ron Wikberg, *Life Sentences: Rage and Survival behind Bars* (New York: Times Books, 1992), p. 75.

60. Abbott, *Belly of the Beast*, p. 106.

61. Michel Foucault, *Discipline and Punish: The Birth of the Prison*, trans. Alan Sheridan (New York: Pantheon, 1977), p. 30.

62. Abbott, *Belly of the Beast*, pp. 13–14.

63. In fact, the first section of Abbott's *In the Belly of the Beast* is titled "State Raised Convict."

64. Abbott, *Belly of the Beast*, p. xi.

65. See Nicholas von Hoffman, *Citizen Cohn* (New York: Doubleday, 1988), for a thorough examination of Cohn's career and private life. On Cohn's relationship to Shine, see pp. 188–93.

66. This denial is fabulously expressed by Tony Kushner in his play *Angels in*

America: Part One, Millennium Approaches (New York: Theatre Communications Group, 1993). Kushner's Cohn says this in response to his doctor, while denying that he is homosexual: "Homosexuals are not men who sleep with other men. Homosexuals are men who in fifteen years of trying cannot get a pissant anti-discrimination bill through City Council. . . . I have sex with men. But unlike nearly every other man of whom this is true, I bring the guy I'm screwing to the White House and Ronald Reagan smiles at us and shakes his hand. Because *what* I am is defined entirely by *who* I am. Roy Cohn is not a homosexual. Roy Cohn is a heterosexual man, Henry, who fucks around with guys" (pp. 45–46).

67. Von Hoffman discusses at length the evolution of social attitudes toward homosexuality in Washington and New York political circles. See *Citizen Cohn*, pp. 228–33.

68. Ibid., pp. 63–64.

69. Ibid., pp. 120–21.

70. See Sidney Zion's *Autobiography of Roy Cohn* (Secaucus, N.J.: Lyle Stuart, 1988). Zion collaborated with Cohn and then finished the book after his death. For reasons having to do as much with Cohn's tax liability as anything else, Zion is listed as the sole author of the work, which he compiled from taped recollections Cohn dictated as he was dying.

71. Von Hoffman, *Citizen Cohn*, p. 283.

72. See Richard Gid Powers, *Secrecy and Power: The Life of J. Edgar Hoover* (New York: Free Press, 1987), pp. 19–20.

73. Ibid., pp. 196–209.

74. Ibid., p. 210.

75. Ibid.

76. Ibid.

77. Rogin, *Ronald Reagan, the Movie*, p. 106.

78. Theweleit, *Male Fantasies*, pp. 410–11.

79. Ibid., p. 412.

80. Powers, *Secrecy and Power*, p. 59.

81. Anthony Summers, *Official and Confidential: The Secret Life of J. Edgar Hoover* (New York: G. P. Putnam's Sons, 1993).

82. Ibid., p. 255.

83. One can only wonder what passages were being read to him. The Bible as a source of pornographic writing is a tendentious dirty joke of the highest order.

84. Ibid., p. 254.

85. For a valuable analysis of the cultural politics of cross-dressing, see Marjorie Garber, *Vested Interests: Cross-Dressing and Cultural Anxiety* (New York: Routledge, 1992). Garber presents a useful discussion of the idea of the "third" term in her introduction. See pp. 10–12.

86. For a discussion of Hoover's antipathy to Ethel Rosenberg on these grounds, see Ronald Radosh and Joyce Milton, *The Rosenberg File: A Search for the Truth* (New York: Holt, Rinehart & Winston, 1983), p. 376. For an excellent discussion of the relationship between Hoover and Ethel Rosenberg, see Virginia Carmichael, *Framing History: The Rosenberg Story and the Cold War* (Minneapolis: University of Minnesota Press, 1993), pp. 202–3.

87. Carmichael, *Framing History*, p. 102.

88. Ibid., p. 103. Carmichael notes that this psychological profile was used repeatedly in various accounts and official reports on the Rosenberg case.

89. Summers, *Official and Confidential*, p. 254.

90. Rogin discusses the obsession with the excremental that informed Richard Nixon's thought. See his chapter on Nixon and Lincoln, "The King's Two Bodies," in *Ronald Reagan, The Movie*, pp. 81–114.

91. For a study of the relationship of Bush to Nixon, see Stanley Blumenthal, *Pledging Allegiance: The Last Campaign of the Cold War* (New York: Simon & Shuster, 1989).

92. The details of Reagan's life are best described by Reagan himself. See Ronald Reagan, with Richard Hubler, *Where's the Rest of Me?* (New York: Karz-Segil, 1965). It is worth noting that Reagan spends a total of two paragraphs discussing his marriage and divorce from Jane Wyman, including the children they had together. Michael, an adopted son, he notes, suffered the most pain. But he doesn't ask why, and doesn't seek to explain himself. On that topic, he states, "I have never discussed what happened, and I have no intention of doing so now" (p. 202). Reagan himself throughout demonstrates his unquestioning attachment to and loyalty for older men who in his mythical rendering unerringly gave him advice on how to advance through life. Never in the entire book does he question authority, except in the context of demonstrating the error of his ways and the goodness of their ways.

93. Michael Shapiro brought this incident to my attention.

94. All quotations from the second presidential debate of 13 October 1988, at Pauly Pavilion at UCLA in Los Angeles, are transcribed from video obtained from Vanderbilt Television News Archive, Vanderbilt University, Nashville, Tennessee.

95. Some have suggested that if Dukakis had responded by saying that he would have wanted to kill the rapist, but that he is thankful that here in the United States rule by law prevails, so that justice prevents private vengeance, he would have turned the campaign around, or at least have held his ground. (Two thoughtful correspondents, George Kateb and Jean Elshtain, made precisely that argument to me in response to a draft of this essay.) But such a response, it seems to me, reflects a nostalgia for a time when we could see such a gap between private and public discourse. I think that few members of the voting public are prepared to accept the legitimacy of a claim such as the one Dukakis might have made.

96. "North's Opinion of CIA Decoded," *Los Angeles Times*, 12 April 1989, sec. 1, p. 4.

97. Susan Page, "A Kinder, Gentler Spate of Quayle Jokes," *Los Angeles Times*, 16 May 1989, sec. 5, p. 1.

98. Adorno, *Minima Moralia*, p. 247.

4. Rodney King, or The New Enclosures

Epigraph taken from Jane Gross, "In Simi Valley, Defense of a Shared Way of Life," *New York Times*, 3 May 1992, p. A12.

1. Slavoj Žižek, *The Sublime Object of Ideology* (New York: Verso, 1989), p. 28.

2. The term "open-air carceral" is one I borrow from Richard Flathman.

3. See Cornel West, "Nihilism in Black America," in *Race Matters* (Boston: Beacon, 1993), p. 19.

4. See Marie-Hélène Huet, "Monstrous Imagination: Progeny as Art in French Classicism," *Critical Inquiry* 17 (Summer 1991): 725. This essay has since been incorporated into her book *Monstrous Imagination* (Cambridge: Harvard University Press, 1993).

5. My knowledge of gangsters is largely derived from Leon Bing, *Do or Die* (New York: HarperCollins, 1992), from conversations with Brenda Bright, who has had more direct encounters with gang members than I have, and from eight months spent living in East Los Angeles. I should add that while living in East Los Angeles, I did not interview gangsters, rather I came to know children in the neighborhood who, I eventually learned, were members of gangs. My remarks concerning gangsters are thus particularly tentative.

6. See George Lipsitz, "Knowing Their Place: Street Artists, Communities, and the Politics of Space," in Donna Graves, ed., *Shared Spaces: Collaboration in Contemporary Public Art in the United States, 1975–1990* (forthcoming).

7. Michael Rogin, *Ronald Reagan, the Movie, and Other Episodes in American Political Demonology* (Berkeley and Los Angeles: University of California Press, 1987), p. 285.

8. Ibid., p. 290. I will contest Rogin's point that women are cast as monsters below. They *produce* monsters, which is an important distinction.

9. Ibid., p. 291.

10. Ibid., p. 207.

11. The recent spectacle in Washington concerning the confirmation of Clarence Thomas in the face of accusations of sexual harassment by Anita Hill is a dense thicket of these complications. For an exposition of these issues concerning the psychosexual grievances of African American men against African American women, see Michele Wallace, *Black Macho and the Myth of the Superwoman* (New York: Routledge, 1991). Also see the Greg Tate review of the Hill-Thomas confrontation, *Village Voice*, 17 October 1991.

12. I use the term ghostly in a very specific sense. See Toni Morrison, *Beloved* (New York: Dial, 1988).

13. The interview occurred on National Public Radio, *Morning Edition*, 20 December 1991.

14. Orlando Patterson, "Race, Gender, and Liberal Fallacies," *New York Times*, "Week in Review," 20 October 1991. The recent book by David Brock, *The Real Anita Hill* (New York: Free Press, 1993), is of a different character altogether. Here the generalized enemy is what the American tough baby considers to be "the left." A conspiracy theory is at the heart of Brock's argument.

15. Public Enemy, *Apocalypse '91: The Empire Strikes Black* (Columbia Records, 1991).

16. For a brief discussion of some of the antebellum antecedents to contemporary racist misogyny, see "Injustice and Violence of Representation" in Chapter 2.

17. Perhaps the first to do so was Daniel Patrick Moynihan in his famous report

on the African American family. See *The Negro Family: The Case for National Action* (Washington, D.C.: U.S. Department of Labor, 1965). In rhetorically attempting to separate the disparaging claims he made concerning an entire race from the logical charge of racism, Moynihan anticipated the form of the argument developed by James Q. Wilson by several years. See Wilson, "The Urban Unease," *The Public Interest* 12 (Summer 1968): 25–39.

18. Huet, "Monstrous Imagination," p. 720.

19. Ibid., pp. 720–21.

20. Ibid., p. 722.

21. Ibid., p. 725.

22. Ibid., p. 737.

23. For a comparative study, see Jacques Donzelot, *The Policing of Families*, trans. Robert Hurley (New York: Pantheon, 1979).

24. See Thomas L. Dumm, *Democracy and Punishment* (Madison: University of Wisconsin Press, 1987), especially pp. 89–96.

25. See "Understanding the Riots" (special series), *Los Angeles Times*, 11–15 May 1992, sec. T.

26. For important instances of the literature that emerged about the time of the L.A. riots, see Derrick Bell, *Faces at the Bottom of the Well* (New York: Basic Books, 1992), and Andrew Hacker, *Two Nations, Separate and Unequal* (New York: Harper & Row, 1992). A book from the previous year, Mike Davis's *City of Quartz: Excavating the Future in Los Angeles* (New York: Verso, 1991), which presented a suitably pessimistic view of the condition of that city, received a nomination for the National Book Award.

27. This way of evading the problem is consistent with the argument developed by Joel Kovel regarding what he calls "aversive" racism, in *White Racism* (New York: Columbia University Press), 1984. Kovel is put to good use in the superb analysis of the Hill-Thomas controversy by Kendall Thomas, "Strange Fruit," in Toni Morrison, ed., *Racing Justice, Engendering Power* (New York: Pantheon, 1992), pp. 364–89.

28. See Connolly, "Democracy and Territoriality," in Frederick Dolan and Thomas Dumm, eds., *Rhetorical Republic* (Amherst: University of Massachusetts Press, 1993).

29. Throughout this essay, I rely on the *Report of the Independent Commission on the Los Angeles Police Department* (Los Angeles: Independent Commission on the Los Angeles Police Department, 1991). For references to the Mobile Digital Terminal (MDT) communications, see pp. 48–55. For specific references to MDT communications by officers who beat King, see pp. 14–15.

30. See Robert Miles, *Racism* (New York: Routledge, 1989), pp. 36–38.

31. Benjamin Rush, "Observations intended to favour a supposition that the Black Color (as it is called) of the Negroes is derived from the LEPROSY," *Transactions of the American Philosophical Society* 4 (1799): 289–97. For a powerful discussion of Rush, see Harold Takaki, *Iron Cages: Race and Culture in Nineteenth-Century America* (New York: Knopf, 1979), pp. 16–35.

32. Rush, "Observations," p. 297.

33. Miles, *Racism*, p. 37.

34. This theme is developed in great detail in Robert Gooding-Williams's analysis of Frantz Fanon's *Black Skins, White Masks*. See "Look, a Negro," in Robert Gooding-Williams, ed., *Reading Rodney King, Reading Urban Uprising* (New York: Routledge, 1993).

35. See James Q. Wilson and Richard Herrnstein, *Crime and Human Nature* (New York: Simon & Schuster, 1985). Wilson, it should be mentioned, was an expert witness (and served as an adviser) to the mayor of Los Angeles's special commission to investigate police brutality, known as the Christopher Commission, which was organized in the wake of the beating of Rodney King (see *Report of the Independent Commission*, Table 2A-2). Herrnstein is currently working on a study of the relationship between race and I.Q. with Richard Murray, a scholar better known for advancing the idea that welfare creates poverty by encouraging a "culture of dependence."

I focus on this book because it is a standard in the field of criminology. In 1985, it summarized the literature in an attempt to develop a general theory of criminal behavior. I also chose it because Wilson has been exceedingly influential on the direction of criminal punishment policy in the United States, a leader in what has been termed the "neo-classical" revival in criminal punishment, which has led to theoretical justification for greater punitiveness in sentencing and the explosive growth of prison populations. Finally, Wilson is not considered merely a "popularizer" of ideas. His work on the study of policy is respected enough in the discipline of political science that the American Political Science Association named him its president for 1992.

36. Wilson and Herrnstein, *Crime and Human Nature*, pp. 71–72.

37. Ibid., pp. 102–3.

38. Ibid., pp. 81–90, but especially pp. 85–86. The development of a "scientific" understanding of what a criminal is, an understanding independent of law, has long been a eugenically inspired utopian impulse in modern criminal discourse. These attempts to reach some essential understanding of "who the criminal is" underlie what Michel Foucault referred to as the establishment of both general categories of "delinquency" and the identification of specific persons as "dangerous individuals," in which the focus is not on criminal acts but on individualized behavior. See Foucault, *Discipline and Punish: The Birth of the Prison*, trans. Alan Sheridan (New York: Pantheon, 1977), especially pp. 290–92. Also see Foucault, "The Dangerous Individual," trans. Alan Baudot and Jane Couchman, with reference to a translation by Carol Brown, in Lawrence Kritzman, ed., *Michel Foucault: Politics, Philosophy, Culture* (New York: Routledge, 1988), pp. 125–51.

39. Wilson and Herrnstein, *Crime and Human Nature*, p. 66. A "slow autonomic nervous system" implies an imperviousness to pain.

40. I will return to this theme of "stillness" later in this essay.

41. On Adorno's reference to "tough baby," see Chapter 3.

42. Foucault, *Discipline and Punish*, especially pp. 28–31.

43. For an analysis of television that influences mine, see Stanley Cavell, "The Fact of Television," in *Themes out of School* (Chicago: University of Chicago Press, 1988), pp. 235–68. I discuss the politics of the spectacle further in the next section.

44. See Richard A. Serrano and Tracy Wilkinson, "All Four in King Beating Acquitted," *Los Angeles Times*, 30 April 1992, p. 2.

45. See Christopher Hill, *The World Turned Upside Down: Radical Ideas during the English Revolution* (Baltimore: Penguin, 1975), especially chap. 3.

46. Ibid., pp. 40–41. Also see Foucault, *Discipline and Punish*, p. 291.

47. Hill, *World Turned Upside Down*, pp. 40–41.

48. Foucault, *Discipline and Punish*, p. 85.

49. See Mike Davis, *City of Quartz*, p. 270.

50. On minority inversions of the dominant automobile culture in the American Southwest, see Brenda Bright, "Mexican American Lowriders: An Anthropological Approach to Popular Culture" (Ph.D. diss., Rice University, 1994).

51. On the political theology of the medieval monarchy, see Ernst Kantorowicz, *The King's Two Bodies: A Study in Medieval Political Theology* (Princeton: Princeton University Press, 1957). This book is put to great use by Foucault in *Discipline and Punish*, pp. 28–29.

52. Serrano and Wilkinson, "All Four in King Beating Acquitted," p. 2.

53. See Jonathan Crary, *Techniques of the Observer: On Vision and Modernity in the Nineteenth Century* (Cambridge: MIT Press, 1990).

54. See Davis, *City of Quartz*, especially "Fortress L.A.," pp. 223–63. By this title Davis himself implicitly acknowledges a shift in the form and function of surveillance, which is not to provide an individuating power, but instead to establish a citadel for those inside, and as he notes in the following chapter, "The Hammer and the Rock," pp. 267–322, to enable the redeployment of militarizing tactics of control for the remainder of the population.

55. See the next section of this chapter for an elaboration on this theme.

56. Crary, *Techniques of the Observer*, especially pp. 17–19.

57. This is one of Crary's important points. Also see the most important theorization of this perspective, Guy Debord, *The Society of the Spectacle*, trans. Donald Nicholson-Smith (Detroit: Red & Black, 1983).

58. The metaphor of waste product is a dangerous one, implying as it does the disposability of those who are waste. I first encountered its use in a review essay by John Langbein, "*Albion's* Fatal Flaws," *Past and Present* 98 (February 1983): 96–120.

59. Davis, *City of Quartz*, p. 246.

60. Ibid., p. 257.

61. Gross, "In Simi Valley, Defense of a Shared Way of Life," p. A12.

62. The classic critique of this form of normalization is Herbert Marcuse, *One-Dimensional Man* (Boston: Beacon, 1964).

63. See François Ewald, "Norms, Discipline and the Law," trans. and adapted by Marjorie Beale, *Representations* 10 (Spring 1990): 138–61. See also Jonathan Simon, "The Ideological Effects of Actuarial Practices," *Law and Society Review* 22, no. 4 (1988): 771–800. I return to the question of the meaning of norms in Chapter 8.

64. Gross, "In Simi Valley, Defense of a Shared Way of Life."

65. Ibid.

66. Ibid.

67. On the erosion of citizen rights of standing in the United States, see Chapter 2.

68. Marc Mauer, *Young Black Men and the Criminal Justice System: A Growing National Problem* (Washington, D.C.: The Sentencing Project, February 1990), p. 3.

69. See Jason DeParle, "Young Black Men in Capital Study Finds 42% in Courts," *New York Times*, 18 April 1992, p. A1.

70. See Sir Leon Radzinowitz and Marvin Wolfgang, eds., *Crime and Justice*, vol. 3, *The Criminal in the Arms of the Law* (New York: Basic Books, 1977), especially, "Ideologies and Crime," by Radzinowitz and Joan King, pp. 442–49.

71. James Q. Wilson, *Thinking about Crime* (New York: Basic Books, 1975), p. 235.

72. "Rodney King's Statement," *Los Angeles Times*, 2 May 1992, p. 3.

73. For a trenchant analysis of the uses to which blackness is put in American culture, see Toni Morrison, *Playing in the Dark* (Cambridge: Harvard University Press, 1992).

74. Edward Soja, *Postmodern Geographies: The Reassertion of Space in Critical Social Theory* (New York: Verso, 1989), p. 246.

5. Barbara Kruger, or "You Really Crack Me Up"

Epigraph taken from Barbara Kruger, *Remote Control: Power, Culture, and the World of Appearances* (Cambridge: MIT Press, 1993), p. 220.

1. Carol Gilligan, *In a Different Voice: Psychological Theory and Women's Development* (Cambridge: Harvard University Press, 1982). I am being too simple here, and I do not want to parody Gilligan. Her point is important. Two recent studies of great use in elucidating her work in reference to political issues are Bonnie Honig, *Political Theory and the Displacement of Politics* (Ithaca: Cornell University Press, 1993), and Stephen White, *Political Theory and Postmodernism* (Cambridge: Cambridge University Press, 1991), especially chap. 6, "Difference Feminism and Responsibility to Otherness."

2. Judith Butler, *Gender Trouble: Feminism and the Subversion of Identity* (New York: Routledge, 1990), p. 33.

3. For a powerful critique of this position, see Anne Norton, "Engendering Another American Identity," in Frederick Dolan and Thomas Dumm, eds., *Rhetorical Republic: Governing Representations in American National Politics* (Amherst: University of Massachusetts Press, 1993).

4. See Nancy Hartsock, "Foucault on Power: A Theory for Women?" in Linda Nicholson, ed., *Feminism/Postmodernism* (New York: Routledge, 1990).

5. See Frederick Dolan and Thomas Dumm, "Inventing America," in Dolan and Dumm, eds., *Rhetorical Republic*. On the concept of strategic essentialism, see Diana Fuss, *Essentially Speaking: Feminism, Nature and Difference* (New York: Routledge, 1989), especially pp. 1–21.

6. Ibid., p. 21.

7. See the discussion in "Jokes" in Chapter 3 herein of the joke told by Gary Gilmore.

8. The term is borrowed from William Connolly. A strong argument against such a move is to be found in Judith Butler, "The Force of Fantasy: Feminism, Mapplethorpe, and Discursive Excess," *Differences* 2, no. 2 (1990). See especially p.120, and note 7.

9. Andrea Dworkin, *Intercourse* (New York: Free Press, 1987), pp. 21–22.

10. Catharine MacKinnon, *Feminism Unmodified* (Cambridge: Harvard University Press, 1987), p. 219.

11. Butler, *Gender Trouble*, p. 6.

12. Joan of Arc is a major hero for Dworkin. See "Virginity," chap. 6 of *Intercourse*.

13. MacKinnon, *Feminism Unmodified*, p. 149. In her footnote, she cites the work of Edward Donnerstein in regard to the relationship of the viewing of pornography to desensitization of young men and presumably their greater brutality against women (p. 267 n.20).

14. See Chapter 3.

15. Susan Stewart, "The Marquis de Meese," *Critical Inquiry* 15 (Autumn 1988): 167.

16. Ibid., pp. 166–67.

17. Ibid., p. 168.

18. Indeed, recently a warden in a Massachusetts prison banned a novel by Dworkin, characterizing it as pornographic.

19. MacKinnon's lecture appears in revised form as "Reflections on Law in the Everyday Life of Women," in Austin Sarat and Thomas Kearns, eds., *Law in Everyday Life* (Ann Arbor: University of Michigan Press, 1993).

20. See the discussion of William Connolly in Chapter 3.

21. Dworkin, *Intercourse*, p. 45.

22. Ibid., p. 122.

23. Charlie Chaplin, "The Idle Class" (First National [Warner Bros.], 1921).

24. See Craig Owens, "The Medusa Effect, or the Spectacular Ruse," and Jane Weinstock, "What She Means, to You," in Barbara Kruger, *We Won't Play Nature to Your Culture* (Basel: Institute for Contemporary Art, Kunsthalle Basel, 1983). Kruger's use of direct address is not unlike the terms of address that I am trying use throughout this book. Who "we" are is not easy to determine, nor is it ever settled by simply drawing attention to it.

25. See Kathy Ferguson, *The Feminist Case against Bureaucracy* (Philadelphia: Temple University Press, 1984), for the argument concerning the structural subordination of men in a managed society, especially chaps. 3 and 4.

26. See Kaja Silverman, *Male Subjectivity at the Margins* (New York: Routledge, 1992), especially chap. 5. Silverman quotes Francis Bacon on perversion, "Women to govern men . . . slaves to govern freemen . . . being total violations and perversions of the laws of nature and nations" (p. 185).

27. Ibid., p. 200. Here Silverman is referring to an analysis made by Leo Bersani in his *Freudian Body: Psychoanalysis and Art* (New York: Columbia University Press, 1986), pp. 38–39.

28. Owens, "The Medusa Effect, or the Spectacular Ruse." He suggests that Kruger tries to "mobilize the spectator" (p. 11). I contend that her work from the mid-1980s does precisely that.

29. Michel Foucault, "Panopticism," in *Discipline and Punish: The Birth of the Prison*, trans. Alan Sheridan (New York: Pantheon, 1977).

30. For a good review of the politics of vision that inform Foucault's work, see John Rajchman, "Foucault's Art of Seeing," *October* 44 (Spring 1988): 88–119.

31. See Hubert Dryfus and Paul Rabinow, *Michel Foucault: Beyond Structuralism and Hermeneutics* (Chicago: University of Chicago Press, 1983), for a discussion of panopticism that relates it to the question of practices.

32. Maurice Merleau-Ponty, *The Phenomenology of Perception*, trans. Colin Smith (London: Routledge, 1981), p. 147.

33. Rajchman, "Foucault's Art of Seeing," p. 89.

34. I do not pretend here to gender neutrality, but instead to a replication of status of the hermaphrodite in the choice of a word that has been used for that other purpose. One might try to claim that there is no such thing as a s/he *other* than as hermaphrodite, but that would demonstrate the same lack of imagination that I want to decry here.

35. Michel Foucault, ed., *Herculine Barbin, Being the Recently Discovered Memoirs of a Nineteenth Century French Hermaphrodite*, trans. Richard McDougall (New York: Pantheon, 1980), pp. viii–ix.

36. Rajchman, "Foucault's Art of Seeing," p. 90.

37. Michel Foucault, *The Birth of the Clinic: An Archaeology of Medical Perception*, trans. A. M. Sheridan Smith (New York: Vintage, 1975), pp. ix–x, and p. xiii.

38. Ibid., p. 120.

39. Foucault, ed., *Herculine Barbin*, pp. 133–35.

40. Ibid., pp. 127–28.

41. See Michel Foucault, *The History of Sexuality*, vol. 1, *Introduction*, trans. Robert Hurley (New York: Pantheon, 1978).

42. Ibid., p. 78.

43. The confusion of vision and reason, I think, has its source here, as Rajchman suggests, in "Foucault's Art of Seeing," pp. 89–90, where he criticizes Martin Jay's essay, "In the Empire of the Gaze: Foucault and the Denigration of Vision in Twentieth-Century French Thought," in David Cousins Hoy, ed., *Foucault: A Critical Reader* (London: Basil Blackwell, 1986).

44. Inclusion/exclusion lines should operate as what Gilles Deleuze would call "segmentary lines." See "Politics," in Deleuze and Felix Guattari, *On the Line*, trans. John Johnston (New York: Semiotext(e), 1983), pp. 69–70. Segmentary lines divide processes of experience into static moments of being as well as give definition to the shape of things. Deleuze has written at length on this problem in his various studies of Henri Bergson, as well as in his "Bergsonian" study of the modern cinema. Another version of this is to be found in Deleuze and Guatarri's *Thousand Plateaus*, trans. Brian Massumi (Minneapolis: University of Minnesota Press, 1987).

45. Alexis de Tocqueville, *Democracy in America*, trans. George Lawrence, ed. J. P. Mayer (Garden City, N.Y.: Anchor, 1967), p. 429.

46. Gilles Deleuze, *Foucault* (Minneapolis: University of Minnesota Press, 1988), p. 120.

47. Ibid., p. 121.

48. Ibid.

49. Paul Bové, "The Foucault Phenomenon," in *Deleuze, Foucault*, p. xxxii.

50. Deleuze, *Foucault*, p. 120.

51. Ibid., p. 123.

52. An important discussion of the political implications of this question can be found in William E. Connolly, *Political Theory and Modernity* (1988; Ithaca: Cornell University Press, 1993), pp. 72–79. The question is posed in de Sade's "Philosophy in the Bedroom."

53. In this sense, Deleuze might be more sensitive and subtle in his understanding of the power of the body than Peter Sloterdijk, who endorses the Greek cynic Diogenes of Sinope's act of shitting in public as having established shit as a "high" theme of philosophy, ethics, and politics. See Sloterdijk, *The Critique of Cynical Reason*, trans. Michael Eldred (Minneapolis: University of Minnesota Press, 1987), p. 151.

54. Craig Owens, "The Discourse of Others: Feminists and Postmodernism," in Hal Foster, ed., *The Anti-Aesthetic: Essays on Postmodern Culture* (Port Townsend, Wash.: Bay Press, 1983), p.77.

55. I first viewed this lenticular photograph in the spring of 1985 at the Museum of Contemporary Art, Houston, Texas. My thanks to Laura Rice-Sayers for first acquainting me with Kruger's work in the summer of 1984 and to Brenda Bright for alerting me to the exhibit.

56. I am exactly paraphrasing Foucault here, only substituting "her" for "him." See *Discipline and Punish*, p. 30.

57. Marjorie Garber, *Vested Interests* (New York: Routledge, 1992), p. 11.

58. On Hoover, see Chapter 3.

59. Michel Foucault, *This Is Not a Pipe*, trans. and ed. James Harkness (Berkeley and Los Angeles: University of California Press, 1983), pp. 32–33.

60. Ibid., p. 54.

61. Deleuze, *Foucault*, p. 121.

62. Deleuze and Guattari, *A Thousand Plateaus*, p. 227.

63. Ibid., p. 231.

6. Joyce Brown, or Democracy and Homelessness

Epigraph taken from Friedrich Nietzsche, *The Gay Science*, trans. Walter Kaufmann (New York: Random House, 1974), aphorism 377.

1. Benjamin's arcade project, or *Passagenwerk*, has been much commented on. My understanding of its meaning is informed most fully, for better or worse, by the work of Susan Buck-Morss. See especially her *Dialectics of Seeing: Walter Benjamin and the Arcades Project* (Cambridge: MIT Press, 1989).

2. Henry David Thoreau, *Walden*, in *Walden and "Civil Disobedience"* (New York: New American Library, 1960), pp. 37–38.

3. On a similar note, see Stanley Cavell, "Introduction: The Idea of Home," to *Home: A Place in the World*, a special issue of *Social Research*, 58 (Spring 1991): 9–10.

4. For a reading of Thoreau in a spirit similar to the one I evoke here, see Jane Bennett, "On Being a Native: Thoreau's Hermeneutics of Self," *Polity* 22 (Summer 1990). Bennett asks, "Can the native still flourish in a world where Walden is a '$2.5 million state erosion control and beautification project that includes construction of a path around the pond?'" (p. 580).

5. See Stanley Cavell, *The Senses of Walden (an expanded edition)* (Chicago: University of Chicago Press, 1992). Cavell writes, "Study of *Walden* would perhaps have not become such an obsession with me had it not presented itself as a response to the question: Why has America never expressed itself philosophically? Or has it—in the metaphysical riot of its greatest literature?" (p. 123).

6. Stanley Cavell, *This New Yet Unapproachable America* (Albuquerque: Living Batch, 1989), pp. 18–19, and also pp. 61–64. For the relevant passage in Wittgenstein, see his *Philosophical Investigations*, 3d ed., trans. G.E.M. Anscombe (New York: Macmillan, 1958), pp. 2e–3e.

7. Don DeLillo, *White Noise* (New York: Viking, 1985), pp. 37–38.

8. See Fredric Jameson's *Postmodernism, or the Cultural Logic of Late Capitalism* (Durham: Duke University Press, 1991). This book expands on the thesis Jameson first presented in an essay with the same title, in *New Left Review*, no. 146 (July–August 1984).

9. See Georges Bataille, *The Accursed Share*, vol. 1, *Consumption*, trans. Robert Hurley (New York: ZONE, 1988), p. 131.

10. Ibid., p. 129.

11. Ibid., pp. 33–35. In this section Bataille explains the relationship of eating animals to the human fear of death. His basic point is one that is now popular among vegetarians who are also "greens," that the production and consumption of meat is incredibly energy inefficient. See also Georges Bataille, "Animality," chap. 1 in *Theory of Religion*, trans. Robert Hurley (New York: Zone, 1989). In exploring Bataille, I am preparing to ask another question. If this intimacy is *external*, can it be compared to an *internal* form of intimacy? Posed as a question rather than as an answer, Emerson's idea of self-reliance might animate contemporary discussions of the possibility of finding a place to be.

12. Bataille, *Accursed Share*, p. 32.

13. For a discussion of how the simple act of counting one's change can trigger a sequence of political engagements and refusals, see the provocative passage in Judith Shklar, *The Faces of Injustice* (New Haven: Yale University Press, 1990), pp. 43–45.

14. Here I am thinking of the distinctions that George Kateb has made between self-reliance as action and as intellectual communication in his first McCloy Lecture, "Self-Reliance as Method" (Amherst College, 22 October 1992).

15. And yet how can I not be ashamed when I realize the profound depth of misery of which my thought is but one termination point? Someone is suffering so that I may think about it. My responsibility, then, is to think. But I remain tempted by yet another path. A hyperpessimism that leads to action, or what Foucault referred to as "hyper- and pessimistic activism" might be the response of a post-

structuralist theorist to a self-reliant thinker. See Foucault, "On the Genealogy of Ethics: An Overview of Work in Progress," in Paul Rabinow, ed., *The Foucault Reader* (New York: Pantheon, 1984), p. 343. Is such an activism *merely* a thought? And this question of self-reliance, when and how will it move from the margins and footnotes to assume its importance to the homeless?

16. For an illustration, see the interview "Baudrillard Shrugs," in William Chaloupka and William Stearns, eds., *Jean Baudrillard and the Disappearance of Art and Politics* (New York: St. Martin's, 1992). For a response to Baudrillard parallel to that which I suggest here, see, in the same collection, "The Invisible Skyline," by Thomas L. Dumm.

17. Judith Shklar, in *Ordinary Vices* (Cambridge: Harvard University Press, 1984), and in "The Liberalism of Fear," in Nancy Rosenblum, ed., *Liberalism and the Moral Life* (Cambridge: Harvard University Press, 1989), flirted with that danger by insisting on the ubiquity and permanence of the ordinary vices. Even as she insisted that modern liberalism is complex, limited, constrained, and constraining in the demands that it places on persons, Shklar did not develop an argument concerning how these vices operate, not on agents, but on bodies, even as she suggested that physical cruelty is worse than mental. See "Putting Cruelty First," chap. 1 of *Ordinary Vices*. For a more extended discussion of Shklar, see Chapter 2.

18. On the idea of secular thought and acceptance of mortality, see William E. Connolly, *Identity/Difference: Democratic Negotiations of Political Paradox* (Ithaca: Cornell University Press, 1991), p. 16. Connolly suggests "We secularists, it seems, know where we are going. We're on the road to nowhere." But do we know? Connolly himself is gesturing toward a song, "We're on the Road to Nowhere," from Talking Heads, *Little Creatures* (David Byrne, Warner Bros. 1986).

19. Buck-Morss, *Dialectics of Seeing*, p. 373. This page presents a photo of a postcard that stamps the number of seconds left until the year 2000 and urges the reader "To pass the time, drink a cointreau!"

20. See Peter Greenaway's 1989 film, *The Cook, The Thief, His Wife and Her Lover*, for the gruesome representation of this theme.

21. Phyllis Rose, "Tools of Torture: An Essay on Beauty and Pain," in *Atlantic*, October 1986, pp. 38–39. I thank Eric Forsman for drawing this essay to my attention.

22. See Chapter 5.

23. Rose, "Tools of Torture," p. 39.

24. See Elaine Scarry, *The Body in Pain* (New York: Oxford University Press, 1985), pp. 40–41.

25. Ibid., p. 35.

26. Ibid., pp. 36–37.

27. Ibid., pp. 37–38.

28. See Walter Benjamin, "Unpacking My Library," in Hannah Arendt, ed., *Illuminations* (New York: Schocken, 1969).

29. See Thomas Hobbes, "Of Persons, Authors and things personated," in *Leviathan*, ed. C. B. MacPherson (Baltimore: Penguin, 1968).

30. For more on this etymological association, see John Wikse, *About Possession: The Self as Private Property* (University Park: Penn State Press, 1977). Wikse might

claim that it is at the extreme of self-possession that one becomes dispossessed, in a manner that makes one seek to turn inward. He argues that Emerson is preparatory to Nietzsche because the political psychology of self-possession leads to self-reliance as a compensation (using that term in what he believes to be Emerson's sense). I follow up on this insight below.

31. Scarry, *Body in Pain*, p. 260.

32. Ibid., p. 279.

33. I take this to be one of the important lessons of Toni Negri. For a precis of his argument see Toni Negri and Felix Guattari, *Communists Like Us: New Spaces of Liberty, New Lines of Alliance*, trans. Michael Ryan (New York: Semiotext(e), 1990).

34. Scarry, *Body in Pain*, pp. 303–4.

35. Ibid., p. 304.

36. Michel Foucault, *Discipline and Punish* (New York: Pantheon, 1977), p. 30. I am paraphrasing here.

37. See Barbara Loyd, "Lost in the woods? All at sea? Help is at hand, via satellites," *New York Times*, 1 February 1992, p. 1B; Laurant Belsie, "Computer sky-track tells where you are," *The Christian Science Monitor*, 22 May 1991, p. 12; and Andrew Pollack, "War Spurs Navigation by Satellite," *New York Times*, 6 February 1991, p. 1C.

38. When I suggest that this experience is possible for a majority of the world's human population, I am emphasizing the fact that the majority of the world's human population lives (or soon will be living) in urban areas. See *The Universal Almanac, 1990*, ed. John Wright (New York: Andrews & McNeel, 1990). "According to the U.S. Census Bureau, 29% of the world's population lived in urban areas in 1950; by 1970, 37% did. The movement of millions of people from rural areas to urban complexes then continued with even greater intensity, so that by 1985, 45% of the world's population were urban dwellers" (p. 352). The urban experience of the twentieth century as constituting a distinctive style of being is a subject that has attracted enormous attention. For my purposes the work of Georg Simmel is of great importance on this topic. For example, see his essay "The Metropolis and Mental Life" (1903), in Donald Levine, ed., *Georg Simmel: Individuality and Social Forms* (Chicago: University of Chicago Press, 1971), pp. 324–39.

39. See Donna J. Haraway, "A Manifesto for Cyborgs: Science, Technology, and Socialist Feminism in the 1980s," *Socialist Review* 80 (1985): 65–108. This has been reprinted as "A Cyborg Manifesto," in Haraway, *Simians, Cyborgs, Women* (New York: Routledge, 1991). Haraway suggests that a cyborg is a hybrid of machine and organism. In this sense, any time a human *touches* a machine (or is touched by a machine) the two combine to form a cyborg. The cyberneticization of the world will occur when all are connected, when all are touched through a common network of machinery.

40. Thomas Pynchon, *The Crying of Lot 49* (New York: Bantam, 1967), p. 95.

41. Celeste Olalquiaga, *Megalopolis: Contemporary Cultural Sensibilities* (Minneapolis: University of Minnesota Press, 1992), pp. 2–3. Olalquiaga herself cites two texts by Paul Virilio on the critique of space and the aesthetics of disappearance: *L'Espace critique* (Paris: Christian Bourgeois, 1984) and *Estetica de la desaparicion* (Barcelona: Anagrama, 1988).

42. For a series of meditations on this question, see Avital Ronell, *Crack Wars* (Lincoln: University of Nebraska Press, 1992). This question is obviously tinged with metaphysical difficulties. At its heart is the question concerning technology as formulated by Martin Heidegger in "The Question Concerning Technology." See his *Basic Writings*, ed. David Farrell Krell (New York: Harper & Row, 1977).

43. This insight can be gathered from Michel Foucault's now famous analysis of Jeremy Bentham's plan for the Panopticon. The constant possibility of being observed paradoxically introduces a core instability into the experience of surveillance because one never knows for certain whether one *is* being observed. See *Discipline and Punish*, pp. 195–228. On the ethics underlying the escape from this form of visibility, see Alexander E. Hooke, "The Order of Others," *Political Theory* 15 (February 1987), especially his proposal for an "anonymous individuality," pp. 55–58.

44. On this process, see Anne Norton, *Republic of Signs: Liberal Theory and American Popular Culture* (Chicago: University of Chicago Press, 1993), pp. 50–51.

45. Again see Haraway, "Manifesto for Cyborgs." She suggests that cyborg imagery is useful for thinking about ways "out of the maze of dualisms in which we have explained our bodies and our tools to ourselves" (p. 108). Sympathetic to the project of resistance Haraway endorses, I would only suggest that she herself too readily relies on the dualisms she criticizes in that very essay. The issue of the body in relationship to the politics of technology is addressed by Foucault in *The History of Sexuality*, vol. 1, trans. Robert Hurley (New York: Pantheon, 1978), and more recently by Judith Butler in *Gender Trouble* (New York: Routledge, 1990).

46. For a primer on the conditions of the homeless I rely heavily on Jonathan Kozol, *Rachel and Her Children: Homeless Families in America* (New York: Fawcett Columbine, 1988), and Alice S. Baum and Donald W. Burnes, *A Nation in Denial: The Truth about Homelessness* (Boulder: Westview, 1993). Kozol's study focuses on the lack of housing that is available to poor people and provides information about the bureaucratic regulation that overwhelms those who lack places to be. Baum and Burnes adopt a more communitarian point of view, arguing that deinstitutionalization, alienation, and other factors associated with the spiritual poverty of late modern life are to blame. Their policy prescriptions are correspondingly more antiliberal.

47. See Cavell, "Introduction: The Idea of Home," pp. 9–10.

48. Ibid., p. 10.

49. Michele Wallace, "Homelessness Is Where the Heart Is," in *Invisibility Blues* (New York: Verso, 1990), p. 61.

50. Ibid., pp. 61–62.

51. Stanley Cavell, "Finding as Founding: Taking Steps in Emerson's 'Experience,'" in *This New Yet Unapproachable America*, p. 116.

52. Wallace, "Homelessness," p. 62.

53. Cavell, "Finding as Founding," p. 118.

54. This is part of the problem that Heidegger identified in his later work. It is a particular theme of his in "The Question Concerning Technology," in which he develops the idea of standing reserve.

55. George Kateb, "Introduction: Exile, Alienation, and Estrangement," in "Home: A Place in the World," *Social Research* 58 (Spring 1991): 135. This is a familar Katebian theme. See his comments on alienation in *Hannah Arendt: Politics, Conscience, Evil* (Totowa, N.J.: Rowman & Allanheld, 1985) and "Hannah Arendt: Alienation and America," in Richard Pourier, ed., *Raritan Reading* (New Brunswick: Rutgers University Press, 1990), pp. 196–221.

56. Kateb, "Introduction: Exile, Alienation, and Estrangement," p. 137.

57. Ibid. "They want more home; they will not grow up and try to become self-reliant."

58. See Kateb's "Active Self-Reliance" (paper presented at the APSA Annual Meeting, Washington D.C., 1993), pp. 67–73. There he suggests that Emerson sees society itself as the difficulty that leads people to lack of courage and conformity, or what Kateb develops in another essay as docility. See Kateb, *The Inner Ocean: Individualism and Democratic Culture* (Ithaca: Cornell University Press, 1992), pp. 222–39.

59. See Jeremy Waldron, "Homelessness and the Issue of Freedom," *UCLA Law Review* 39 (1991): 295–323.

60. Ibid., p. 301.

61. Ibid., p. 302.

62. Ibid., p. 323. Waldron only outlines the material conditions, but he is supplemented in the issue of the *UCLA Law Review* with an article by Mike Davis, "Afterword—a Logic Like Hell's: Being Homeless in Los Angeles," *UCLA Law Review* 39 (1991): 325–31. Davis describes an eery scene in the Skid Row of L.A. of thousands of homeless people wandering the streets, rarely sitting because of the likelihood of police harassment.

63. Ibid., p. 304.

64. Ibid., p. 321.

65. See George James, "Burning Dollar Bills on the Sidewalk," *New York Times* 29 October 1987.

66. Josh Barbanel, "In Hospital Courtroom, Plea for Freedom," *New York Times*, 6 November 1987.

67. Ibid.

68. Ibid.

69. Ex parte motion part., "In the Matter of the Retention of Billie Boggs," Supreme Court of New York County, 136 Misc.2d 1082, p. 411 (Judge Robert D. Lippman, 12 November 1987).

70. And her story has an ending that is happy only up to a point. Where is she now? Sometime after this case was heard, she was living again with her sisers, people whom she had wanted to avoid in the first place.

71. Dale Maharidge, "The Last of the Old-Time Hobos," *Nation*, 9–16 August 1993, p. 166.

72. Maurice Blanchot, *The Unavowable Community*, trans. Pierre Joris (Barrytown, N.Y.: Station Hill, 1988). The idea of this "immanence" to which Blanchot refers is developed in Jean Luc Nancy's essay *La Communauté desoeuvreée* (Paris: Christian Bourgeois, 1986). Blanchot's essay is a response in part to that earlier

essay. A further discussion of the question of immanentism is to be found in Philippe Lacoue-Labarthe, *Heidegger, Art and Politics*, trans. Chris Turner (New York: Basil Blackwell, 1990), pp. 70 and 75.

73. The utopia of a cybernetic blending of animal and machine that would allow recontesting the meaning of humanity, in Haraway's vision, does not account for this aspect of the technological, as far as I can tell. On the implosion of meaning see Michael Weinstein, *Meaning and Appreciation* (West Lafayette, Ind.: Purdue University Press, 1978).

74. See Hannah Arendt, *The Origins of Totalitarianism* (New York: Harcourt, Brace, Jovanovich, 1973), pp. 477–78.

75. Alex Hooke, in "The Order of Others," suggests the style of resistance to such naming. "Anonymous individuality incites a type of self-consciousness insofar as it seeks to offer a resistance to those forces that proliferate through their ingenuity of finding a name for everything we do and designating a place for everything we are" (p. 58). For a genealogy of the legal concept of personal law that traces its demise as personality itself becomes more prominent, see Marianne Constable, *The Law of the Other: The Mixed Jury and Changing Conceptions of Citizenship, Law, and Knowledge* (Chicago: University of Chicago Press, 1994).

76. See Michel Foucault, "The Masked Philosopher," in Lawrence Kritzman, ed., *Michel Foucault* (New York: Routledge, 1988).

77. Foucault, "Maurice Blanchot," in *Foucault/Blanchot*, pp. 23–24.

78. On this perplexing question of constitution, see Bonnie Honig, "Declarations of Independence," in Frederick Dolan and Thomas Dumm, eds., *The Rhetorical Republic: Governing Representations in American Politics* (Amherst: University of Massachusetts Press, 1993).

79. Heidegger, "The Question Concerning Technology," p. 306.

80. Blanchot, *Unavowable Community*, p. 6.

81. On the fabulous character of constitutive moments, see Jacques Derrida, "Declaration of Independence," trans. Thomas Keenan and Thomas Pepper, *New Political Science* 15 (Summer 1986), and Bonnie Honig's "Declarations of Independence." For a fuller analysis of the fabulous, see Thomas Keenan, "Freedom, the Law of Another Fable," *Yale French Studies* 79 (1991).

82. Foucault, "Maurice Blanchot," p. 35.

83. Norton, *Republic of Signs*, pp. 139 and 174.

84. Foucault, "Maurice Blanchot," p. 33.

85. Ibid., pp. 34–35.

86. Anne Norton elucidates this point brilliantly. See her conclusion to *Republic of Signs*.

87. Foucault, "Maurice Blanchot," p. 38.

88. See Wikse, *About Possession*, chap. 1, for a discussion of the production of idiocy.

89. See Scarry, *Body in Pain*. If only Scarry would use pain to comprehend torture, and not the other way around!

90. Maurice Blanchot, *Writing of the Disaster*, trans. Ann Smock (Lincoln: University of Nebraska Press, 1986), p. 18.

91. This phrase is taken from Don DeLillo, *White Noise*, p. 38.

92. This ethic of care is developed by Foucault in his late works, especially *The History of Sexuality*, vol. 3, *The Care of the Self*, trans. Robert Hurley (New York: Pantheon, 1986).

93. David Bromwich, "Alienation and Belonging to Humanity," in "Home: A Place in the World," *Social Research* 58 (Spring 1991): 139–57. One might object that Wordsworth is an English poet, and hence what he has to say cannot be so easily placed in the context of *our* united states. But the conditions he describes, especially the factories and poorhouses, are not so foreign to our history and might, in fact, be described as shared by the English, French, and Americans.

94. Ibid., p. 144 (lines 99 to 101), cited by Bromwich on p. 149.

95. Ibid., p. 151.

96. Ibid., p. 150.

97. Ibid., p. 151.

98. Ibid., p. 144 (lines 123 to 125), cited by Bromwich on p. 153.

99. Ibid., p. 153.

100. Ibid., p. 154.

101. Ibid., p. 141.

102. David Rothman, *The Discovery of the Asylum: Social Order and Disorder in the New Republic* (Boston: Little, Brown, 1971), pp. 180–205. See Michael Ignatieff, *A Just Measure of Pain* (New York: Columbia University Press, 1978).

103. Bromwich, "Alienation and Belonging to Humanity," p. 146 (lines 179–82), cited by Bromwich on p. 152.

104. See Thomas L. Dumm, *Democracy and Punishment: Disciplinary Origins of the United States* (Madison: University of Wisconsin Press, 1987), especially chaps. 4 and 5, for a discussion of the role that the shift from isolate to congregate punishment had on theories of character and their relation to habit.

105. William Corlett is perceptive on this matter of reassurance. See *Community without Unity: A Politics of Derridian Extravagance* (Durham: Duke University Press, 1989).

106. Kateb, "Active Self-Reliance," p. 71.

107. Ibid., pp. 58–61.

108. Ibid., p. 72.

109. In an essay that closely parallels this one, I have suggested that Emerson without God is Kafka. Thomas L. Dumm, "Spare Parts: Political Theory as Compensation" (manuscript).

110. Kateb, "Active Self-Reliance," p. 73.

111. Ralph Waldo Emerson, "Compensation," from *Essays: First Series*, in *The Selected Writings of Ralph Waldo Emerson*, ed. Brooks Atkinson (New York: Modern Library, 1992), p. 155.

112. Ibid.

113. Ibid., p. 156. Kateb suggests that "Compensation" is a companion to "Circles." He writes, "At the start of 'Circles,' Emerson says that the form of the circle is read to us all our lives. The moral drawn from that fact in 'Circles' is that 'every action admits of being outdone.' But a different and adversarial moral can be

drawn from 'the circular—character of every human action.' It is that a circular action is not progressive but compensatory" (Kateb, "Active Self-Reliance," p. 34).

114. Ralph Waldo Emerson, "Circles," from *Essays: First Series*, in *The Selected Writings of Ralph Waldo Emerson*, ed. Brooks Atkinson (New York: Modern Library, 1992), p. 252. "Our life is an apprenticeship to the truth that around every circle another can be drawn."

115. Emerson, "Compensation," p. 156.

116. Ibid., p. 159.

117. Ibid.

118. Michel Foucault, *Discipline and Punish: The Birth of the Prison*, trans. Alan Sheridan (New York: Pantheon, 1977), p. 30.

119. Emerson, "Compensation," p. 168.

120. Ibid.

121. Ibid., p. 169.

122. Ibid., p. 170.

123. Ibid.

124. Kateb, *Inner Ocean*, p. 171.

125. See George Kateb, "Individualism, Communitarianism, and Docility," in *Inner Ocean*, p. 239. "Admirers of Foucault should worry more about communitarianism than individualism. Indeed, they should work to rehabilitate individualism."

P.S. (I Love . . .) Television in Wartime

Epigraph taken from Laurie Anderson, *United States* (New York: Harper & Row, 1984), part 1, "Say Hello."

1. See Craig Owens, "Sex and Language: In Between," in Jane Kardon, ed., *Laurie Anderson* (Philadelphia: University of Pennsylvania, Institute of Contemporary Art, 1983). Owens writes, "This is, of course, an image of sexual difference, or rather of sexual differentiation according to the distribution of the phallus—as it is marked and re-marked by the man's right arm, which appears less to have been raised than erected in greeting" (pp. 49–50).

2. Ibid., pp. 51–52. Owens suggests that a major feat of Anderson is her ability to historicize what had been, for Derrida and de Man, "a fundamental ambiguity inscribed within language itself." By pointing to the digital, to the development of cybernetics as a mode of "communication," and showing its effects, Anderson shows us the circulation of signs as a "scramble system."

3. Ibid., p. 50. "In this picture, chosen to represent the inhabitants of Earth for the extraterrestrial Other, it is the man who speaks, who represents—stands for—mankind. The woman is only represented, spoken for; she stands by her man."

4. For her preliminary study of television as shock absorber, see the reflections of the Rodney King case in Avital Ronell, *Finitude's Score* (Lincoln: University of Nebraska Press, 1994).

5. Here I am thinking especially of Avital Ronell, "Support Our Tropes," in Frederick Dolan and Thomas Dumm, eds., *Rhetorical Republic: Governing Representations in American Politics* (Amherst: University of Massachusetts Press, 1993), and

James Der Derian, "Cyberwar, Videogames, and the Gulf War Syndrome," chap. 8 in *Anti-Diplomacy: Spies, Terror, Speed, and War* (New York: Basil Blackwell, 1992).

6. See Avital Ronell, *The Telephone Book: Technology, Schizophrenia, Electric Speech* (Lincoln: University of Nebraska Press, 1989).

7. Instant replay: Eddie Murphy as Buckwheat being assassinated on *Saturday Night Live*, the shooting of JR on *Dallas*.

8. Don DeLillo, *Libra* (New York: Viking Penguin, 1988), writes in an author's note to the novel which was dropped from the paperback edition, "But because this book makes no claim to literal truth, because it is only itself, apart and complete, readers may find refuge here—a way of thinking about the assassination without being constrained by half-facts or overwhelmed by possibilities, by the tide of speculation that widens with the years."

9. Stanley Cavell, "The Fact of Television," in *Themes Out of School* (San Francisco: North Point, 1984), p. 250.

10. Ibid., p. 251.

11. Ibid., p. 239.

12. Ibid., p. 241.

13. Ibid., p. 245.

14. Ibid., pp. 246–49.

15. Ibid., pp. 251–52.

16. Ibid., p. 253.

17. See Todd Gitlin's introduction to Gitlin, ed., *Watching Television* (New York: Pantheon, 1986), p. 6.

18. Cavell, "The Fact of Television," p. 255.

19. Ibid., p. 257. One might also reflect upon this question, posed by Emmanuel Levinas: "Is not the face given to vision?" See *Totality and Infinity*, trans. Alphonso Lingis (Pittsburgh: Duquesne University Press, 1969), p. 185.

20. Cavell, "The Fact of Television," p. 258.

21. Ibid., p. 257.

22. See William Corlett, "Pocock, Foucault, Forces of Reassurance," *Political Theory* 17 (February 1989): 79. In each of the three categories, Corlett cites (respectively), Plato and Husserl, Aristotle, and Heraclitus. The only slightly hidden hand of the critique of seriality here is Jacques Derrida's critique of *presence*.

23. See Thomas L. Dumm, "From Danger to Fear," in *Democracy and Punishment: Disciplinary Origins of the United States* (Madison: University of Wisconsin Press, 1987), for a gloss. See also Thomas Dumm, "Fear of Law," in Austin Sarat and Susan Silbey, eds., *Studies in Law, Politics, and Society*, vol. 10 (Greenwich, Conn.: JAI, 1990).

24. See Alphonso Lingis, *Excesses: Eros and Culture* (Albany: SUNY Press, 1983), pp. 113–14.

25. Ibid., pp. 14–15.

26. See Walter Benjamin, "The Work of Art in the Age of Mechanical Reproduction," in *Illuminations*, ed. Hannah Arendt (New York: Schocken, 1969), pp. 239–41. I work from a "corrected" translation of the English text, informally done by an old friend. I rely on the alternative translation when it seems to make better sense.

27. Ibid., p. 240.

28. In this, Benjamin has strong affinities with Georges Bataille. I address the question of excess, as conceived by Bataille, in Chapter 8.

29. Benjamin, "Work of Art," p. 242.

30. Der Derian, *Antidiplomacy*, p. 183.

31. As an academic, I was also in a community where attention was paid to this war through a variety of sources, including (for the first time) electronic mail networks, which tried to provide alternative sources of information to the coverage provided by the corporately owned news sources. Moreover, the day-to-day schedule suddenly included helping to organize and attend meeting after meeting with antiwar faculty and students in order to try to protest. I was also secretly relieved when a moratorium resolution that I supported failed in the Amherst College faculty, simply because the further disruption of my regularly scheduled programming it would involve would increase my level of nervous exhaustion. But my relief should not be interpreted as simple acquiescence. Instead, it might be read as a symptom of the debilitation that is associated with and is companion to the politics of televideo dissemination of news.

32. Der Derian, *Antidiplomacy*, p. 187.

33. *The Camera Never Blinks* is the title of the ghostwritten autobiography of Dan Rather (New York: Warner, 1977).

34. We had a rather stormy class meeting that day. I had asked the students to read a debate that had occurred between Chomsky and Michel Foucault in the early 1970s. (It can be found as "Human Nature: Justice Versus Power," in Fons Elders, ed., *Reflexive Water: The Basic Concern of Mankind* [London: Souvenir, 1974].) In his comments to the class, Chomsky accused Foucault of being a Nazi, suggested that one of the Puerto Rican students in the class must be from "the ruling class" to be attending a school like Amherst, and generally exhibited an intolerance for student questions, rhetorically asking at one point if they could tell the difference between a rock and a cow. All in all, he exhibited the downside of the Enlightenment project that day, its presumption of clear and certain knowledge about human nature and its willingness to condemn those who question its certainty.

35. Later the act of protest was to be contested as such. At the spot, people started leaving mementos, and area activists staged a vigil. Talk began about a permanent memorial, and others in town began to discuss ways of removing the people who were there. The site became contested, in a minor way.

36. I once thought that a comparison of Chomsky and Jean Baudrillard on the war would end up making Baudrillard look worse. This is still the view of Christopher Norris. See his *Uncritical Theory: Intellectuals and the Gulf War* (Amherst: University of Massachusetts Press, 1992). But I have changed my mind. Baudrillard's *faux* embrace of stoicism should not distract from the fact that he thinks about the forces that enable the sorts of dissimulations that allowed the Gulf War to operate so smoothly as a cultural war machine.

37. Der Derian, *Antidiplomacy*, p. 187.

38. One might argue it is the schedule of the prison. See Michel Foucault, *Discipline and Punish: The Birth of the Prison*, trans. Alan Sheridan (New York: Pantheon, 1977), pp. 6–7, a work schedule that bears a formal resemblance to a

television schedule, to the point of containing summary descriptions of what happens when.

39. One might protest that CNN news is continuous, an exception to the rule. But CNN's format is no different from that of the half-hour news programs. It is a chain of half-hour programs that is able to pretend to be more because few people watch it for more than twenty minutes at a time. The only "real" exception to the rule is the CNN service channel, C-Span, which fulfills the function of monitor spectacularly. This regulation, through regularization, of time explains why George Bush had such an enormous advantage over Dan Rather when Rather agreed to a live interview of Bush on the *CBS Evening News*, during the 1988 presidential campaign. All Bush had to do was to keep talking, and Rather was in deeper and deeper trouble.

40. Steven Erlanger, "In Moscow, Relief and Resignation," *New York Times*, 5 October 1993, p. A1.

41. See Paul Virilio, "The State of Emergency," in *Speed and Politics* (New York: Semiotext(e), 1986), pp. 133–51.

Index